M000073922

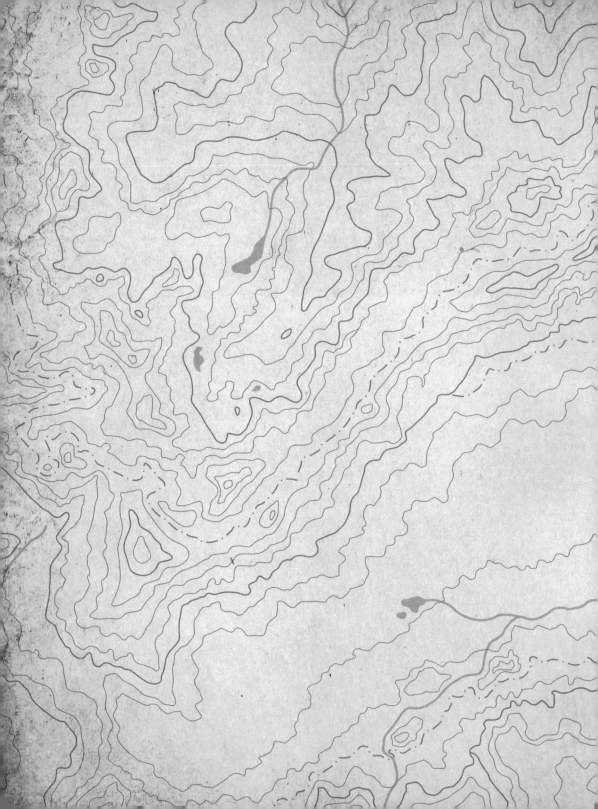

TO

_____

FROM

_____

Summerside Press™

Minneapolis, MN 55438

www.summersidepress.com

NIV Teen Devotional Journal

© 2011 by Zondervan Publishers, Inc.
Selections are taken from *The NIV Teen Devotional Bible* and are used
by permission.

ISBN 978-1-60936-103-7

M'Cheyne Bible Reading Plan by Scottish minister, Robert Murray
M'Cheyne (1813-1843).

Compiled by Jill Olson.

Cover and interior design by faceout studio | faceoutstudio.com.

Summerside Press™ is an inspirational publisher offering fresh,
irresistible books to uplift the heart and engage the mind.

Printed in China.

NIV :: TEEN

DEVOTIONAL

JOURNAL

A 365 Daily
Devotional Journal

summerside

Trust in him at all times...pour out your
hearts to him, for God is our refuge.

PSALM 62:8

The *NIV Teen Devotional Journal* has been compiled to help you understand what the Bible has to say about the questions you have about life and eternity. And there's room to record your own thoughts, questions, and prayers each day.

Based on the *NIV Teen Devotional Bible*, the daily entries have been taken from devotions written by teenagers (you'll see their names and ages on the entries), as well as a few written by youth leaders. Included for each day is a Bible reading, a selected verse, the devotion, and (on most entries) questions to inspire further thought and journaling.

The Bible is like a special letter from God to you. When you read it, you'll get to know Him better. A Bible reading plan is included in the back of the book to help you do that. By following the daily guide, you can read through the whole Bible in one year. Although they may complement each other, the reading plan is independent of the daily devotions. Used together they are great tools for spiritual growth and understanding.

READ GENESIS 1:26-28

Who Do You Look Like?

God created man in his own image, in the image of God he created him; male and female he created them.
GENESIS 1:27

There are lots of times when other people's opinions lead me to believe I'm somehow not important. When I get teased or picked on at school, it changes my image of myself. But when I read this verse, it brings things back into perspective. As long as I'm living the way God wants me to, it doesn't matter what people think about me. I am made in God's image, and I can feel good about who I am.

Being made in God's image means that God made me exactly the way he wanted me to be. Knowing that God loves me so much helps me feel better about myself. That makes me want to learn more about him and let him shine through me so other people will see him in me.

WHAT ABOUT YOU?

:: *Do you ever put yourself down for the way you look? What are you saying to God when you put down what he made?*

:: *Create something that tells people something about you—a painting, a poem, a song. How do you feel about your creation? What do you want people to learn about you through your creation?*

:: *Thank God for 1 or 2 things that make you who you are.*

A Real Guilt Trip

Then the man and his wife heard the sound of the LORD God as he was walking in the garden...and they hid from the LORD.

GENESIS 3:8

I remember the first time I lied to my parents. I knew what "sin" meant before that, but it was the first time I really felt like I had sinned. It was horrible.

I hated feeling so guilty, and I told myself I'd never lie again. But then I told another lie. I felt bad, but not quite so bad as the first time. Before I knew it, I was lying all the time.

Even though lying got easier and easier, the guilty feeling never totally went away. That's when I learned that guilt isn't always a bad thing. The bad feeling made me want to stop lying.

Finally, I asked God to forgive me and help me stop lying. When I apologized to my parents and told them the truth, the horrible feeling went away. I definitely learned a lesson about sin and how important it is to ask for forgiveness. I just wish I hadn't had to learn it the hard way.

WHAT ABOUT YOU?

:: *Think about when you've felt guilty and why.*

:: *Are there any people you need to ask for forgiveness from? Tell them you're sorry and ask for their forgiveness today.*

JANUARY :: 3

READ GENESIS 4:1-16

Can Brothers and Sisters Be Friends?

The LORD said to Cain, "Where is your brother Abel?". "I don't know," he replied. "Am I my brother's keeper?"
GENESIS 4:9

Since I'm the youngest of 5 kids, I know what it's like to fight with siblings. One of my sisters and I used to argue over the littlest things. And sometimes I wonder if I'll ever learn to love my brother....

But in the last few years, I've learned that fighting with my brothers and sisters is only one part of our relationship. Three of them have finished high school and moved away. When I think about them, I don't think about the arguments and the silly fights we had. I think about the fun we had together. I think about how much I miss them and love them.

When you get right down to it, brothers and sisters are some of the best friends you'll ever have. No matter how much you can't stand them sometimes, one day it'll hit you how important they are to you.

WHAT ABOUT YOU?

:: What are 3 things you can do that will help you get along better with your brothers and sisters?

:: Think of several ways you can show love to them. Do one of those things for them today.

:: Ask God to help you all get along.

JANUARY :: 4

READ GENESIS 6:9-14

Taking a Stand

Noah was a righteous man blameless among the people of his time, and he walked with God.
GENESIS 6:9

My dad isn't a Christian, and he yells at me a lot. When I try to show him a Christian response by not yelling back, he calls me self-righteous and accuses me of having a stuck-up attitude....

I'm glad I'm not the only one who's ever had this problem. Noah did too. He got criticized by everybody when he was building the ark. But he did what God asked him to do anyway....

When I'm struggling to stand up for what's right, I can think about Noah and know that I'm doing the right thing. If I'm obedient, I know God will always provide a safe place for me too.

WHAT ABOUT YOU?

:: *Think about a time someone made fun of you when you tried to do the right thing. What helped you stay strong?*

:: *Write a letter of encouragement to someone who's been yelled at or put down (it could even be you). If you need ideas, check out Matthew 5:10-12.*

:: *Pray for the strength to take a stand for your faith even when it's not easy.*

JANUARY :: 5

AMY, AGE 13

READ GENESIS 9:12-17

Rainbow Reminder

Whenever I bring clouds over the earth and the rainbow appears in the clouds, I will remember my covenant between me and you.
GENESIS 9:14-15

I've always known that God keeps his promises and listens when we pray. But these verses give me even more faith in God and his promises. Sometimes I need that extra faith, like when it feels like God isn't hearing my prayers, or when he answers them in a different way than I had hoped for.

Even though God is always listening to us and helping us out, we often can't see with our eyes exactly what he's doing. That's why a rainbow is so cool—it's something we can actually see that reminds us God is there. And because rainbows come after storms, they show us that God's there even when our situation looks bad. He's always there for us; no matter what happens, he'll keep his promises.

WHAT ABOUT YOU?

:: *What do you think of when you see a rainbow?*

:: *Pull out a bunch of different colored clothes from your closet. Lay them on the floor in the shape of a rainbow. Think about God's faithfulness while you are making your rainbow.*

:: *Thank God for being so faithful to you.*

JANUARY :: 6

READ EPHESIANS 5:1-2; 6:1-4

Family Ties

Be imitators of God, therefore, as dearly loved children and live a life of love, just as Christ loved us and gave himself up for us as a fragrant offering and sacrifice to God.
EPHESIANS 5:1-2

This week's devotions from Genesis prove that even in Bible times people struggled to get along with their families. Hasn't changed much in a few thousand years, has it?

It might seem hopeless in your house sometimes, but God gave us families so we could take care of each other. Heather struggled with her brothers and sisters—but realized later that she loved them. Zack lied to his parents and was afraid of their response—but found out just how much they cared about him.

"Honor your father and mother..." Ephesians says. "Honoring" can be tough, especially if your mom and dad aren't perfect, which of course they aren't. But neither are you. Think of one thing that your parents need to be honored for. Remember that the Bible tells us to do it—and gives us a nice promise for the future if we follow the instructions.

WHAT ABOUT YOU?

:: *Think of one thing you can do this weekend to help your parents—then do it!*

:: *Ask God to help you remember to see your family as friends who take care of each other. Thank him for giving you people to live with and care about.*

JANUARY :: 7

READ GENESIS 8:20-22

Sacrificial Thanks

Then Noah built an altar to the LORD, and taking some of all the clean animals and clean birds, he sacrificed burnt offerings on it.
GENESIS 8:20

One way people show thanks to someone else is by giving him or her a gift. Noah gave God a thank-you gift. It's called a sacrifice because it means giving up something that's yours that you could use for yourself. Sometimes it's not easy to give things up, but it's a way to show God you appreciate him. Noah gave his best animals and birds to God as an expression of thanks. We can give to God also. We can give our money, time, and talents as thank-you gifts to God.

But we shouldn't give good things or do good stuff to earn God's love or approval—we already have his approval if we accept Jesus' sacrifice. We are made right not by the good stuff we do, but by having true faith in God. So doing good stuff is our way of saying a big thanks!

JANUARY :: 8

READ GENESIS 12:1–7

The Right Move

So Abram left, as the LORD had told him.
GENESIS 12:4

I was really having trouble with some other students at my school, so my parents moved me to a different school. I think God helped my parents make this decision, because changing schools has been one of the best things that's ever happened to me. For once in my life I feel like I belong somewhere, and I'm actually happy to go to school.

Change can be scary, but change can also be really good. We can find the courage to make big changes by knowing God will be with us wherever we go. That's how Abram had the courage to move his family miles and miles away from home. He loved God, and God loved him. Abram knew God only wanted the best for him. God wants the best for every one of us. When we know that, we can be brave enough to do anything.

WHAT ABOUT YOU?

:: *What has been the biggest change in your life in the last year? How did God help you through it?*

:: *Make a timeline showing important changes in your life. Think about how God was with you through each change.*

:: *Thank God for guiding you through life.*

JANUARY :: 9

MARK, AGE 13

READ GENESIS 18:12-14

His Word on It

Is anything too hard for the LORD?
GENESIS 18:14

When my little brother was born prematurely, he had a lot of health problems. One of the major problems was a hole in his heart. I didn't have much faith that God was really in control of the situation, because I was scared my brother might die. But God helped me see that nothing is out of his hands—not even a hole in the heart. Now my brother is 4 years old and doing fine.

I can understand why Sarah, Abraham's wife, doubted that she would have a child. After all, she was 90 years old! In verse 14, he asked Abraham, "Is anything too hard for the LORD?" Then God said he would come back in a year to visit Abraham and Sarah—and their new baby! God wants us to trust him. There are a ton of promises in the Bible that tell us God is in control of every situation. We know that's true, because we have his word on it.

WHAT ABOUT YOU?

:: *Even with all of God's promises in the Bible, why is it sometimes hard to trust God?*

:: *Thank God for taking care of the people and things you're concerned about.*

JANUARY :: 10

READ GENESIS 22:1–18

The Hardest Test

Take your son, your only son, Isaac, whom you love, and go to the region of Moriah. Sacrifice him there as a burnt offering on one of the mountains.
GENESIS 22:2

As a Christian, I need to be brave and obey God no matter what the risk might be. Maybe other kids will make fun of me. Maybe I won't understand what God wants me to do. Maybe I'll have to give up what I want to do because God wants me to do something else. But if Abraham could trust God enough to obey his command about Isaac, I know I can too.

I do need to remember, though, that Abraham had known God a long time already when God tested him with Isaac.... The more time I spend reading my Bible and praying, the more I learn to trust God and follow him. He really does want what's best for me.

WHAT ABOUT YOU?

:: *Think about a time when it was hard to trust in God, but you did it anyway. What did you learn from this experience?*

:: *Memorize Psalm 118:6: "The LORD is with me; I will not be afraid. What can man do to me?" Use it to help you trust God when you are scared.*

:: *Ask God for the strength to trust and obey him no matter what.*

READ GENESIS 27

Biting Off More Than You Can Chew

Jacob said to his father, "I am Esau your firstborn."
GENESIS 27:19

One time my brother ate over half a package of Oreos. When my parents asked him about it, he lied and told them he hadn't eaten the cookies. But finally he told them the truth. As punishment, my parents wouldn't let him eat any dessert for a week. I'm not sure what my brother learned, but I realized that it doesn't pay to deceive people.

In Genesis 27, Jacob pretended to be his older brother Esau so he could get the blessing from their father Isaac. And he did get the blessing! But Jacob lost his brother's trust. In fact, Esau swore he would kill Jacob.

That's the way lying is—in the end, you find yourself stuck in a bigger mess than you know how to get out of. Worst of all, you make God unhappy.

WHAT ABOUT YOU?

:: *When are you tempted to lie or cheat? What can you do to avoid giving in?*

:: *Think of a recent lie you told. What were the consequences, if any? What would have been different if you'd told the truth?*

:: *Ask God to help you be honest, even when it's hard. Thank him for his grace when you make mistakes.*

JANUARY :: 12

JOEL, AGE 13

READ GENESIS 32:22-32

All-star Wrestling

Your name will no longer be Jacob, but Israel, because you have struggled with God and with men and have overcome.
GENESIS 32:28

This past summer, I had a major pain in my left side. My mom thought it might be appendicitis, which would need to be operated on right away, so she rushed me to the doctor.... I was really frustrated with God for letting me be in all this pain.

But then I realized the best thing I could do was pray and ask God to help me. When I got to the doctor's office, they took some X-rays that showed I didn't have appendicitis. They gave me some medicine for the pain and sent me home.

Even though I wanted to fix the situation, I couldn't. The only One who can completely control any-thing is God. Whenever I try to do things my own way, God usually shows me that I have to turn to him with my problems. Just like Jacob wrestled with God and realized God is always in control, it took some pain and fear for me to remember that God's in charge of everything.

WHAT ABOUT YOU?

:: *Have you ever felt like you were "wrestling" with God—trying to make him work things out your way? What happened?*

:: *Ask God to help you give him control of your life.*

JANUARY :: 13

What a Relief

LORD, how many times shall I forgive my brother when he sins against me?
MATTHEW 18:21

Have you ever been wandering around the mall and bumped into someone you treated poorly? You know, that former friend you ditched, only because your other friends thought she was a real loser? So to save face, you dropped the friend you really liked a lot.

A few days ago, Megan talked about the story of Jacob and Esau (remember, the stolen-birthright brothers?). Did you know that Jacob later bumped into his brother Esau in the middle of nowhere? Jacob thought he was going to get the tar beat out of him, but instead Esau embraced him. In that moment Jacob experienced the wonder of forgiveness.

Imagine how it would feel if that former friend in the mall looked at you with forgiveness in her eyes instead of revenge. It would feel good, wouldn't it? Now it's your turn.

WHAT ABOUT YOU?

:: *Who is one person you have been holding a grudge against? What would happen if you chose to forgive that person?*

:: *Write down what you could do or say that would let this person know that you want to forgive them.*

:: *Pray that God will help you forgive that person for the wrong they did to you.*

JANUARY :: 14

The Great Gift

I canceled all that debt of yours because you begged me to. Shouldn't you have had mercy on your fellow servant just as I had on you?
MATTHEW 18:32-33

Have you ever been caught doing something you knew was wrong? That knot you felt in your stomach was your guilt. Adam and Eve were the first people to experience guilt after they ate the fruit from the wrong tree. They hid from God because they knew they were in trouble, and they felt ashamed.

Genesis gets things started: God invents a perfect world, Satan gets the first humans to mess it all up. This book has it all: BIG stuff (creation), BAD stuff (the world's first sin), WET stuff (Noah's cruise), TALL stuff (the Babel Tower disaster), and a lot of really good stuff about God. He never gives up trying to pull us humans back to him.

Jesus came and died so we can be forgiven. This means we don't have to hide from God when we feel guilty; we need to come to him and ask to be forgiven.

In today's passage, Jesus' story of the unforgiving servant gives us some pointed words about forgiving other people. We're supposed to forgive other people over and over and over again. Has anyone ever forgiven you for something you did? Didn't it feel great?

JANUARY :: 15

READ GENESIS 39

Run Away

How then could I do such a wicked thing and sin against God?
GENESIS 39:9

One day I was out skating and I saw these older kids skating nearby. They were awesome skaters! So I went over and started talking to them. They seemed nice and said I could skate with them.

Then they pulled out some weed. It totally shocked me to see these kids smoking marijuana. They asked if I wanted any, and when I said no they started making fun of me and calling me a pansy. I just left. When I read the story of Joseph running away from temptation, I can relate. God is going to be there for us and reward us for doing the right thing.

WHAT ABOUT YOU?

:: Imagine yourself saying no to something you know is wrong. What's the worst thing that could happen? What's the best thing?

:: If you had a glass of Kool-Aid, and you left a piece of paper in it for a minute, what would happen to the paper? How is this an example of what happens when we give in to a "little" temptation?

:: Read 1 Corinthians 10:13. The next time you face temptation, stop, pray, and ask God to show you a way to escape.

JANUARY :: 16

NOAH, AGE 12

Happy Endings

You intended to harm me, but God intended it for good.
GENESIS 50:20

When my grandpa died, I felt like the worst thing in the world had happened. But the more I thought about it, the more I realized God did something great for my grandpa: God ended Grandpa's pain and brought him to heaven. Even though I still miss my grandpa, I know he's happy spending eternity with God.

The story of Joseph is a great example of how God can take a bad situation and bring good out of it. Joseph lost everything—his family, his friends, and his freedom. But God worked through Joseph to help the people of Egypt survive a drought and a famine. Joseph saved thousands of lives. He trusted God the whole time he was a slave. He never forgot that God loved him and was in control of everything. God loves all of us, and he has a purpose for everything that happens.

WHAT ABOUT YOU?

:: *What was one time in your life that God turned something from bad to good?*

:: *When you get your immunization shots, you're actually given a little tiny bit of the bacteria or virus that causes the illness! Think about how bad things can strengthen your relationship with God.*

:: *Ask God to help you trust him when life seems confusing.*

JANUARY :: 17

CHRIS, AGE 12

READ EXODUS 1:22-2:4

Never Fear! God's Here!

She got a papyrus basket...placed the child in it and put it among the reeds along the bank of the Nile.
EXODUS 2:3

One thing the story of Moses proves is that God is always there to help people through hard times. Moses' mother was scared that her baby would be killed, so she sent him down the river in a basket. She probably couldn't have done that if she didn't trust God to take care of her baby.

It's not easy to trust God when you're scared. And fear can make people do things that aren't very smart. When I was really little, my sisters played a trick on me. I was sitting on top of a table when my sisters turned off the lights and ran out of the room. I was so scared that I didn't know what to do. Finally, I decided to jump off the table. I hit the door of our stereo cabinet, which was glass. I ended up needing stitches! I got hurt because I panicked. I would have been fine if I'd stayed calm and called for help.

WHAT ABOUT YOU?

:: What are some things you worry about? Why is it sometimes hard to trust God to take care of the difficult situations in our lives?

:: Ask God to help you trust him always—even in difficult times.

JANUARY :: 18

JULIE, AGE 12

Following God

Who gave man his mouth? Who makes him deaf or mute? Who gives him sight or makes him blind? Is it not I, the LORD?
EXODUS 4:11

When God asked Moses to lead the Israelites out of Egypt, Moses tried to get out of it by using a lame excuse. Moses said he wasn't a good enough speaker to lead God's people. God basically told him that he knew what Moses' mouth could do. After all, he was the One who created it!

God gives us the abilities that we need to obey him, and he'll always be there to help us out when things get tough. "I can't" doesn't cut it with God.

God wants to use all of his children as witnesses for him. So even if I don't think I'm very good at talking with other people about my faith, God still wants me to give it a try. Obeying God might make me feel really uncomfortable sometimes, but I know it's what God wants from me.

WHAT ABOUT YOU?

:: *Why is it sometimes hard to talk with other people about God?*

:: *Make a list of some of your talents. How can you use these to be a witness for God?*

:: *Tell God you're willing to follow him and trust him to give you everything you need to be a witness for him.*

JANUARY :: 19

ANNA, AGE 17

READ EXODUS 16:1-12

No Worries

Then the LORD said to Moses, "I will rain down bread from heaven for you."
EXODUS 16:4

A couple of years ago my dad almost lost his job. Instead of being laid off, his salary was cut big-time. But God provided everything we really needed, like food and shelter. It wasn't the most comfortable time for my family, but we never had to worry about the basics. God had them covered.

    I knew God would provide for us because he always provides for his people. Even when the Israelites whined and complained and disobeyed God's rules about the manna in the desert, God never said, "Well, these people didn't do what I said, so now I'll just let them starve." He kept sending bread in the morning and meat at night. God will always be there for me in hard times like he was with the Israelites. He'll be there for me in good times too. Just knowing how much he loves me makes me want to love him more.

WHAT ABOUT YOU?

:: What do you see that's similar between the Israelites in the desert and your own behavior?

:: Ask some Christian adults (possibly parents or grandparents) to tell you about a time they experienced serious money problems and what God taught them.

JANUARY :: 20

Which Way?

If any of you lacks wisdom, he should ask God, who gives generously to all without finding fault, and it will be given to him.
JAMES 1:5

A few days ago, Noah reminded us in his devotion that God works things out for the best. Later in the week, Chris and Anna talked about trusting God to take care of us. Today James (in the Bible) tells us to do several things, including asking God to give us wisdom.

When we face tough decisions about which direction to go, it's not always obvious to us which road to take. But we still have to make a decision, and trust that God will be with us whatever we decide. Guess what? That's exactly what God does! So if you're facing a decision with no obvious answer, don't choose the option of no decision at all. Ask God for wisdom, then make a choice and trust God for the best!

WHAT ABOUT YOU?

:: *What decision are you struggling with right now? Write down the choices you have. List the good and bad points about each, then write a date by which you have to make a decision. Make sure you go ahead and decide by this date!*

:: *Spend a few moments in prayer asking God for wisdom to help you make a good decision. Then thank him in advance for taking care of you regardless of your choice.*

READ EXODUS 14

Great Escapes

Moses answered the people, "Do not be afraid. Stand firm and you will see the deliverance the LORD will bring you today."
EXODUS 14:13

It's amazing how God got his people out of some really big jams. Like in Exodus 14, when the Israelites were trying to get away from Pharaoh's army. They were backed up to the shore of the Red Sea with nowhere to run. It looked like the end of Israel. But Moses stuck out his staff and the sea split wide open, creating a dry escape route! The Israelites saw their chance and took it. When the Egyptian army came after them, the walls of water crashed down on Pharaoh's soldiers. And that was the end of that.

God was also the master of these great escapes:

>> Jonah escaped drowning by being swallowed by an enormous fish. Before all that fishy stomach acid turned Jonah into fish food, God helped Jonah escape again with the help of a whale of a belch. (Jonah 1:15–2:10)

>> Three buddies escaped becoming toast in a blazing furnace. Their death-defying feat had something to do with a mystery guest who joined them in the oven. (Daniel 3:19–27)

>> Daniel escaped becoming lion food when an angel muzzled the ferocious felines. (Daniel 6:16–22)

WHAT ABOUT YOU?

Can you think of some ways that God has gotten you out of a big jam?

_____

_____

_____

_____

_____

_____

JANUARY :: 22

KATIE, AGE 12

READ EXODUS 20:1-17

God's Cool Rules

I am the LORD your God, who brought you out of Egypt, out of the land of slavery. You shall have no other gods before me.
EXODUS 20:2-3

By giving us the Ten Commandments, God lets us know that he isn't just some guy who sits back and says, "As long as you say you believe in me, you can do whatever you want."

What's really great about God's rules is that they make sense. We don't just have to follow them because he says so, even though that would be good enough reason. Following the Ten Commandments, makes our lives better too.

Like the one about honoring your parents. Life at home is a lot nicer when you obey Mom and Dad, isn't it? Or the commandment about coveting. Coveting just makes you want more and more until you're never satisfied. If you follow God's rules, you don't have to feel that way.

God really does know what's best for us. Obeying his commandments might seem frustrating sometimes, but it'll make us a lot happier in the end.

WHAT ABOUT YOU?

:: *Pick a commandment you have trouble keeping. What's happened when you've chosen not to obey this rule?*

:: *Rewrite the Ten Commandments in your own words and tape up a copy where you'll see it every day.*

:: *Ask God to help you be more obedient.*

J A N U A R Y :: 2 3

JONATHAN, AGE 14

READ EXODUS 32

Get Back Here

When the people saw that Moses was so long in coming down from the mountain, they gathered around Aaron and said, "Come, make us gods who will be before us."
EXODUS 32:1

It's so easy to turn away from God! Sometimes we get impatient, like the Israelites did when they were waiting for Moses to come down from the mountain. Sometimes we get frustrated because God does things his own way instead of the way we want him to. Sometimes we make idols too. Not golden cows! But we worship money, music, sports, trophies, and other "treasures."

God doesn't like it when we turn away from him. But he forgives us if we're sorry for our sins because he understands that we're not perfect. Sinning is part of human nature—even strong Christians can occasionally turn away from God. When we mess up we need to ask God for forgiveness and trust him to help us get back on track. And he will.

WHAT ABOUT YOU?

:: List 5 reasons why you think people your age turn from God.

:: Write a list of things you sometimes put ahead of God. Pray for strength to get rid of these "idols." Now throw the paper away as a sign you're "throwing away" the idols in your life.

:: Ask God to strengthen your faith and help you not turn away from him.

JANUARY :: 24

KEVIN, AGE 13

READ EXODUS 34:29-35

Time to Shine

When Moses came down from Mount Sinai with the two tablets of the Testimony in his hands, he was not aware that his face was radiant because he had spoken with the LORD.
EXODUS 34:29

Talking with God and spending time with him makes us feel radiant, kind of like how it made Moses radiant. People can see we're different when we've been spending time with God. We act different; we think different. If we really want to represent God to our friends, we need to spend quality time with God. I'm not always motivated to read my Bible, but these verses are a great reminder of how much I can change when I take time to really talk to God and listen to what he has to say to me.

WHAT ABOUT YOU?

:: *When was the last time you really spent time with God—not just a quick prayer, but real, quality time with God? How did you feel for the rest of that day?*

:: *What do you think other people see when they look at you? Do they see someone who's excited about life? Do they see someone who knows he or she is loved by God? What can you do to "radiate" God's love?*

:: *Try to pray for a full 10 minutes. Concentrate on really having a conversation with God. Tell him what's going on in your life—what you're worried about, excited about, bored with, whatever.*

JANUARY :: 25

JESSICA, AGE 14

The Scapegoat

He is to cast lots for the two goats.
LEVITICUS 16:8

When my parents got divorced, I felt angry and bitter. I blamed all my hurt on everyone else. I hated the world, and I hated God. Because I didn't think anyone could understand my pain, I just kept it to myself.

In Leviticus 16, God tells Aaron to lay all the blame for the people's sins on one goat—the scapegoat—and let the other one go free. This passage helped me realize that if I had laid all my hurt on Jesus' shoulders instead of carrying it myself, I wouldn't have felt so alone. My heart would have healed a lot faster, and I could have forgiven my parents sooner. We don't have to take everything on ourselves. We can give our burdens to Jesus, and, like the scapegoat, he carries them.

WHAT ABOUT YOU?

:: Why do you try to hide your hurts? What good things can happen when you let others know you're hurting?

:: On a small piece of paper, write down something that's really hurting you. Ask Jesus to take your hurt upon himself. Remember that Jesus knows you and loves you. Thank him for caring about your needs.

:: Tell God about other hurts in your life right now. Ask him to help you heal.

JANUARY :: 26

MELISSA, AGE 16

READ LEVITICUS 19:3; EPHESIANS 6:1–3

A Little Respect

Each of you must respect his mother and father.
LEVITICUS 19:3

Everyone knows that God expects us to obey and honor our parents. But it's not always easy. When my mom and I fight, it's so tempting for me to yell at her. But whenever I do, I get in more trouble than if I would have shown her respect.

God put us in our families for a reason. Even when I'm having a hard time getting along with my mom, I have to remember that she is one of God's blessings to me. Yeah, sometimes it seems like my parents must be a "blessing in disguise," but the truth is, God knows what he's doing and can teach us a lot through our relationships with our parents. I think the most important thing I've learned is that obeying my mom is a lot like obeying God: It might not always be what I want, but it's what's best for me.

WHAT ABOUT YOU?

:: Think about some people in your life who deserve respect. What is one way you can show respect to others?

:: Thank God for your parents.

JANUARY :: 27

READ EXODUS 20:2-3

Time for the Rules

You shall have no other gods before me.
EXODUS 20:3

Earlier Katie wrote "God's rules make sense" and went on to say that obeying God's commandments will "make us happier in the end." Katie is one sharp cookie! She understands a tough idea.

Most of us, at least sometimes, don't *feel* like God's laws and rules make sense. You know those times—when you know that lying will keep you out of trouble with your parents. Or when looking at the smartest kid's paper during a test will help you pass. Or when talking behind someone else's back is really fun. These are the times when it is easier, and sometimes more fun, to do the wrong thing.

Katie was right, especially when you think of life in terms of the long run. Over time, you'll be far happier and have better friendships if you trust the only true God to teach you how to live.

WHAT ABOUT YOU?

:: What is the hardest thing for you about trusting and obeying God's commandments?

:: Which of the Ten Commandments is the toughest for you to follow? Talk to someone you trust and ask them to help you find some ways you can do better at obeying it.

:: As you pray, ask God to help you obey that commandment.

JANUARY :: 28

READ EXODUS 13:13; NUMBERS 6:22-27

Bought and Blessed

The LORD bless you and keep you; the LORD make his face shine upon you and be gracious to you; the LORD turn his face toward you and give you peace.

NUMBERS 6:24-26

In the days of slavery, some people bought slaves just so they could set them free. In the same way, the Israelites bought their firstborn sons back from God. The sacrifice of a lamb was the price that needed to be paid. Did you know God bought us also? We would be separated from him forever if he hadn't paid the price for us. He sacrificed his Son, Jesus, as a payment for us so we could have freedom and a relationship with him.

Not only has he bought us, he has also blessed us. The word bless means "to give a good word." This blessing is still used today as God's "good words" to us. God is doing those things for you right now. God is talking about you ("bless you") and is making sure you are being protected ("keep you"). God is even shining on you, and being cool ("gracious") to you. He's looking right at you, right now, and he's trying to give you a deep, inside calm. Wow! Do you feel his blessing?

JANUARY :: 29

Whiner Warning

Why is the LORD bringing us to this land only to let us fall by the sword?... Wouldn't it be better for us to go back to Egypt?
NUMBERS 14:3

Imagine that you're trying to plan a fun game for some little kids. But before the game even starts, the kids start complaining that it's taking too long and the game's going to be dumb anyway. Pretty soon nobody's having any fun at all. If the kids would have just trusted you to make the game fun, they could have had a great time. But their bad attitudes ruined the whole thing.

God had a plan for the Israelites too, but they ruined it with their whining and complaining. To punish them, God didn't let any of the complainers see the land he had promised them!

If we have the same bad attitude today, we can miss the good stuff God wants for us. Even when it seems like we have a lot to complain about, we need to trust that God will work everything out the best way possible.

WHAT ABOUT YOU?

:: Why is complaining so easy? Why do you think God doesn't like it?

:: Think of something you really don't like—cleaning your room, doing homework, babysitting your little brother, whatever. Then write down 5 good things about it.

:: Ask God to help you resist complaining.

JANUARY :: 30

Keep Your Cool

Balaam answered the donkey, "You have made a fool of me! If I had a sword in my hand, I would kill you right now."
NUMBERS 22:29

This passage reminds me of the time one of my teachers embarrassed me in front of the whole class. I misspelled a word on a test. When she handed back the test, she said, "Jeremiah, come here and spell this word correctly." Well, I got so angry, I just sat at my desk and wrote "I hate this teacher!" over and over again in my notebook. Instead of just calmly fixing my error, I let my embarrassment turn into anger and made a big deal out of nothing.

Balaam did the same thing. When his donkey wouldn't stay on the path, he got embarrassed and then angry. Instead of just staying calm, he hit his donkey and made a big fool of himself.

The next time I get embarrassed, I hope I can remember this story and stay calm. That's a whole lot better than acting foolish like Balaam did.

WHAT ABOUT YOU?

:: How do you usually handle embarrassing situations? Does your reaction make the situation better or worse?

:: Think back to the last time you were really embarrassed. What could you have done differently, and what would the result of that have been?

:: Ask God to help you stay calm when you feel embarrassed.

JANUARY :: 31

WADE, AGE 13

READ DEUTERONOMY 3:21-29

Judgment? No Joke!

Look at the land with your own eyes, since you are not going to cross the Jordan.
DEUTERONOMY 3:27

Wherever Moses and the Israelites went, they disobeyed God and suffered the consequences. Take Moses. He didn't even get to see the Promised Land. Things really haven't changed much since then. There's plenty of sin at my school. It's everywhere! Lucky for me, I don't have to fight sin by myself. Only God can do that. What I can do is help people to know that Jesus will forgive their sins if they ask him to. People who learn about Jesus and become Christians don't have to think the end of the story is God's judgment. Sure, God doesn't like it when Christians mess up, and sometimes he lets them suffer the consequences for their choices, but he is always merciful if we ask his forgiveness.

People who live without faith in God have a lot to fear. People who live with faith in God have a lot to be thankful for. I know I'm thankful. Are you?

WHAT ABOUT YOU?

:: *Why do you think God is such a good judge?*

:: *Confess your sins to God and thank him for the forgiveness you have through Jesus.*

READ DEUTERONOMY 6:4–9

The Best Kind of Studying

These commandments that I give you today are to be upon your hearts.... Talk about them when you sit at home and when you walk along the road, when you lie down and when you get up.
DEUTERONOMY 6:6–7

If you're a Christian, it makes sense that you'd want to learn as much as you could about Jesus Christ and his Word. You can do that by talking about the Bible with your friends and family, writing down verses or memorizing them. You can also learn by going to church and listening to what your pastor or youth leader says.

Think about it—of all the things you learn in your life, what's the most important? It's not algebra or biology! Although studying these subjects is important and necessary, the most important thing is to know who God is and what he wants you to do in your life. And the more you learn about him, the more you feel secure and have strength for whatever challenges you have to face. Reading the Bible is the best kind of studying!

WHAT ABOUT YOU?

:: *Think of a time you really enjoyed reading the Bible. What made you so excited about it?*

:: *Write down your favorite verse from the Bible. Then put it someplace where you'll see it every day.*

:: *Thank God for giving us the Bible.*

JENNIFER, AGE 13

READ DEUTERONOMY 8:10-18

Thankfulness

Praise the LORD your God for the good land he has given you.
DEUTERONOMY 8:10

What do you do when your mom comes home from the store with groceries? Look through the bags for your favorite snack? Maybe, if you're in the right mood, help her put things away? Do you ever stop to say "thank you"? I know I hardly ever do.

There must be days when my mom really doesn't want to go to the store. But she does it anyway—she gives up what she wants to help me out. And then I forget to even say thank you.

I don't do much better when it comes to thanking God. I mean, God's the One who gave me so many good things. By thanking God for everything he's done, I'll also get better at thanking other people, starting with my mom. She'll be so surprised!

WHAT ABOUT YOU?

:: *How do you feel when someone thanks you?*

:: *Think of 3 people who help you a lot. Say "thank you" to them this week.*

:: *Thank God for all the ways he helps you.*

FEBRUARY :: 3

READ NUMBERS 22:29–34

About-face

Balaam said to the angel of the LORD, "I have sinned. I did not realize you were standing in the road to oppose me. Now if you are displeased, I will go back."
NUMBERS 22:34

In an earlier devotion, Jeremiah helped us see, from Balaam's story, that it's important to keep calm and ride out the storm when we get embarrassed.

But there is more to the story of Balaam. God knew that Balaam had a hidden agenda. When Balaam saw God's angel, he "fell facedown."

Think about it: Why would Balaam fall down on his face? Do you think he just tripped? No, Balaam knew his own motives weren't pure, and he was afraid and ashamed and felt trapped. When God reminded him, Balaam was truly sorry, and God sent him on his way once again.

When you are selfish or embarrassed or angry, God wants to get your attention. The key is to be willing to admit you're wrong when you blow it. God will always help you when you sincerely ask him to.

WHAT ABOUT YOU?

:: Do you sometimes have a hard time admitting when you're wrong? If so, when?

:: See if you can think of one wrong thing you have done that you feel a little bit bad about. Is there someone you can ask to help you make the wrong right?

:: Ask God to bring to mind any wrong you have done and then ask his forgiveness.

FEBRUARY :: 4

READ DEUTERONOMY 2:14-15; 11:1

"Obey"—That Dirty Word

Love the LORD your God and keep his requirements, his decrees, his laws and his commands always.
DEUTERONOMY 11:1

God promised the Israelites a new land and a new life. He showed them the land and told them to go for it. But the people were afraid. They were more afraid of doing what God told them to do than they were afraid of God himself. That made God ticked. He knew what he was doing, but the people were too scared and stubborn to trust him.

The people told God, "Forget it—we're not going into that scary land!" (Even the toughest dudes were shaking in their boots!) So God said, "Fine! Whatever! I'll make you guys walk around for 40 years, and I'll wait until you guys croak; then I'll give your kids the choicest lots around."

When you have to obey someone, doesn't it make your skin crawl? Maybe that's because we think obeying means we don't matter and don't have any say. But when God tells us to obey him, he means that he wants us to love him. The big part about loving God is trusting that he knows what he's doing. To obey God is cool, because his way of living is the best, most awesome, and greatest way to live.

FEBRUARY :: 5

READ DEUTERONOMY 16:1-8

A Major Celebration

Celebrate the Passover of the LORD your God, because...he brought you out of Egypt by night.
DEUTERONOMY 16:1

If there's one thing we don't do enough of, it's celebrating. Think of all the things God has done for us: He provides us with food, a place to live, people who love us, and, best of all, life with him forever. That's a lot to be excited about!

God has given us so much, and he wants us to thank him for it. How? By celebrating! God wants us to enjoy his goodness and remember how much he's done for us. When we do, we will start to feel happier about life. And when we think about all God has done for us, we'll want to start doing things for other people too.

After all, who wants to celebrate alone?

WHAT ABOUT YOU?

:: *Think about some of the things God has done for you. Why is it so easy to take those things for granted? What would your life be like without God's many gifts?*

:: *Make a top 10 list of what you're thankful for, then party with some of God's wonderful gifts—yummy food, awesome music, and great friends.*

:: *Write a thank-you note to God, praising him for all he's given you.*

FEBRUARY :: 6

ASHLEY, AGE 14

Rebel Child

Then all the men of his town shall stone him to death.
DEUTERONOMY 21:21

Before I moved to California, I chose some wrong friends and did some things I knew I was not supposed to do. I tried drugs and alcohol, I hardly came home, and I was a D student. When my parents told me to do something, I would never do it.

These verses remind me that rebellion is a big deal in God's eyes. In Old Testament times, a rebellious child could be stoned to death by a whole town! I know that would never happen to me, but it sure makes me think twice about not obeying my parents.

Avoiding punishment is one reason why I obey my parents, but it's not the biggest one. Rebelling against my parents is sin—it's not what God wants me to do. Thinking about it that way helps. I want to obey my parents because I want to obey Jesus.

WHAT ABOUT YOU?

:: Why do you think obeying your parents is so important to God?

:: Try to see your parents' rules from their side. If you honestly don't get the reasons for some of them, ask your parents to help you understand.

:: Thank God for your parents and ask him to help you obey them.

FEBRUARY :: 7

KENT, AGE 13

READ DEUTERONOMY 24:19-22

Care and Share

When you harvest the grapes in your vineyard, do not go over the vines again. Leave what remains for the alien, the fatherless and the widow.
DEUTERONOMY 24:21

When I'm eating lunch in the cafeteria, sometimes I see that someone else has forgotten their lunch or forgotten to bring money to buy one. Often I think, If *I share my lunch, then I'll be hungry later.* But that's really no excuse. If I *don't* share my lunch, then the other kid will definitely be hungry later. I need to think about other people, because God cares for them as much as he cares for me. And if God cares, I should care too.

There are actually lots of good things that can come from sharing with other people. Once I start caring for people who have less than I do, I bet I'll want to do it more. And maybe other people will watch what I'm doing, and they'll want to do their part too.

WHAT ABOUT YOU?

:: Why does God want us to help take care of people who are less fortunate than we are?

:: Put an extra something in your lunch tomorrow—an orange, chips, even a candy bar. Look for a person you could give it to in the lunchroom. Make their day!

:: Ask God to help you be more generous.

FEBRUARY :: 8

DAN, AGE 14

READ JOSHUA 1:1-9

Strong on Faith

Be strong and very courageous.
JOSHUA 1:7

I think a lot about my future. For instance, I really want to go to a good college. But to do that, I have to get great grades from now on. That means I have to work hard in school.

The problem is that I have a bad habit of watching too much TV. And when I watch TV, I don't get my homework done. If I don't get my homework done, I don't get good grades. See the problem?

God doesn't want me to be lazy or waste my brain. He wants me to do what's right, whether that's doing my best in school or following his commandments in other parts of my life.

God gave us the Ten Commandments so that we'd know how to live. He wants us to be strong in our faith and work hard at living by his commands.

WHAT ABOUT YOU?

:: What are some things that hold you back from living your faith to the max?

:: Ask your youth leader to help you make a plan for overcoming the things that hold you back.

:: Ask God to help you be strong and courageous about your faith.

FEBRUARY :: 9

SCOTT, AGE 13

READ JOSHUA 4:4-9

Nothing's Impossible

In the future, when your children ask you, "What do these stones mean?" tell them that the flow of the Jordan was cut off before the ark of the covenant of the LORD.... These stones are to be a memorial to the people of Israel forever.

JOSHUA 4:6-7

Sometimes I'm afraid to talk to my friends about God. Some of them just seem like they're not interested at all. But these verses make one thing clear: If God can stop a raging river, he can definitely change a person's heart.

Joshua wanted his men to get stones from the Jordan River so they would remember God's power. The stones were a reminder of what God had done in the past...and a promise of what God could do in the future.

When something seems impossible, we only have to look at the "impossible" things God did throughout history to know that God can take care of anything.

WHAT ABOUT YOU?

:: *Name something God did for you this week. Now take a little more time and think about what God has done for you in the past month and year.*

:: *Now that you have those things in mind, write 'em down. Tuck that into the book of Joshua. Think of it as your own personal history of God's faithfulness. Look at it every time something seems "impossible."*

_____

_____

_____

_____

_____

_____

FEBRUARY :: 10

Rules = Gifts?

Do not deprive the alien or the fatherless of justice.
DEUTERONOMY 24:17

We have looked at celebrating life, honoring parents, giving to others, being strong in our faith and remembering that nothing is impossible with God. God's laws are really all about celebrating, loving, honoring, caring, and trusting him.

The verse above reminds us that we have this little tendency to clobber each other whenever it suits us. But God wants us to know how much he cares, *especially* for those who are the most beaten-down and sad. Just like God knew about the Israelites' trouble when they were in Egypt, he knows you sometimes feel down. God cares for you, and he knows your troubles. So, when you think of the rules in the Bible, remember that they are a great gift. They're one of the ways God helps you to know that he really cares about you.

WHAT ABOUT YOU?

:: *Is it hard for you to think of the rules and laws in the Bible as a gift? Why or why not?*

:: *Can you remember a time when you were really sad or lonely or scared? How does it help to know God cares about you, especially when you are feeling like that?*

:: *Pray for someone in your life who needs God's loving care right now.*

FEBRUARY :: 11

READ JOSHUA 6:1-20

Wacky Weapons

When the trumpets sounded, the people shouted, and...the wall collapsed; so every man charged straight in, and they took the city.
JOSHUA 6:20

Okay, you're a soldier guarding the city walls of Jericho. Say you look over the wall one day and see a bunch of guys marching around, making a lot of noise with their old beat-up horns. *Oooh, scary!* you'd think to yourself while laughing at the horn-blowing hacks. But then something weird happens: The wall you are guarding starts to crumble, and you're face to face with a brassed-off horn player. Now who's laughing?

Trumpets aren't the only weird weapons you'll find in the Bible. Check out the following war stories:

>> Samson used foxes and torches to scare away the Philistines. (Judges 15:3–5)

>> Gideon used trumpets, torches, and jars to whup a huge army of Midianites. (Judges 7:16–21)

>> Jael used a glass of milk and a tent peg to take out the commander of the enemy army. (Judges 4:18–21)

>> Samson wielded a donkey's jawbone to kill a thousand men. (Judges 15:15)

>> Moses used his stick (and God's power!) to drown the Egyptians in the Red Sea. (Exodus 14:19–31)

Thank God for using the weak and unlikely to do the impossible.

FEBRUARY :: 12

READ JOSHUA 24:14–15

Who's Number One?

Now fear the LORD and serve him with all faithfulness.
JOSHUA 24:14

Sometimes people get so obsessed with something they like—an object, a sport, a famous person, or whatever—that they just don't leave time for God. For example, a guy in my small group at church told us he was so into skateboarding that his relationship with God was slipping. He realized he had to change some of his priorities. That got me thinking about my own favorite activities, and I realized I had to make some changes too.

Just like people in Joshua's day, people today have a choice of who or what is number one in their lives. If we seek God first, everything else will fall into place the way God wants it to.

God makes it very clear that we should live our lives for him, above anything or anyone else. Joshua put God first in his life. Have you?

WHAT ABOUT YOU?

:: *Why do you think it's so tempting to live for something or someone other than God?*

:: *Draw a picture of a clock. For each hour of the day, write down one thing you can do to show God he's your top priority.*

:: *Tell God you want to put him first, and ask him to help you do that.*

FEBRUARY :: 13

JON, AGE 14

READ JUDGES 4

No Problem Is Too Big

At Barak's advance, the LORD routed Sisera and all his chariots and army by the sword, and Sisera abandoned his chariot and fled on foot.
JUDGES 4:15

There have been some times in my life when I thought a situation was totally hopeless. One time my dog ran away. Since we live in a big city, I thought I'd never see him again. I prayed about the situation, but I wasn't very hopeful.

A few days later, I heard a report on the radio that someone had found my dog. I couldn't believe it! Just when I was about to give up, God came through and brought him back.

Okay, maybe that's nothing compared to the way God defeated Sisera's army in this chapter. And I know that even if my dog had never come back, God would still have been in control. But I think it's pretty clear that God can do anything. No barriers are too great for him to overcome, and no problems are too small for him to care about. Things don't always go the way we think they should. But God promises he always has a plan.

WHAT ABOUT YOU?

:: Name 2 or 3 situations when you've felt hopeless. How did God help you get through them?

:: Write yourself a letter describing something that's challenging you right now. Next month at this time, open the letter and think about the ways God has helped you with your situation.

:: Thank God for helping you deal with life's challenges.

FEBRUARY :: 14

ROBYN, AGE 13

READ JUDGES 6:11-16

Who, Me?

When the angel of the LORD appeared to Gideon, he said, "The LORD is with you, mighty warrior."
JUDGES 6:12

When I started 7th grade last year, I felt that God was telling me to be a witness for him at my school. The thought of that scared me to death! After all, I was struggling with my own Christian life.

Even if we don't know what it is or how we can possibly do it, God has a job for each of us. Gideon thought of himself as the least important person in all of Israel, but God used him to lead his country to victory. It was difficult for Gideon to believe he could be used by God in such an awesome way, but God kept his word.

Sometimes I find it hard to believe that God can use me to spread the word about his love, but stories like Gideon's remind me that God can—and does—use all of us!

WHAT ABOUT YOU?

:: *Think of a time when God helped you accomplish something you didn't think you could do. Thank him for that experience.*

:: *Do you have a friend who feels like he or she is failing at something? Encourage your friend to look to God for help.*

:: *Remember the story of Gideon, and tell God you're willing to go wherever he leads you.*

FEBRUARY :: 15

DAN, AGE 14

God Is #1

So he told her everything. "No razor has ever been used on my head," he said, "because I have been a Nazirite set apart to God since birth. If my head were shaved, my strength would leave me."
JUDGES 16:17

When I read the story of Samson and Delilah, I get frustrated with Samson. He puts his own desires in front of God's plans for him. And you can see where that gets him—weak, blind, and eventually dead!

The really frustrating part is that I do kind of the same thing. One of my biggest struggles is with my possessions. Sometimes they become more important to me than God. But when I think of them as gifts from him, it's a lot easier for me to put God first.

God and Samson had a special bond, even though Samson messed that up when he told Delilah. I know God has a special bond with me too, and with all of his people. When I make God first in my life, that bond stays strong.

WHAT ABOUT YOU?

:: Think about a time when you've made something else more important than God. What happened? How did you feel?

:: Make a list of things that are important to you. What can you do to make sure God is always first on your list?

:: Pray that God will help you make him the most important part of your life.

FEBRUARY :: 16

READ RUTH 1:16-18

I'm Going Too

Don't urge me to leave you or to turn back from you. Where you go I will go, and where you stay I will stay. Your people will be my people and your God my God.

RUTH 1:16

In this passage, Ruth is explaining to Naomi that she loves her and will stick with her through thick and thin. Now that's a great friend!

Not long ago, I heard a rumor about a friend of mine. People said she was talking about me behind my back. That really upset me and made me mad. I guess I believed the rumor about my friend without even stopping to think it might not be true. She had always stuck with me and been nice to me. There was no reason for me to doubt her friendship, except for this false rumor.

A real friend is a friend forever, not just for a summer or until you get out of the class you have together. And a real friend is loyal and faithful. God is that kind of friend. He never leaves us. Ruth understood this kind of faithfulness. I think that's why she wanted to do for Naomi what God had done for her.

WHAT ABOUT YOU?

:: Think about 2 of your closest friends. What do you like about them? What do you think they like about you?

:: Thank God for faithful friends.

FEBRUARY :: 17

READ RUTH 3:1–6

"Whatever You Say..."

"I will do whatever you say," Ruth answered.
RUTH 3:5

We have been learning about trusting and obeying God. Carissa wrote that "we should live our lives for him," and Robyn reminded us that "God has a job for each of us." But obeying someone else is hard. The older you get, the more you want to make your own decisions, your own friends, and your own plans.

But look at Ruth. She left home and married into a family in a new land. Her husband died. Then her brother-in-law, the last man in the family (really, really important in those days), kicked the bucket too. Even her sister-in-law ended up leaving. So Ruth was left with Naomi, her mother-in-law.

The quality that has made Ruth such a well-known and deeply loved heroine of the Bible was her willingness to listen to and obey Naomi. If Ruth hadn't listened to Naomi, she would never have met Boaz, her future husband (who was a totally cool guy, by the way!).

Sometimes the best way to obey God is to obey your parents (ouch).

WHAT ABOUT YOU?

:: *Make a commitment to try total obedience (no arguing or grumbling) for one week! Just try it!*

:: *Pray for your parents (or guardian), and ask God to give you the ability to listen to them and to do what they say.*

FEBRUARY :: 18

READ RUTH 4:13-22

A Great Story

The women living there said, "Naomi has a son." And they named him Obed. He was the father of Jesse, the father of David.
RUTH 4:17

When Ruth married Boaz, she became a member of his tribe—Judah. It was a pretty popular tribe. Eventually it became the name of the whole country and rubbed off on the names of the region (Judea), religion (Judaism), and the people themselves (Jews).

Judah also became the royal tribe. Starting with Ruth's great-grandson David, most of the nation's kings came from this bloodline. Many centuries after David died, when the kingless Jews were being bullied by the Romans, they were hoping and praying for someone to rescue them like David did. They were looking for a king. To them, that meant someone from the tribe of Judah. They were looking for a descendant of David.

And that's exactly where King Jesus came from! Jesus' mom was married to Joseph, a great-great-great-...(you get the point) grandson of King David himself. And just to make sure no one missed the significance of this fact, God made sure that Jesus was born right when Joseph and Mary just happened to be visiting Bethlehem, the city of David, the capital of the good old tribe of Judah, right where Ruth and Boaz fell in love. Pretty amazing, isn't it?

READ 1 SAMUEL 1

Someone Who Really Listens

I prayed for this child, and the LORD has granted me what I asked of him.
1 SAMUEL 1:27

A few months ago, I was praying for my friend Annie. She had a serious back problem called scoliosis, and she was scared she might have to have surgery.

Well, a few weeks later, Annie's back started to get better. We were at camp and people were praying for her. The pain she'd felt for months started to go away. Now she doesn't have to have surgery, and she feels so much better.

That whole experience proved to me that God really does answer prayers. We're not talking to a brick wall when we pray—we're talking to Someone who really listens.

WHAT ABOUT YOU?

:: In this chapter, Hannah tells God she's sad and angry. When was the last time you were completely honest with God? Why do you think we are sometimes afraid to ask God for what we really want?

:: For the next few days write down the things you pray about. Keep those notes handy. Whenever you feel like God has answered one of your prayers—and the answer might be no—write that down on the same list. (Remember, you might not be able to check everything off your list—God works in his time, not ours.)

:: Think of your prayers as a chance to be really honest with God about what you want out of life. Then trust God to give you his best.

FEBRUARY :: 20

MICHELLE, AGE 14

Believe It or Not

Now appoint a king to lead us, such as all the other nations have.
1 SAMUEL 8:5

About a year ago, I had doubts about my faith. I would always be asking myself, *Is God really real? And if he is, why doesn't he ever show me signs of him being here?*

The Israelites felt sort of the same way. They wanted an earthly king, just like the other nations. They didn't have enough faith to believe that God was the best ruler for them. God quickly reminded them that he is the ultimate King, the only ruler Israel needed.

I think that all of us wonder where God is sometimes. We want someone we can see. But God wants us to trust him and have faith in him, even when we can't see him.

WHAT ABOUT YOU?

:: Have you ever felt like God wasn't around? How did God eventually let you know that wasn't the case?

:: For the next week, watch the weather. Think about how God is like the moon; some days he's easy to see, some days he's not, but no matter what, he's always there.

:: Ask God to help you see him working in your life.

READ 1 SAMUEL 16:7-13

Looks Don't Count

Man looks at the outward appearance, but the LORD looks at the heart.
1 SAMUEL 16:7

A new kid came to our school last year, and he was a little on the heavy side. No one gave him a chance to show what kind of person he was; instead, everyone judged him by his weight. Unfortunately, I did too. Later in the year, many of us got to know him better, and he turned out to be really cool. I felt so guilty about the way we acted earlier, and I wish we hadn't judged him because of his appearance.

I'm sure everybody has treated someone unfairly at one time or another. And most of us can be kind of shallow and sometimes judge people by how they look. But God is never shallow. He cares about all of us—not because of what we look like, but because of who we are.

WHAT ABOUT YOU?

:: *Try to remember a time you judged someone unfairly because of the way they looked. How did you feel about it later?*

:: *Flip through your school yearbook. Pay special attention to all the different kinds of people you see. Why do you think God made each person unique?*

:: *Thank God for the unique way he's made you. Thank him for the way he's made other people too.*

FEBRUARY :: 22

AMY, AGE 14

READ 1 SAMUEL 18:1-4

Friends Forever

Jonathan became one in spirit with David, and he loved him as himself.
1 SAMUEL 18:1

David and Jonathan had a great friendship that lasted because they truly loved God and each other. They went through some hard times together, but their friendship stayed strong.

My best friend and I have a relationship based on the Lord too. I'd do anything for her, and she feels the same about me. I know she'll warn me if I'm doing something I shouldn't. I know she'll help me grow in my faith. And I know she'll always tell me the truth about myself, even when I don't want to hear it.

Being a good friend means treating her with love and respect. It means not letting jealousy or little arguments come between us. Being a friend means loving my friend as much as I love myself. Sure, we have fights and don't always agree on everything. But because we both love God, we know we need to love each other too. That helps our friendship grow, even through difficult times.

WHAT ABOUT YOU?

:: *Think of some hard times you've been through with your friends. How did you get through them?*

:: *Is there someone you know who needs a good friend? What is one thing you can do to reach out to that person?*

:: *Ask God to help you be more loving, patient, and caring toward your friends.*

FEBRUARY :: 23

CHIP, AGE 16

READ 1 SAMUEL 24:1-13

Don't Fight Back

May the LORD judge between you and me. And may the LORD avenge the wrongs you have done to me, but my hand will not touch you.
1 SAMUEL 24:12

When some guys from school smashed my car window and stole my guitar, CD player, and all my CDs, fighting back was exactly what I wanted to do. My friends even told me to find those guys and beat them up. It sure seemed like they deserved it!

In the passage for today, I know David must have been tempted to get Saul back for his evil deeds. After all, Saul had gathered 3,000 men to hunt David down—and this wasn't the first time he had tried to kill David. But David knew God wanted him to forgive Saul, and that's exactly what David did.

I was really angry when those guys at school trashed my car and took my things. But I didn't try to beat them up. And since they didn't hurt me, I decided not to press charges as long as they returned my stuff. It was up to God, not me, to do what he wanted with those guys. My job was to forgive.

WHAT ABOUT YOU?

:: Is there someone you need to forgive? Even if that person hasn't apologized to you, make a point of offering him or her your forgiveness as soon as you can.

:: Ask God to help you forgive people who hurt you.

FEBRUARY :: 24

READ 1 SAMUEL 20

Best Buds

Jonathan said to David, "Whatever you want me to do, I'll do for you."
1 SAMUEL 20:4

You've read about the incredible friendship between David and Jonathan. Jonathan's dad, Saul, hated David. Saul was jealous of David's looks, popularity, and the way people treated him. So Jonathan was torn between his dad and his best friend. When push came to shove, Jonathan proved to be a really committed friend and even helped David to trying to talk Dad out of murder.

Life is tough, and there are so many "enemies" around (enemies like loneliness, fear, distrust, to name a few) that we all need a good friend. The Bible gives us a great picture of what a friend is—not just someone to help you out, but someone you can help. Sometimes your friends need you a lot more than you need them (in today's passage David sure needed Jonathan more than Jonathan needed David!). And that's okay, because we all go through times when we need somebody to come through for us and don't have much to give back.

Let David and Jonathan teach you what it means to be a great friend.

WHAT ABOUT YOU?

:: What are the top 5 things you want and need in a friend? Now ask yourself whether you are that kind of friend to others.

:: Pray for your friends, asking God to help you be better friends to each other.

FEBRUARY :: 25

READ 1 SAMUEL 3:4-10

Hello, This Is God

The LORD came and stood there, calling as at the other times, "Samuel! Samuel!" Then Samuel said, "Speak, for your servant is listening."
1 SAMUEL 3:10

Would you recognize God's voice if he spoke to you? Do you expect the telephone to ring, or to receive an e-mail? Or maybe you check to see what's going on at www.God.com? Look at verses 4 through 10 and see how God called Samuel. It's comforting to see that even Samuel didn't know God's voice at first. But he learned to hear from God and became his mouthpiece.

Up to this point, God acted as Israel's King as he spoke through the prophet Samuel. But the Israelites wanted to be like everyone else. They wanted a human king—you know, the crown, the velvet robe, the whole works. They just didn't realize they already had the King of Kings. Soon they had a king who wasn't as interested in listening to their true King as he should have been.

Samuel's instructions were simple—destroy all the Amalekites and every single thing they own. The Amalekites were a group of raiders who attacked Moses unprovoked. God had declared that they were to be wiped out (see Exodus 17:8-16), but Saul spared their king and the best of their livestock.

WHAT ABOUT YOU?

:: *Tell about a time you felt you heard from God.*

_____

_____

_____

_____

_____

_____

_____

FEBRUARY :: 26

KELLY, AGE 15

READ 2 SAMUEL 12:1-14

Sin's Baggage

Then David said to Nathan, "I have sinned against the LORD."
2 SAMUEL 12:13

A few weeks ago, a family friend committed suicide. As I sat at the funeral, I saw this person's family crying in the front row of the church. The pain they felt was incredible, and they'll have it for the rest of their lives. His family has to live with the consequences of what he did.

King David's story is about living with sin's consequences. He slept with another man's wife, got her pregnant, then had her husband killed. David repented and was forgiven, but he still had to live with the results of his sin. And those results were awfully painful.

Sometimes people think sin is no big deal. They figure they can do what they want, ask for forgiveness and be off the hook with God. But every sin has consequences.

The story of David makes me think about my own decisions. If I do something I shouldn't, I know God will forgive me if I ask him to. But I also know I'll have to live with the consequences, no matter how painful they might be.

WHAT ABOUT YOU?

:: Is there someone you've hurt in the past? What can you do to help heal your relationship?

:: Are there sins you need to be forgiven for? Tell God you're sorry and ask for his forgiveness

FEBRUARY :: 27

DERRICK, AGE 13

READ 2 SAMUEL 18:9–18

Too Stuck-up

I just saw Absalom hanging in an oak tree.
2 SAMUEL 18:10

I remember when we were playing another school in basketball. The first time we'd played them I had a great game and scored somewhere between 15 and 20 points. But when it was time for the second game, I was full of pride and played cocky. I ended up with 4 or 6 points, and we lost by about 25.

Absalom had a different problem: He was stuck-up about his appearance, especially his hair. He must have been growing it out for a long time if he had enough of it to get caught in a tree. He probably thought he looked all handsome until he was hanging in midair. Then I bet he looked pretty stupid.

No matter what it is you're overly proud about, that attitude's going to hurt you eventually. Besides, pride is totally opposite from what God wants us to be like. He wants us to be humble and not draw attention or glory to ourselves. Instead, we should glorify him.

WHAT ABOUT YOU?

:: *Make a small sign that says GOD'S GIFTS and stick it on your mirror. Remember that everything you see in the mirror is a gift from God and should be used to glorify him.*

:: *Ask God to help you get rid of any pride in your heart.*

FEBRUARY :: 28

READ 2 SAMUEL 23:8-23

The A-team

So the three mighty men broke through the Philistine lines, drew water from the well near the gate of Bethlehem and carried it back to David.... Such were the exploits of the three mighty men.

2 SAMUEL 23:16-17

I wish I had read this passage last year when I was cut from the basketball team. I was crushed then, but now I know that God can use me even if I'm not the best at everything—even when I feel like the biggest loser, and I'm sure I'm not skilled at anything. Even then he can use me.

Just look at David's mighty men. They did all kinds of great deeds and became famous. But I doubt that they were always that way. I bet some of them even got cut from their high school, uhh, warrior team. But it didn't keep them down.

My name, Laura, means "victorious." And that's the way God sees me. I may never be a star basketball player, but I'll always have a place in his lineup.

WHAT ABOUT YOU?

:: You probably aren't great at everything (no one is), but you're probably good at 1 or 2 things. What is something you do well?

:: What does your name mean? Look it up. Why is your name important? Remember, God knows you by name, and he has a plan just for you.

:: Ask God to help you discover and develop your talents.

FEBRUARY :: 29

READ 1 KINGS 3:5-15

Wise Guy

I am only a little child and do not know how to carry out my duties.... So give your servant a discerning heart to govern your people and to distinguish between right and wrong.
1 KINGS 3:7, 9

If God ever came to me and said I could have anything I wanted, I sure hope I'd ask for wisdom like Solomon did. He wanted to be a good king who would follow God and make good decisions. God gave Solomon just what he asked for and a lot more: God made Solomon the wisest man who ever lived, plus one of the richest and most honored.

All of us could use a little more wisdom. Most people have a hard time making good decisions, and a lot of Christians struggle to follow God. When we ask God to help us grow closer to him and live for him, he'll give us exactly what we need to do it.

WHAT ABOUT YOU?

- *Be honest. If you could ask God for anything, what would you want? How would getting that thing help you follow God?*

- *When you have trouble making a decision, create a "Pro and Con" list. By studying both lists, you'll probably have a good idea of what to do.*

- *Ask God to help you be a wise decision maker.*

MARCH :: 1

CARISSA, AGE 14

READ 1 KINGS 8:27-28

Everywhere You Go

But will God really dwell on earth? The heavens, even the highest heaven, cannot contain you.
1 KINGS 8:27

During the Christmas season my youth group went downtown to watch the Christmas play, The Nut-cracker. We wore our nicest clothes and goofiest slippers. (The play is all about dreaming, right?) While waiting in line outside the theater, we sang Christmas carols. Lots of people noticed us, and some of them even joined in. It felt great to witness to them about the birth of Jesus through our songs—and we were nowhere near a church building!

God is everywhere, and we need to tell people about him wherever we go. Church is still important, but most of our witnessing will be in other places—at school, on a sports team, even on a sidewalk outside a theater. You never know what opportunities you'll have. But you can be sure that whatever and wherever they are, God wants you to use these moments to tell others about him.

WHAT ABOUT YOU?

:: Of all the places you spend time, think of 2 where you can be a witness for God.

:: Ask some Christian adults (like your parents or youth leaders) about unusual witnessing opportunities they've had.

:: Pray and tell God you're willing to be his witness wherever he wants you to go.

M A R C H :: 2

READ 2 SAMUEL 11:2-5

One Thing After Another

Isn't this Bathsheba...wife of Uriah the Hittite?
2 SAMUEL 11:3

Kelly's devotional a few days ago was a story about a friend's suicide and how much pain this one action caused. The point of Kelly's story was not the suicide itself but the tragic path that choices sometimes travel.

Take King David, for example. The king was at first attracted, then lustful, and finally had to "have" Bathsheba. He didn't plan any of the next steps—pregnancy, murder, and pain.

Sin has a way of doing that. You make one little choice (a bad one) and try to cover it up or even ignore it, and you end up getting caught in a bigger sin. How would David's life have been different if, after the first sin (sex with Bathsheba—well, okay, technically *lusting* after Bathsheba and *planning* the sex was the *first* sin, and the sex was the *second*), he had confessed his sin and accepted the consequences?

This may sound harsh, but it's true: Stop the cycle of sin in your life. It can become a habit.

WHAT ABOUT YOU?

:: Decide whether or not you want to live differently from King David and not let one sin turn into several. If so, write out 1 John 1:9 on a note card and put it in your Bible, reading it every day this week.

:: Pray that God will give you the courage to admit your wrongs right away, instead of trying to cover them up.

MARCH :: 3

Totally Undevoted

As Solomon grew old, his wives turned his heart after other gods, and his heart was not fully devoted to the LORD his God, as the heart of David his father had been.
1 KINGS 11:4

In a dream, the young king Solomon asks God for wisdom. God is so pleased that he grants the request and throws in wealth and honor besides. Solomon immediately invests his gifts to build a strong national government, good relationships with foreign countries, and a permanent temple in downtown Jerusalem. In the Old Testament, the temple was the one place God wanted people to come to him.

But Solomon's bunch of foreign women (he had 300 wives!—not to mention 700 concubines—a polite word for someone who's somewhere between a wife and servant) and their wacky religions become his downfall.

God was sad, mad, and knew that Solomon was leading the whole nation down the drain with him. Bummer! After Solomon turned his back on God, the Lord let the Israelite kings continue their evil ways. King after king denied God and ignored the truth.

If Solomon would have been able to keep a note card of 1 John 1:9 and follow its instruction, what would his confession sound like?

NIKKI, AGE 15

What Matters Most?

"What have I done wrong," asked Obediah, "that you are handing your servant over to Ahab to be put to death?"

1 KINGS 18:9

A lot of people whine about their lives. They complain, "Why me?" or "It's not fair." I admit, sometimes I'm like that too.

I was playing in a doubles tennis match recently when the other team cheated to try to win. I got so frustrated with them calling fair balls "out." They were beating us so badly that I felt like giving up. But my partner and I got over our frustration and decided to play even harder. And we knew it was better to lose honestly than cheat. In the end, we won the match!

That time, our decision to follow God's rules and be honest was rewarded right away. But sometimes life isn't like that. Sometimes you do everything you're supposed to and still don't win. That's just the way life is. What matters is obeying God and doing your best.

WHAT ABOUT YOU?

:: What are 2 reasons why we sometimes lose confidence in God?

:: Look out the window toward the place where the sun rose today, yesterday, and the day before. How can you be confident that it will come up again tomorrow? Can you have confidence in God for some of the same reasons?

:: Ask God to help you trust him.

MARCH :: 5

KATE, AGE 12

READ 1 KINGS 19:9-13

Listening for Him

After the fire came a gentle whisper. When Elijah heard it, he pulled his cloak over his face and went out and stood at the mouth of the cave.
1 KINGS 19:12-13

When we pray to God, we don't really know how he'll answer us. We might be waiting for a big voice to say, "Do this!" Or we might look in all the wrong places, expecting to find a big billboard sign with the answer on it. Most of the time we have to wait patiently to find out what God says.

While we're waiting, it's really important to listen. Even though God is super-powerful, he can speak in a very quiet voice. Sometimes the answer to your prayer is just a little whisper in your heart. God can also "speak" through Bible reading, the pastor's sermon, or even the advice of a friend.

It may take a while for you to figure out what God wants you to do. And when you do get an answer, it might not be the one you were hoping for. But God knows what he's doing, and we can know it too, if we listen.

WHAT ABOUT YOU?

:: Ask some Christian adults, like your parents or your youth leaders, about the different ways God has answered their prayers.

:: Take 2 minutes of prayer time just to listen to God. Thank him for all the ways he guides you.

MARCH :: 6

READ 2 KINGS 4:8-37

Part of His Plan

When she reached the man of God at the mountain, she took hold of his feet.... "Did I ask you for a son, my LORD?" she said. "Didn't I tell you, 'Don't raise my hopes'?"
2 KINGS 4:27-28

My aunt recently died of cancer, and at first I couldn't understand why God would take away someone I loved. It all seemed like a big mistake.

Don't you think the Shunammite woman in this story felt the same way when her son died? She had waited almost her whole life to have a baby, but when she finally had one, he didn't even live very long. Why would God let that happen?

What the Shunammite woman learned was that God has a purpose for everything—even her son's death. It brought her closer to God because it gave her the chance to see a miracle. She learned a lot about God's power and goodness.

My aunt's death must be part of God's master plan too, even though I'm not sure how it all fits together. He doesn't make mistakes, and he never wants to hurt me. It's my mistake when I forget that.

WHAT ABOUT YOU?

:: *Have you ever asked God why he allowed something bad to happen in your life? Looking back, what did you learn from that experience?*

:: *Ask God to give you patience when you don't understand his plan.*

MARCH :: 7

KAREN, AGE 12

READ 2 KINGS 23:19-25

Give 100%

Neither before nor after Josiah was there a king like him who turned to the LORD as he did.
2 KINGS 23:25

Loving God the way King Josiah did isn't easy. Josiah had to take on the evil things that were happening in his whole country. I don't have a whole country to look after, thank goodness, but even changing my own life takes a lot of effort. Every day I see more ways I need to be obedient to God.

But however hard it is for me to get close to God, nothing I do could be harder than what he's already done for me. After all, he sent Jesus to die for me. When I think about it that way, I really want to love God with all my heart and soul and strength. That's the best way I know how to give back a little of the amazing love he's given me.

WHAT ABOUT YOU?

:: What does it mean to be committed to God?

:: Write down 1 way you need to be more obedient to God. For the next week, give yourself a grade in that area every day.

:: Praise God for the way you are growing in this area of your life.

MARCH :: 8

READ 1 CHRONICLES 5:23–26

Looking Inside Out

They were brave warriors, famous men, and heads of their families. But they were unfaithful to the God of their fathers.
1 CHRONICLES 5:24–25

I couldn't believe it. I turned on the TV and found out my favorite actor was dead. I'd always thought this guy had everything going for him. He seemed so cool, so fun, like he didn't have any problems. But when he died, all the news stories and interviews with his friends made it clear that he was a pretty unhappy, messed-up guy.

Sometimes I get worried about what people think of me. I want them to like me, to think I'm cool. But that really doesn't matter as much as what's going on inside me. If I don't have a strong relationship with God, it doesn't matter if other people think I'm cool or popular. The only thing that matters is staying true to God and living my life for him.

WHAT ABOUT YOU?

:: *Think about some of the people the world considers successful. What do you really know about these people? How have they earned success?*

:: *Think of people who have personal qualities you admire. How can you develop those traits in yourself?*

:: *Ask God to help you see people as they really are. Ask him to bring positive role models into your life.*

MARCH :: 9

Be a Gatekeeper

The four principal gatekeepers...were entrusted with the responsibility for the rooms and treasuries in the house of God.
1 CHRONICLES 9:26

Many of our recent devotions talked about listening to God and loving him with boldness. In the passage you read today, you see that there were some people who had the job of being a "gatekeeper" in the temple. The gatekeepers in Israel's day were treated with respect and honor; they were looked up to and trusted by everyone.

As a follower of Jesus, you're a gatekeeper too. Your actions are a big key to what people think about Christians, the church, and even Jesus himself. As the apostle Paul wrote to his "son in the faith," Timothy: "Don't let anyone look down on you because you are young, but set an example for the believers in speech, in life, in love, in faith and in purity" (1 Timothy 4:12).

WHAT ABOUT YOU?

:: *How do you feel about being a "gatekeeper" for Jesus? (Remember that God hasn't left you alone as a gatekeeper. He's promised to be with you, giving you the power and love to be an incredible gatekeeper!)*

:: *Think of one person who needs to see God. What's one way you can help that one person by living as a gatekeeper?*

:: *Try to pray every day for a whole week for that person, and see what God does.*

MARCH :: 10

Snapshot

Then King David went in and sat before the LORD, and he said, "Who am I, O LORD God, and what is my family, that you have brought me this far?"
1 CHRONICLES 17:16

First and 2 Chronicles represents a snapshot of history, but not a videotape of history. The lists in this first book were important to the Israelites because they helped people understand things about the temple and where their kings came from. They were not trying to talk about everything and everybody, just the most important stuff. Through these lists God shows that he remembers the past, and his work is connected to people from the past, like David.

King David was great—the greatest leader in Israel's history. He was strong, smart, powerful, and people loved him. He had every reason to get stuck-up and full of himself, thinking he was Mr. Cool. But the reason why David was loved by God was that he knew who he was—an ordinary guy who had been lifted up by an extraordinary God.

God has always been active in the world, using regular people. He is active now!

WHAT ABOUT YOU?

:: *What would a snapshot of your life show about how God has been active in your life?*

READ 1 CHRONICLES 21:1–8

A Big Head?

Satan rose up against Israel and incited David to take a census of Israel.
1 CHRONICLES 21:1

I really want to be a rapper. One Sunday morning I performed at my church. After the service, nearly everyone I knew told me I did a great job. Even people I had never seen congratulated me and told me it was awesome. I appreciated all the compliments, and I almost let their praise go to my head. But I tried to shake off the temptation of pride by acknowledging the truth: God has given me a talent, and all I can do is thank him for it. God hates selfish pride. He has given us everything.

King David was a powerful guy, and he let it go to his head. But once he remembered that God is in control of everything, David was like, *Whoa, what was I thinking?* He had let pride get the best of him.

Whenever I'm tempted to be proud and think I'm really talented, I need to remember that God deserves all the credit for everything I do.

WHAT ABOUT YOU?

:: *What are some of the talents God has given you? How can you give him credit when you do something well?*

:: *Thank God for the talents he's given you and ask him to help you use them to show his love to others.*

MARCH :: 12

KATE, AGE 13

READ 1 CHRONICLES 29:14–19

Liar, Liar

I know, my God, that you test the heart and are pleased with integrity.
1 CHRONICLES 29:17

God knows who's telling the truth and who's not. But sometimes it's tough for us to figure it out. When I was in 6th grade, there was this girl who no one trusted. It was impossible to tell whether she was being honest or lying. I'd say that's a terrible reputation to have. I definitely don't want to be that kind of person!

We should take David's example and follow God's rules for living, because God never lacks integrity. When we do that, God will help us to be "real" Christians—people who listen to God's Word and try to live out what we believe.

David was a man after God's own heart. I want to be a girl after God's own heart. If I'm that kind of person, I won't have to worry about my reputation, and I won't be a dishonest person.

WHAT ABOUT YOU?

:: *Why is it tempting to stretch, hide, or twist the truth? Think of the last time you did this. How did you feel? How do you think God felt?*

:: *Ask God to help you be a person of integrity.*

MARCH :: 13

BRIAN, AGE 14

READ 2 CHRONICLES 5:11–14

Sing It!

Accompanied by trumpets, cymbals and other instruments, they raised their voices in praise to the LORD.... Then the temple of the LORD was filled with a cloud...for the glory of the LORD filled the temple of God.
2 CHRONICLES 5:13–14

I used to wonder why singing during youth group was such a big deal. So what if I kept talking to my friends when the leader was trying to lead songs? I thought singing was just something to do between games and the devotional—basically, a waste of time. I can't remember what changed my mind, but I finally realized that the songs were part of our worship. Singing wasn't supposed to entertain me. It was supposed to help me get closer to God.

Now I'm one of the song leaders for my youth group, and I watch some of the other students goofing off like I used to. I just keep reminding them, "You're not singing for yourself—you're singing for the Lord. It doesn't even matter if you have a good voice. If you're singing with your heart, you sound great to him!"

WHAT ABOUT YOU?

:: God didn't have to give us music. But why do you think he did?

:: Sing your favorite praise song as a prayer to God.

MARCH :: 14

RYAN, AGE 14

READ 2 CHRONICLES 24:1-2

Too Young?

Joash was seven years old when he became king, and he reigned in Jerusalem forty years.
2 CHRONICLES 24:1

Some people think you have to be an adult in order to serve Jesus Christ. But I think being young opens up all kinds of doors for me to share my faith with other people. For example, most people make decisions about religion when they're young. And most of the people at my school would rather talk about faith with someone their own age. That means teenagers like me have a big responsibility to share our faith. This verse says that Joash was only 7 years old when he became king! It also tells us that he did what was right in God's sight.

We can be like Joash and stand up for God when we're young. God used this young king, not an adult, to show Israel how to live right. The world may not think we're qualified, but God does. He can, and will, use anyone who wants to serve him.

WHAT ABOUT YOU?

:: *When was the last time you got discouraged because of your age? What did you do about it?*

:: *Brainstorm some ways you can serve God at your school or in your neighborhood. What are 2 things you can do that your parents or other adults can't?*

:: *Ask God to show you creative ways to serve him, no matter what your age.*

MARCH :: 15

JEFF, AGE 14

READ 2 CHRONICLES 26:16–23

Tough on Sin

After Uzziah became powerful, his pride led to his downfall.
2 CHRONICLES 26:16

God didn't go easy on King Uzziah. The king had gotten so proud that he thought he could break God's rules. But when Uzziah crossed the line, God punished him. God showed that even though he's patient and forgiving, he has his limits and will draw the line when it comes to punishment.

This story reminds me that God gets tough on sin, but it also tells me that, even when God punishes, he's still merciful. At the end of the story, Uzziah got to be buried in the royal cemetery with all the other kings. Uzziah definitely paid for his pride, but his punishment didn't last forever. God forgave even him.

Sometimes I forget that mercy doesn't mean that God makes everything perfect again after I sin. I might have to pay some serious consequences. That's why it's so great to know that Jesus has already paid the most serious consequence—the death that I deserve. God's mercy will always be bigger than my sin.

WHAT ABOUT YOU?

:: How would your idea of God be different if he didn't punish sin? How would your life be different?

:: If someone has hurt you by their sin, what can you do to show them forgiveness?

:: Thank God for his rules and for his mercy.

MARCH :: 16

Is Your Belief Yours?

Ahaz was twenty years old when he became king.... Unlike David his father, he did not do what was right in the eyes of the LORD.

2 CHRONICLES 28:1

A few days ago Kate talked about trying "to live out what we believe." Sometimes it's hard to know what you believe. It's pretty normal for teenagers to still be figuring this out (and that's okay!).

King Jotham was a hero of Israel who "did what was right in the eyes of the LORD" (2 Chronicles 27:2). But his son, Ahaz, "did not do what was right in the eyes of the LORD" (2 Chronicles 28:1). Just because your mom or dad loves Jesus, or doesn't love Jesus, doesn't necessarily mean that you'll follow in their footsteps. Everyone has to choose for themselves who (or what) they're going to believe.

So, when you're trying to live out what you believe, whose belief is it? Yours?

WHAT ABOUT YOU?

:: *Do you see your faith as something you have "inherited" from your parents? Or is it your own faith? How do you know?*

:: *Talk with your parents and ask them about their faith. Then talk to them about your faith.*

:: *Decide what is true about your faith, and tell God what you want in your faith. Then be quiet and let him comfort you as his own special child, apart from your family, friends, and church.*

MARCH :: 17

READ 2 CHRONICLES 36:22-23

Rebuilding

The LORD, the God of heaven...has appointed me to build a temple for him at Jerusalem in Judah. Anyone of his people among you—may the LORD his God be with him, and let him go up.
2 CHRONICLES 36:23

Second Chronicles starts with the story of David's son Solomon. Solomon, the builder of God's temple, gets lots of coverage in the first part of the book. The rest of the book covers the subsequent kings, going light on their sins and heavy on their successes. The book ends with the best news the Jews have had in a century: The king of Persia (who's now boss of the Babylonians too) gives the Jews permission to return to Jerusalem to live and rebuild God's house—you know, the temple.

Solomon's temple, which was destroyed 70 years prior, when the Israelites were taken into captivity, was incredible—gold and expensive jewels everywhere, huge pillars, 3-D carvings, and statues of little angels all over the place. You could make big bucks just charging admission. (But they didn't; they wanted people to come and worship God.) It was one of the world's most impressive buildings. But the best thing about it was that God was present there.

WHAT ABOUT YOU?

:: *Why do you think it was such good news to the Jews that they were allowed to go back home and rebuild the temple?*

MARCH :: 18

TIM, AGE 14

Being a Better Witness

Ezra had devoted himself to the study and observance of the Law of the LORD, and to teaching its decrees.
EZRA 7:10

I really could have used this passage a few years ago. I had some friends who weren't Christians, but I had no idea how to witness to them.

Those old friends were caught up in swearing, sex, drugs, and whatever else they could find to fill the emptiness of not having Jesus in their lives. If I had known the Bible better, at least I could have tried to help them know Jesus.

During the time of Ezra, the Israelites were coming back from Babylon after living as captives. Their children no longer knew God's law. Ezra felt called to help get Israel back on track, but instead of just teaching others about God's law, he spent time studying it himself. He made sure *he* understood it before trying to tell others about it. God blessed Ezra for his faithfulness and hard work.

WHAT ABOUT YOU?

:: *Think over some questions non-Christians might have about God. Study your Bible and talk with your parents or youth pastor to find some answers.*

:: *Ask God to help you live out the things you learn as you read your Bible.*

READ NEHEMIAH 4:1–3

Better Than Popularity

He ridiculed the Jews...he said, "What are those feeble Jews doing?"
NEHEMIAH 4:1-2

Reading these verses in Nehemiah reminds me that God's children were criticized for doing what was right even thousands of years ago!

Doing what God wants isn't always popular. But it's a mistake to think that being popular and cool is the most important goal in life. In fact, what my peers think of me is one of the worst ways to determine my self-worth. Being criticized by them isn't nearly as bad as disappointing God.

God desires and expects us to take a stand for him every day of our lives. Sometimes this might be really hard, but we don't have to do it alone. God helped the Jews keep working on the wall when everybody was making fun of them for it. I know he'll help me obey him too, no matter what other people say.

WHAT ABOUT YOU?

:: *Put a rock in a place where you can see it every day. When people give you a hard time about doing what's right, think about how God can help your faith be as solid as a "rock."*

:: *Ask God to help you bless the people who criticize you (see Luke 6:27–28).*

MARCH :: 20

CARISSA, AGE 14

READ NEHEMIAH 8:9-12

Party On!

Go and enjoy choice food and sweet drinks, and send some to those who have nothing prepared.
NEHEMIAH 8:10

I've been to parties that made me feel really horrible and low because everybody there was getting all worried about how they looked and who paid attention to them. I've also been to parties that made me feel really happy because people were just being themselves and having a ton of fun. Most of the fun parties were youth group parties—but when I tell my other friends how much fun I had, they don't believe me!

Some of my friends think of God as a head honcho who sits on a big throne and orders people to "be good." I used to think of God that way too. But youth group activities, and verses like this one in Nehemiah, show me that God wants us to have fun too. I guess you could say he created fun. It's all part of the great life he wants us to have.

WHAT ABOUT YOU?

:: *If you could plan the ultimate youth group activity, what would it be?*

:: *Get a group of Christian friends together for a party. Be sure to invite non-Christian friends!*

:: *Thank God for fun!*

MARCH :: 21

READ ESTHER 4:14-16

When the Going Gets Tough

Who knows but that you have come to royal position for such a time as this?
ESTHER 4:14

When my best friend moved away, I couldn't understand why God allowed it to happen. I mean, I know God has a plan and wants the best for us, but it seemed like he wanted to mess up my life. I doubted that anything good could come of the situation.

Thousands of years ago, Esther and her cousin Mordecai were in a bad situation too—way worse than mine. The Jews' lives were in danger, and it would have been easy for them to complain and get discouraged. But Mordecai reminded Esther that God does have a purpose, even when everything seems to be falling apart.

When I read these verses, I realized that since God has come this far with me, he'll stay with me and guide me no matter what happens. This is especially true in difficult times when we can't figure out what God's up to. All of us are here on earth for a reason—not just to live and die. We can trust God's purpose for us.

WHAT ABOUT YOU?

:: *Think about a time you doubted that God could work in a bad situation. What did God do next?*

:: *Tell God about anything that's discouraging you. Ask him to remind you of his presence in your life.*

M A R C H :: 2 2

Be Quiet!

No one said a word to him, because they saw how great his suffering was.
JOB 2:13

Often when I'm mad about something, I want to get my feelings out by talking things over with friends or even talking out loud to myself. Actually, now that I think about it, I never like to be quiet, no matter what mood I'm in. I guess it's just easier to make noise than to be silent.

When all kinds of terrible things happened to Job, he couldn't find any words to say for a whole week. Even his friends kept quiet. From this verse I can see that there are times when it's best for me just not to talk, that I should just listen instead. God wants me to know I can come to him anytime. I need to learn to listen to him, and that often means keeping my mouth shut—at least for awhile.

WHAT ABOUT YOU?

:: *Sometimes talking about how we feel is a good thing. But think about how being quiet can help you sort out your feelings.*

:: *Take 5 minutes each day this week to simply sit and think about God. To give your mind a jump-start, pretend that you are interviewing him. At the end of the week, jot down what you learned about God.*

:: *Ask God to help you listen as he speaks to your heart.*

MARCH :: 23

READ JOHN 16:31-33

That's Just the Way It Is

In this world you will have trouble. But take heart! I have overcome the world.
JOHN 16:33

In the last week you've been reading all about problems: Tim's friends making poor decisions; Emile's lessons in handling criticism; Christina's best friend moving away. Did you know that Jesus actually promised you problems? God does discipline his kids when they veer off course, but sometimes problems come not because you've done something bad, but because you've done something good.

Think about it. If Ezra didn't want to teach God's Word...if Nehemiah didn't want to rebuild Jerusalem...if Esther didn't want to save her people...if Job hadn't been so squeaky-clean, their lives would have been much easier! Things got messy because they followed God fully. That's just the way it is.

Do your best to live a life of obedience to God. And remember Jesus' promise: "Take heart! I have overcome the world!"

WHAT ABOUT YOU?

:: What are your biggest problems right now? Do you think you brought them on yourself or have they come from another source?

:: What is one good choice God is calling you to make that could result in trouble coming your way?

:: Ask God to give you the courage to be completely devoted to him, so you can take the heat for being his disciple.

MARCH :: 24

READ JOB 13:1; 42:12-17

God Is In Control

The LORD blessed the latter part of Job's life more than the first.
JOB 42:12

Imagine having everything you've ever wanted: tons of cool clothes, the best video games and computer stuff, more CDs than you could ever listen to, a bedroom to die for. Add to that an awesome family and a healthy body.

Now imagine all that stuff being zapped. All of it—gone!

That's what happened to Job. He had land-o-plenty, tons of cows and other animals, a bunch of really swell kids, and felt like a hundred bucks. And even though Job loved to obey God, God allowed Satan to take it all away.

Because of that he "cursed the day of his birth." No, Job didn't need his mouth washed out with soap. Instead, he wished he had never been born. He was getting so much bad news that he wanted to give up. But he didn't— God got him through the tough stuff! In the middle of all this, Job learns a great lesson about God: Even when it doesn't feel like it, God is in control.

WHAT ABOUT YOU?

:: *Ask God to show you a glimpse of the good plans he has for your future, then write what you feel he is telling you .*

MARCH :: 25

READ JOB 19:25–27

Filling in the Gaps

I know that my Redeemer lives.
JOB 19:25

After my dad died, a huge part of my life died with him. The pain was almost too much to handle. But God helped me. Through my dad's death, I learned that no matter what happens, God will always be there for me. I could lose everything I think is important, but I won't ever lose God—not as long as I'm a Christian. I'm not afraid of losing my possessions or of surviving life's hard times, because I know God will fill in the gaps like he has in the past.

No matter where we go, no matter what we do, God is with us. He loves us and cares about us and will never leave our side. We can lose everything else, but we just can't lose God.

WHAT ABOUT YOU?

:: *Why is it hard to have faith when things aren't going well? Where do you find encouragement in the hard times?*

:: *Start writing down the ways God has helped you through some rough spots. Read back through them the next time you're struggling.*

:: *Thank God for helping you deal with difficult times.*

MARCH :: 26

CHRIS, AGE 14

READ JOB 31:1-4

Hormones in Check

I made a covenant with my eyes not to look lustfully at a girl.
JOB 31:1

Sometimes it seems like I'm surrounded by beautiful girls. And since I'm a teenage guy, it would only be normal for me to drool over them, right? Well, sort of.

As a Christian, I have to remember that God told guys not to lust after girls. And even though it's not always easy to follow that commandment, I know that's what God wants me to do.

I think that's why Job made a "covenant with [his] eyes." It's not enough to say to myself, *I won't look* when my friends pass around a pornographic magazine or want me to check out a pretty girl. I also have to promise myself to stay away from the kind of stuff that might tempt me. And I have to make sure my friends know where I stand.

I can't hide lust from God or pretend it didn't happen. Life is full of temptations. But God wants us to follow him, not our hormones.

WHAT ABOUT YOU?

:: What does it mean to make a "covenant" with yourself? How can you keep the promises you make to yourself?

:: List 3 ways you can show respect to a guy (if you're a girl) or a girl (if you're a guy).

:: Ask God to help you resist sexual temptation.

MARCH :: 27

CATHERINE, AGE 12

READ JOB 41-42

Who Do You Think You Are?

Then Job replied to the LORD: "I know that you can do all things; no plan of yours can be thwarted."
JOB 42:1-2

Do you ever have a hard time trusting God? I do. I sometimes think I can handle life all by myself, like I'm the only one who really knows what I need. I forget that God is the One who's really got things under control. In these chapters, God goes into detail about all the things he can do. He reminds Job that everything that happens in the world is in God's control. It's almost like God's asking Job, "Hey, who's the boss here, buddy—you or me?"

I hope I never have to suffer like Job did. But even if I do, I hope I'll remember that God will always help me through my problems in one way or another. I can trust God with everything, because he is ultimately in control of the whole universe.

WHAT ABOUT YOU?

:: Why is it sometimes hard to trust that God is in control?

:: Thank God for being in control of your life and everything around you.

MARCH :: 28

AARON, AGE 14

Warning Signs

Blessed is the man who does not walk in the counsel of the wicked.
PSALM 1:1

It would be easy to jump into the wrong crowd at school and get into all kinds of bad stuff. But Psalm 1 reminds me that the way of the wicked is a road to destruction.

Of course, that road might look really good. When I think about it, I imagine wet cement. Usually you can't tell that cement is wet unless there are signs to warn you. As Christians, we need to look at the "warning signs" God gives to help us avoid the way of the wicked—like the ones found in Psalm 1. We should watch out for people who don't take God seriously and make sure we don't join in their sinful activities. Instead, we should be sure our words and actions are pleasing to God.

This passage tells us that those who meditate on God's laws will experience God's blessing. Now that's something you know you can stand on!

WHAT ABOUT YOU?

:: How do you think God helps you choose the right way?

:: For the next few days, be on the lookout for warning signs—road signs, computer warnings, anything you can find. If you could post warning signs on the road of life, where would you put them and what would they say?

:: Ask God to help you do what is right.

M A R C H :: 2 9

READ PSALM 9:1-2, 7-11

All My Heart!

I will praise you, O LORD, with all my heart; I will tell of all your wonders.
PSALM 9:1

I'm a member of the boys' choir at my church, and we're supposed to praise God with our songs. The problem is, some of the boys don't even sing. They just act like they're singing. Or they talk and goof around the whole time. Some of the ones who do sing probably just come for the candy we get after choir practice is over.

There are times when my mind wanders and I don't think about what I'm singing. But God wants my whole attention—and not just when I'm singing. I should praise him with "all my heart" when I'm reading my Bible, sitting in church, or wherever I am.

One of my favorite songs is "Our God Is an Awesome God." God is awesome! We should let him know that we really believe it.

WHAT ABOUT YOU?

:: *How can we make sure we're really worshiping God when we sing in church? Besides singing, what are other ways we worship?*

:: *Write your own praise song to God. You don't have to show anybody, and you don't even have to sing it. Just tell God what he means to you. Then read, sing, or pray the song to God.*

:: *Ask God to help you give him your full attention.*

MARCH :: 30

READ 2 CHRONICLES 20:1–30

What Happens When We Worship?

As they began to sing and praise, the LORD set ambushes against the men...who were invading Judah, and they were defeated.
2 CHRONICLES 20:22

Yesterday Malachi reminded us to worship with all our hearts, which makes good sense. After all, it would be weird to go to a roller rink and not skate. Or to go to a game and not cheer. Or to go to church and not sing. We've got to get into it, heart and soul.

But why is it so important? What happens when we worship? Here are four great things:

>> First, *God* loves nothing better than to hear his kids belt out his praises.

>> Second, *believers* get in touch with God through worship; they sing words that strengthen their faith.

>> Third, *outsiders* are drawn to God when we worship.

>> Fourth, *enemies* are defeated. In 2 Chronicles 20, when God's people knew they couldn't win by swinging swords, they launched worship warheads—and it worked.

So worship hard this weekend—who knows what may happen as a result!

WHAT ABOUT YOU?

:: Take a big risk the next time you're at church—worship God with your whole heart. Pretend no one else is there. If you usually don't sing, then sing. If you sing but don't clap, then clap. Try doing something new to really get into worshiping God.

:: Ask God to make himself real to you as you worship.

MARCH :: 31

Tell Me How You Really Feel

Trust in him at all times...pour out your hearts to him, for God is our refuge.
PSALM 62:8

A psalm is a song. Psalm. Song. Same thing. Poetry put to music. The book started as a diary of the prayers and emotions of King David and others (yes, the same David who, as a young man, tossed a rock at and cut the head off of the Philistine champion, Goliath). Here are some songs he wrote and prayed to God: "When I feel lonely" (Psalm 22), "When I'm caught in the web of sin" (Psalm 51), "When so-called friends lie about me behind my back" (Psalms 62 and 64), "When I need forgiveness" (Psalm 69), "When I get ticked off at my enemies" (Psalms 109 and 137).

The psalms remind us that we can be (and should be) honest with God. He doesn't want to hear sugarcoated words if we have super frustrated hearts. Tell him the truth. The psalms also teach us that praying for the defeat of evil is good, especially if our desire is to see God's goodness win. Scholars call such prayers "imprecatory psalms." (Use the term, impress your pastor!)

WHAT ABOUT YOU?

:: Write your own psalm to God about what has been on your heart lately.

Cross Your Heart?

LORD, who may dwell in your sanctuary?... He whose walk is blameless and who does what is righteous, who speaks the truth from his heart.
PSALM 15:1–2

Once I promised a friend I wouldn't tell her secret, but then I broke my promise. My friend got so mad at me! And I really can't blame her. I would have been mad too if someone blabbed my secrets all over the place.

My only excuse for telling the secret was that this other friend of mine was really begging me to tell her. At first I said no, but eventually I gave in. So basically I had a choice: I could have one friend upset with me for telling, or I could have the other one upset with me for not telling. I made the wrong choice.

Psalm 15:4 shows us that God likes it when we keep our word—even when that's hard for us to do.

WHAT ABOUT YOU?

:: Think of a time when it was hard to keep a promise. Did you make the right choice or the wrong choice? How might you handle the situation differently if it came up again?

:: Write a note reminding yourself of one promise you want to keep. Post it on a mirror, the refrigerator, or someplace where you'll see it every day.

:: Ask God to help you be a trustworthy person.

APRIL :: 2

BECKY, AGE 13

READ PSALM 19:1-6

Look Around!

The heavens declare the glory of God; the skies proclaim the work of his hands. Day after day they pour forth speech; night after night they display knowledge.
PSALM 19:1-2

If I'm ever tempted to think that maybe there's no God at all, all I have to do is look around and see the beauty of nature everywhere. Just by looking at people, trees, the sun, and everything else in the world, I know there is a God.

God doesn't try to hide from people. He wants us to "see" him in his creation. And he wants Christians to remind nonbelievers that there is a God. God has shown himself to everyone—but some people just don't (or won't) notice until someone tells them where to look.

It's incredible that God created everything—even me! The world God made shows me so much about him: that he's creative, that he's beautiful, and that he cares about everything he's made. Most of all, God's creation helps me see that he's real.

WHAT ABOUT YOU?

:: What do the things in your bedroom say about you? Besides the things Becky says in the last paragraph above, what does God's world say about him?

:: Praise God for his power and majesty.

APRIL :: 3

Holding On

My God, my God, why have you forsaken me?
PSALM 22:1

I was in a musical based on the Psalms, and I sang a song called "My God, My God," based on the first few verses of Psalm 22. It was a pretty intense (and almost depressing) song with lots of questions and complaints to God. David was in bad shape when he wrote Psalm 22. And I can understand why Jesus quoted from this psalm when he was at his lowest point—dying on the cross.

But that's not the end of the psalm, or the end of the story. The ultimate message of the psalm is that God never leaves us—even when other people say he has, or when it seems like we're totally alone. He never abandoned David. He never abandoned Jesus. And he'll never abandon you or me.

WHAT ABOUT YOU?

- What was the loneliest time in your life? How did God help you get through it?

- Write down some similarities between David's psalm and Jesus' death. (You can read about the crucifixion in Matthew 27:32–56.)

- Thank God for always hearing your cries for help.

A P R I L :: 4

READ PSALM 29:10–11

Get a Grip

The LORD gives strength to his people.
PSALM 29:11

I don't handle stress well. When I was in 7th grade, I got behind on my schoolwork. I got super worried about missing due dates and turning reports in late. I was too stressed out to concentrate, so the work just piled up. I couldn't sleep very well, I felt sort of sick all the time, and I even got into fights with my friends.

I finally figured out I needed God's help to deal with all my stress. And sure enough, God helped me calm down and get a grip on my life again.

No matter how stressful my life gets, I know I can handle it with God's help.

WHAT ABOUT YOU?

:: What causes stress in your life? How do you handle stress?

:: When you feel stressed out, make a list of what's on your mind. Then write down what you can do about those things. Take care of the stuff you can control, and don't worry about the stuff you can't.

:: Ask God to bring you a sense of peace when you start to lose it.

APRIL :: 5

EMILY, AGE 13

READ PSALM 33:1-5

Music to His Ears

Sing joyfully to the LORD, you righteous; it is fitting for the upright to praise him.... Sing to him a new song;
play skillfully, and shout for joy.
PSALM 33:1, 3

You know how hearing your favorite song always makes you smile, even if you're having a bad day?
Or how certain situations remind you of different songs? When my dog died, a song from church kept
running through my mind. As I hummed it, I started to feel better. Sometimes music's rhythm and joyful
notes make me feel so much better.

Well, when God hears us singing praises to him, it's like he's hearing his song. So if music is the
way you like to praise God, that's great with him. Keep on singing!

WHAT ABOUT YOU?

:: What's your favorite church song? How does it make you feel to sing it?

:: This week as you go to worship, look closely at the words to the songs you sing. What do they tell
you about God? What do they tell you about being a Christian? Sing them as prayers to God.

:: Thank God for the gift of music.

A P R I L :: 6

READ PSALM 90:10–12

All the Time You Need

Teach us to number our days aright.
PSALM 90:12

A teacher once brought a one-gallon can into his classroom. He placed 5 large rocks in the can, filling it to the brim. He asked his students, "Is this can full?" They all nodded yes.

"No it's not," the teacher said. Then he took out a bag of gravel and a bag of sand and poured them into the nooks and crannies around the rocks. Finally, he pulled out a bottle of water and slowly poured it in the can until it reached the top.

"Now the can is full," the teacher said. "But here's the real question: What does this teach you about your busy schedule?"

One girl said, "It shows you that no matter how full your schedule, there's always room for more."

"That's not quite it," the teacher responded. "It should teach you that unless you put in the big rocks first, they'll never fit."

WHAT ABOUT YOU?

:: What would you say are your 5 "big rock" priorities for next week? Get your activity calendar and make sure these fit in first.

:: Pray Psalm 90:12 every day for the next week. Ask God (and your parents) to help you put the big rocks where they should be.

APRIL :: 7

READ PSALM 11:5; 40:6

God Hates Sin

The LORD examines the righteous, but the wicked and those who love violence his soul hates.
PSALM 11:5

Think about your parents or someone else who loves you. Because they love you very much, they hate things like drugs and bad language and not trying in school. They can't stand anything that is against your best. God is the same way. He loves us all, but he hates our sinful behavior. Although he is patient and does not always punish sin right away, God will not put up with it forever.

Like a bunch of nasty blood-sucking worms, sin will sap the life right out of you. David found this out after his sexual sin with Bathsheba. When he tried to hide what he'd done, it almost killed him. It cut off the spiritual strength David drew from his relationship with God, and he felt the effects physically. Only through open, honest confession could the leech of David's sin be pulled from his soul.

In Psalm 40, David says God has pierced his ear. In Bible times, slaves who wanted to show life-long devotion to their masters would have them pierce their ear (See Exodus 21:6). In other words, David is a fired-up, sold-out, God-follower forever.

WHAT ABOUT YOU?

:: *God wants loyal love. Is there any sin leech in your life that you need to confess to come back into a right relationship with God?*

APRIL :: 8

JEFF, AGE 13

PSALM 37:1–4

No Fair!

Do not fret because of evil men.... Trust in the LORD and do good.
PSALM 37:1, 3

Sometimes life just doesn't seem fair! My little brother goofs up a lot, and whenever he gets in trouble, it seems like I get punished too. I think my mom likes to cover all the bases. But it makes me mad, because I haven't done anything wrong.

I need to remember that God sees everything. Even when life seems unfair, God's going to make everything work out in the end. And if I keep my mind on all that God's done for me, maybe I won't get so upset when my life doesn't go how I think it should. I can still "trust in the LORD and do good," knowing God's got it all under control. It's never fun when we're treated unfairly, but it helps to know we're not alone.

WHAT ABOUT YOU?

∷ *Think about a time you were treated unfairly. How did you react? How might you have reacted differently?*

∷ *The next time you play a game with some friends, try this: Play fair and don't complain about anything! Even if you feel cheated, don't complain. How did your "little experiment" affect your friends? How did it affect you?*

∷ *Ask God to help you trust him when life doesn't seem fair.*

APRIL :: 9

CHRIS, AGE 14

READ PSALM 39:1-3

Temper, Temper

I said, "I will watch my ways and keep my tongue from sin; I will put a muzzle on my mouth."
PSALM 39:1

Do you ever get so mad at someone you just have to yell? Me too. Sometimes, when someone really makes me angry, I go beyond yelling. I swear and tell that person exactly what I think of them.

You'd think it would make me feel better to get all that rage out. But it doesn't. I feel guilty for not controlling my temper, or for hurting the person's feelings, or for doing something I know I shouldn't have done.

Even though I know swearing and yelling at other people is wrong, I think the part I really need to work on is controlling my anger in the first place. God can help me do that. Instead of getting angry about things I really can't change, I can ask God to change *me*. I know God can help me be a calmer person. And when I'm not so angry, I probably won't swear as much.

WHAT ABOUT YOU?

:: *What really makes you angry?*

:: *Think of 3 things you can do to calm down.*

:: *Ask God to help you let go of anger.*

APRIL :: 10

READ PSALM 42

Thirst-quencher

As the deer pants for streams of water, so my soul pants for you, O God. My soul thirsts for God, for the living God. When can I go and meet with God?
PSALM 42:1-2

Life isn't always easy, and sometimes we can really get discouraged. But even in those times, we can be excited about God. This psalm helps me remember how amazing God really is.

When my dad died a few years ago, I needed comfort and hope. Nothing in the world could give it to me. The only time I felt any peace was when I was singing or praying or reading God's Word. I was thirsty for comfort, and only God could quench my thirst.

Despite the things that go wrong in our lives, we must seek God. He is our Rock, our Savior. He is all we need.

WHAT ABOUT YOU?

- Think about a time when you needed God's comfort. How did God take care of you?

- Try to go all afternoon without drinking anything. How long can you last without really craving something to drink? Once you do drink something, concentrate on how great it tastes and how much better you feel after you've quenched your thirst.

- Talk to God. Tell him what's in your heart and ask him to fill you with his love.

APRIL :: 11

KRISTIN, AGE 12

READ PSALM 51

The Best of Friends

Have mercy on me, O God, according to your unfailing love.

PSALM 51:1

When I make a mistake, my first reaction is to cover it up. Once, when my brother and I were fighting, I told my mom it was my brother's fault. She yelled at him and sent him to his room. Well, then I felt guilty. So I told my mom it wasn't all my brother's fault—I was partly to blame too.

When King David sinned against God, he ignored his conscience and pretended nothing was wrong for a while. But God sent the prophet Nathan to tell David to confess his sins, and David finally owned up to his guilt.

After I talked to my mom about the situation with my brother, I knew what I had to do to make things right: Ask God for forgiveness and apologize to my brother. That's exactly what I did. And guess what? God forgave me, because he doesn't want sin coming between us. He wants me to be as close to him as a best friend.

WHAT ABOUT YOU?

:: *Imagine what it would be like trying to talk to a friend with a cement wall between you. Kind of hard to talk, huh? How is this like your relationship with God when sin comes between you?*

:: *Ask the Holy Spirit to show you your sins. Thank God for forgiveness.*

APRIL :: 12

JENNA, AGE 13

READ PSALM 55:12-16

A Friend to the End

But I call to God, and the LORD saves me.
PSALM 55:16

Imagine you're walking down the hall at school. You spot some of your friends hanging around in front of their lockers. You walk over to say hi. But when you get there, they all walk away. There you are, alone and rejected. It's the worst feeling in the world.

Earlier this year, some of my friends turned against me for no reason. I was so hurt and confused. I didn't know what to do. They wouldn't talk to me about what was going on, and I felt so helpless. But the experience taught me that even though my friends might turn against me, God never will. Even when I felt more lonely than I ever had before, I knew I could trust God to listen to me and comfort me. And he did. When I felt like no one cared, God did. When I felt like I was all alone, God was there.

So when your friends let you down, remember that God is still there, ready to listen to you and help you get through hard times. He will be a friend to the end.

WHAT ABOUT YOU?

:: *Why does it hurt so much when friends reject you?*

:: *Is there someone you've turned against? How can you repair your friendship with that person?*

:: *When you feel rejected, ask God to comfort you and to show his love to you.*

APRIL :: 13

Are You Really Sorry?

Let the wicked forsake his way.... Let him turn to the LORD, and he will have mercy on him.
ISAIAH 55:7

When you've been hurt there's nothing worse than an insincere apology. A "friend" mocks you with words that cut like razors. "Hey, don't be hurt. Sorry! I was just kidding!"—that's not exactly the apology you're looking for.

We can't control how others apologize, but we can make sure our own "sorrys" are sincere so we can experience full forgiveness. Here's how:

FACE IT. Take full responsibility for your actions, the way David did in Psalm 51.

FEEL IT. Stop and think about how you hurt the other person, and God!

FIX IT. Truly sorry people make amends.

FORSAKE IT. It's not enough to merely confess; we must repent. To repent means to turn away from our sins and go a different direction.

WHAT ABOUT YOU?

:: *How often this week did you say a quick, casual "sorry"? Do you need to offer a real apology?*

:: *For each person you've hurt this week, make a list of words that describe their feelings about what you did. Think about those feelings and "feel their pain" before you talk to them—God included.*

:: *Tell God what you did wrong and how you feel about it. Then ask him to forgive you and give you the ability to make things right with the other people involved.*

APRIL :: 14

Getting Slimed

He lifted me out of the slimy pit...and gave me a firm place to stand.
PSALM 40:2

Everybody gets slimed. Things happen that are neither fun nor your fault. Your parents split, your uncle dies, your house burns, your boyfriend or girlfriend dumps you. This verse reminds us that God rescues slimed (and slimy) people, wipes the goo from their shoes, and gives them firm footing in him. Even when your outward life is in the mud, your inward life can be secure in God, the Rock.

In Psalm 61:4 God tells us he gives us shelter under his "wings." God doesn't really have wings, but he has a huge span of care. This not only tells us of God's strength but also his tenderness. Jesus once wept over Jerusalem, saying he longed to gather its people like a hen gathers her chicks. There's no safer place than under his "wings."

When boulder-sized problems block your way, thank God anyway. Thank him for loving you. Thank him for being with you. Let him know that your confidence in him is bigger than your sadness. And don't brush off God's affection or his protection. Before you know it, God will come to help you.

Read Psalm 50:23, then write a "thank offering" to God to prepare the way for him to show you his salvation.

APRIL :: 15

CRISTINA, AGE 14

READ PSALM 69

I Messed Up

You know my folly, O God; my guilt is not hidden from you.
PSALM 69:5

Stupid, guilty, and sick to my stomach—that's how I felt when I went out with a guy while I was going steady with someone else.

I don't know what I was thinking. I really cared about my boyfriend, but I liked this other guy too. And I felt horrible about it. I hurt him, I hurt the other guy and I hurt myself. I got myself into a huge mess, and I didn't know how I would ever get out of it.

I wish I would have read this psalm then. It would have helped me to see that I could lean on God and he'd be there for me, even though I was in major trouble. God could have comforted me and given me the strength to try and make things right with my boyfriend.

The next time I mess up—and I'm sure there will be a next time—I'll know I can talk to God about it.

WHAT ABOUT YOU?

:: *Think about a time you were in big trouble. How did God help you get through?*

:: *Take another look at Psalm 69, especially verses 1–5 and 13–18. How would you put those verses in your own words?*

:: *Thank God for always being there to talk to.*

APRIL :: 16

Words from the Wise

Even when I am old and gray, do not forsake me, O God, till I declare your power to the next generation.
PSALM 71:18

A lot of people think the only thing older folks do well is boss others around and yell at them. Well, I think that too sometimes, but it really isn't true. What older people say is important.

These verses show me that I should respect the wisdom of my elders. They've been around a while, so they've seen more of God and more of life than I have. They might even help me avoid making unnecessary mistakes if I listen carefully.

Think about this: God has been around longer than anyone else. He never even had a beginning, and he'll never have an end! And when I've got gray hair, I know he'll still be teaching me and showing me new things.

WHAT ABOUT YOU?

:: *Think of a time you had less respect for an older person than you should have. Why does God tell us to listen to our elders?*

:: *Talk to a grandparent, great aunt or uncle, or an older person in your church. Ask them about some things God has taught them over the years and what he's teaching them now.*

:: *Thank the Lord for the older people in your life.*

APRIL :: 17

AMY, AGE 13

Tall Tales?

Your path led through the sea, your way through the mighty waters.
PSALM 77:19

God is powerful! I take that for granted sometimes when I get too focused on myself. But when my family was caught in a dangerous rainstorm not long ago, I had no choice but to admit that God is awesome. We were so scared, but God was in control the whole time.

In Psalm 77, David remembers how God's people suffered "storms" in the past. There were times when they didn't know where God was taking them. I'm sure they felt fearful and small too. But God took care of them, just like he took care of my family.

The more I see God lead our family safely through all kinds of situations, the more I learn to trust him. The more I trust him, the more I want to do what he says, and the more I see his faithfulness.

WHAT ABOUT YOU?

:: How has God been faithful to you over the past year? How has he taken care of your family?

:: Pray for 3 different people or families as they face "storms." Ask God to comfort and help them.

:: Thank God for being faithful to you in the past, present, and future.

APRIL :: 18

NATHAN, AGE 13

READ PSALM 91:1-4

In the Pilot's Seat

I will say of the LORD, "He is my refuge and my fortress, my God in whom I trust."
PSALM 91:2

My dad is a pilot. One day when he was flying a small plane, something went wrong. He was coming in to land, but the landing gear didn't come down. He radioed the tower, and they sent out emergency crews in case he crashed. All my dad could do was pray.

His only choice was to land without the landing gear, so he brought the plane in and skidded down the runway. He came to a stop and climbed out of the plane, unhurt. I really believe God did just what these verses promise: God protected my dad and wrapped his "wings" around him like a shield.

A lot of scary things happen in the world. But as long as I know God is there, I feel more secure and peaceful. We can trust God to be our shelter and our shield. Just ask my dad.

WHAT ABOUT YOU?

:: *Trusting in God's protection doesn't mean nothing bad will ever happen to you. Think about what it really means to say that God is our shelter and our shield.*

:: *Whenever you're facing hard times, remember that God is there, and, like a winter coat, he'll wrap you up in his love.*

APRIL :: 19

READ PSALM 103:2-3, 11-12

Great Big Love

Praise the LORD, O my soul, and forget not all his benefits—who forgives all your sins.
PSALM 103:2-3

One of my friends and I got into an argument a long time ago, and our friendship has never been the same since. We used to get along great, but now I get angry with him all the time. It seems like we fight over stuff that just doesn't matter. After reading this passage, I realize how many times God has forgiven me. And it reminds me that I need to be forgiving too.

I've always known that God forgives me. But I don't always think about what a huge and amazing thing forgiveness really is. I mean, God's love and forgiveness are pretty incredible. And if God can forgive us for the thousands of things we do wrong, it sure seems like we can learn to forgive other people.

WHAT ABOUT YOU?

:: How do you feel when someone forgives you?

:: Go for a walk someplace where there's sand or dirt you can write in with a stick. Write something you'd like to be forgiven for. Tell God you're sorry and ask him to forgive you. Now, use water or the stick to erase what you've written. What does this tell you about God's forgiveness?

:: Thank God for his repeated forgiveness.

APRIL :: 20

Two Kinds of Care Packages

My grace is sufficient for you, for my power is made perfect in weakness.
2 CORINTHIANS 12:9

You've read two stories of God's awesome power. He brought Amy and her family through a raging storm and enabled Nathan's father to safely land a plane without the landing gear. The Bible calls this deliverance

But deliverance is only one of God's care packages. The other is called perseverance. Perseverance is the power to hang in there, to keep going, to stick with it through tough times. And the power to persevere comes from God too—just as much as his miracle-working power does.

The passage for today describes the care package God sent Paul when he prayed for healing from his "thorn in the flesh" (some kind of illness he had). Three times Paul prayed for deliverance—he wanted to be healed. But each time God sent perseverance, the power to put up with the problem. Paul realized that God's help can come in 2 different packages.

WHAT ABOUT YOU?

:: Write a "perseverance plan" for the biggest problem in your life. If God were to give you the power to put up with this problem, what would you have the power to do? What attitudes and actions would you be able to take?

:: You're still allowed to ask for miracles—for deliverance. But also ask God for perseverance and the ability to accept it if that's what he sends.

_____

_____

_____

_____

_____

_____

APRIL :: 21

Alphabet Songs

Glorify the LORD with me; let us exalt his name together.
PSALM 34:3

Several of the psalms are acrostic poems. It'd be like a guy named Buzz writing this mini-psalm:

>> Always God watches me (I'm Buzz).

>> Before the world was, God was.

>> Creation is his gift, for free.

>> Darkness does not frighten me.

...and so on. Besides the goofy rhyme, you can see how each line begins with the next letter of the alphabet. If you think for a moment, you can see the purpose behind writing songs like this...yes, they're easier to memorize! You can see acrostic songs in Psalms 25, 34, 37, 111, 112, 119, and 145. But, uh, you might not recognize the alphabet—since it's the Hebrew alphabet!

Psalm 119 is really different. This chapter has the most verses of any chapter in the Bible, and every verse is about the Word of God. The first 8 verses all begin, in Hebrew, with the letter aleph. The next 8 verses (9–16) all begin with the Hebrew letter beth, and so on.

Try this: Choose any 4 consecutive letters of the alphabet, and write a mini-psalm/song of your own to God. It doesn't have to rhyme, but it can if you want it to; you just have to start each line with the next letter in the alphabet.

APRIL :: 22

MANDY, AGE 13

READ PSALM 116

Wiping the Tears Away

I love the LORD, for he heard my voice; he heard my cry for mercy.
PSALM 116:1

There are some times in our lives when we feel all alone. When a good friend of mine died, I was filled with so much grief and sorrow that I thought nobody could understand. I didn't even think God was listening. But Psalm 116:6 says, "The LORD protects the simple hearted; when I was in great need, he saved me." As I read that, I realized that because God loves me, he will take care of me in every situation. I can trust him.

God does hear us when we're in pain. He was there when I cried out to him about my friend, even though I couldn't hear his voice. He always answers us, though the answers aren't always what we want them to be.

WHAT ABOUT YOU?

:: *Think back on a time you couldn't "feel" God's presence in your life. How did you start to sense his presence in your life again?*

:: *Psalm 116 says the world is full of God's presence. We know that God is all around us. How does that change how you feel about him?*

:: *Ask God to heal your hurts. Thank him for being there, even when you're feeling pain.*

APRIL :: 23

READ PSALM 119:105-112

God's Flashlight

Your word is a lamp to my feet and a light to my path.
PSALM 119:105

When I was in preschool, I was afraid of the dark. I thought that if there wasn't any light in a room, it wasn't safe to go in. I'm not so afraid of the dark now, of course, but I'm not crazy about it either.

Walking in the dark can be dangerous. Walking off the path God wants us to follow is dangerous too. But the Bible shows us the right path and helps us stay on it. It's kind of like having a flashlight at night. It helps you feel safe and keeps you out of trouble.

WHAT ABOUT YOU?

:: *Think of a time when you were struggling. In what ways was the Bible "a light for [your] path"?*

:: *Roam around your house in the dark. Think about why darkness can be so scary. Then turn on the lights. Makes quite a difference, huh?*

:: *Thank God for giving us his Word to light our path.*

APRIL :: 24

READ PSALM 133

Keep the Peace

How good and pleasant it is when brothers live together in unity!
PSALM 133:1

Sometimes I do some really stupid things that hurt my relationships with other people. Like the time I did something I shouldn't have and blamed it on my sister. I was scared my parents would yell at me. Since I'm older, my parents believed me and got mad at my sister. As punishment, they wouldn't let her go to her friend's house. I felt a little bad, but to be honest, I was really thinking, *Hey, I didn't get into any trouble.*

But a few days later my parents found out I was the one who did it and got really mad at me. They weren't all that angry about the original thing I did; they were upset with me for lying. My sister was mad at me too. And I started to realize that I'd messed up my relationships with 3 people I love, just to avoid getting into trouble.

God wants us to get along with each other. Life is so much better when we live the way God wants us to and show each other love.

WHAT ABOUT YOU?

:: Write down 3 things you can do to help strengthen your relationships with your family, your friends, or your youth group.

:: Ask God to help you be someone who makes your relationships better, not worse.

APRIL :: 25

RACHEL, AGE 12

READ PSALM 136

God's Forever-love

Give thanks to the LORD, for he is good. His love endures forever.
PSALM 136:1

God loves you no matter what. Even when you sin or turn away from him, he'll always forgive you, if you confess that you've sinned and rebelled (see 1 John 1:9). God will never leave you.

You might not think of him this way, but God really should be your best friend. He's someone you can tell your innermost secrets to, and he's someone you can be accountable to. He'll help you out of tough situations, like he helped the Israelites get away from Pharaoh. And he loves you more than anyone else will, ever. His love never goes away—it just seems to get bigger the more you know him.

WHAT ABOUT YOU?

:: Much of this psalm is like a time line, with the Israelites remembering all that God had done for them in the past. Write your own "time line psalm" with memories from your life, and make every other line "His love endures forever."

:: Verse 1 says, "Give thanks to the LORD, for he is good." When you pray today, thank the Lord for all the good things he has done for you.

JONATHAN, AGE 14

READ PSALM 139:13-16

Handmade by God

I praise you because I am fearfully and wonderfully made; your works are wonderful, I know that full well.
PSALM 139:14

I've been really short all my life, and I'm not exactly built for sports. Sometimes I feel very self-conscious at school, especially around people who are super-athletic. I look at them and think, *Why did I have to be so small and weak?* Or when I'm around people who are really popular, I feel like I don't measure up.

Lucky for me, God doesn't judge me by how handsome or strong I am. He doesn't care how well I play sports or how popular I am. He loves me for who I am. And he's happy when he looks at my heart, because he sees a person who loves Jesus and is trying to do what's right.

So to anyone else who sometimes feels like a klutz or a nerd, I'd say, "God made you, and he loves you. Don't worry about who you aren't—praise God for who you are!"

WHAT ABOUT YOU?

:: How do people at school judge who's "the best"? How do you think God judges who's "the best"?

:: Write down 10 things you like about the way God made you.

:: Praise God for creating you and loving you just the way you are.

_____

_____

_____

_____

_____

_____

_____

APRIL :: 27

How Important Is the Bible?

Let the word of Christ dwell in you richly.
COLOSSIANS 3:16

Back in Psalm 119, the psalm that Julia wrote about, we find 3 verses that help us figure out whether the Bible is as important to us as it should be.

Verse 72 says, "The law from your mouth is more precious to me than thousands of pieces of silver and gold." Is God's Word more important to you than money—even big stacks of it?

Verse 103 says, "How sweet are your words to my taste, sweeter than honey to my mouth!" Is the Bible more important to you than food?

Verse 148 reads, "My eyes stay open through the watches of the night, that I may meditate on your promises." Is God's Word more important to you than sleep?

When our lives prove that the Bible holds more value to us than money, food, or sleep, we know it is dwelling in us richly, changing our lives and lighting our path.

WHAT ABOUT YOU?

:: *When was the last time you made a sacrifice to get God's Word into your life? Try "fasting"—or skipping one meal this week—in order to have more time to read your Bible.*

:: *Ask God to help you to fall in love with his Word so that you'll read it not because you have to but because you want to!*

APRIL :: 28

READ PSALM 150:1-6

Rock On!

Praise him with resounding cymbals. Let everything that has breath praise the LORD.
PSALM 150:5-6

The book of Psalms is a collection of old, Jewish songs, contributed by King David and other song-writers. It became the Hebrew national songbook—a hymnal for 3,000 years of Jewish worship, and a source for lots of newer Christian songs too.

Jews still sing these psalms during worship, holy days, and festivals. Christians have been singing these ancient songs too—though often put to contemporary music instead of harps and organs.

Songs can be pretty boring when they're just read, because songs are meant to be sung. Just reading the lyrics can be as boring as just reading the script of a play. To feel the range of passions in these psalms—the joy, sadness, anger, peace—they've really got to be sung.

Psalms ends on a high note, with a call to wild, energetic praise. In addition to using the usual hymnbook and organ, we need to praise God in every way imaginable. Psalm 150, carefully chosen to close out the Worship Book of the Bible, calls for horn blasts, cymbal crashes, and waves of sound.

WHAT ABOUT YOU?

:: *Can you think of a way to kick it up a notch when you praise God?*

APRIL :: 29

MEGAN, AGE 14

Good Enough for God

Do not plot harm against your neighbor, who lives trustfully near you.
PROVERBS 3:29

I've said some things in my life that I've regretted. One of the biggest things I regret saying involves a girl I hardly knew. When I was with a bunch of my friends at a slumber party, I started gossiping about this girl—talking about her behind her back and saying things about her that just weren't true. Eventually she found out, and I lost the chance to ever be her friend. I tried to make things right, but she never said another word to me.

Proverbs 3:29 says that I should not do any harm to the people around me. When I gossiped about this girl, I hurt her, and I hurt God too. God created each person in a special way. When we make fun of someone, it's like we're telling God, "That girl or guy isn't good enough for me." And how can we do that when that person is good enough for God?

WHAT ABOUT YOU?

:: *Name a person you find it easy to make fun of. Write down 5 qualities you admire in that person. The next time you see that girl or guy, focus on the things you like about him or her.*

:: *Thank God for loving you the way you are. Ask him to help you see what's special in others.*

Living on the Edge

Can a man scoop fire into his lap without his clothes being burned?... So is he who sleeps with another man's wife; no one who touches her will go unpunished.
PROVERBS 6:27, 29

Imagine looking through a store window at something you really want. But the store is closed. Would you break the window and steal it? Of course not!

No one in their right mind would go for that! But it's kind of like that with sexual temptation. If you give in, you might be happy for a few minutes, or even a few days, but in the end there are real consequences. The guilt starts to set in. So does the regret.

Satan does a good job of tricking us when it comes to sexual temptation. Often, he blinds us so we can't even see the danger. All of us need the wisdom of God and the voice of the Holy Spirit to help us avoid this dangerous trap.

WHAT ABOUT YOU?

:: *Have you ever been tempted to think or act in a way that you knew would be a sin? What did you do? What helped or could have helped you resist?*

:: *Why do you think the author of Proverbs compares sexual temptation to fire?*

:: *Thank God for giving you the strength to resist temptation. Pray that the Holy Spirit will help you make wise decisions.*

MAY :: 1

More Than Anything Else

Wisdom is more precious than rubies.
PROVERBS 8:11

It's easy to get hung up on worldly treasures. I mean, silver and gold and rubies are pretty valuable things. Most people my age aren't into jewels, but we've got our own treasures—CDs, video games, and clothes, for instance. It's okay to have that stuff, but it's not what's truly valuable in life.

In today's passage, God says wisdom and instruction are worth more than anything else we could have. That's because those things actually help us live the right way. I know I don't look for wisdom and instruction enough. I should read my Bible more and pray when I'm wondering how to live everyday life. And I shouldn't look for answers in worldly treasures, because the answer isn't found there. When I talk to God, I know he's listening and he's got the right answers.

WHAT ABOUT YOU?

:: What are your most valuable worldly treasures? Why do you think God's wisdom and instruction are worth so much more?

:: Thank God for his good gifts to you. Thank him especially for wisdom and instruction.

MAY 2

READ PROVERBS 10:1; 17:21

Good Grief!

A wise son brings joy to his father, but a foolish son grief to his mother.
PROVERBS 10:1

I've always thought sin was one of those things that was just between me and God. I mess up, I ask for forgiveness, God forgives me and I try not to mess up again. But this verse says my sins don't just affect me and God. They affect other people too. Especially my parents.

When I do something good, I know my parents are proud of me and happy for me. But I never really thought about how they must feel when I do something bad. It must hurt them when I disobey. And since my parents are Christians, I know they must be disappointed when I ignore God's commandments.

This verse has helped me grow closer to my parents. Now I see things from my parents' point of view too, instead of just my own.

WHAT ABOUT YOU?

:: Think about a time your parents were upset with you. Why do you think your actions bothered them?

:: Ask your parents how they feel when you do something wrong. The next time you're tempted to sin, think about what they said.

:: Ask God to help you bring joy to your parents, not grief.

MAY :: 3

READ PROVERBS 12:17–19

A Put-down

Reckless words cut like a sword, but the tongue of the wise brings healing.
PROVERBS 12:18

One of my friends used to brag about how great she was at sports. But the truth was that she really wasn't a very good athlete. Finally, my other friends and I told her what we really thought, and we weren't very nice about it. Sure, we told the truth, but we didn't do it to be honest with her. We did it to put her in her place. She was crushed.

We could have been a lot nicer about how we told her the truth. One of us could have said something to her in private, so she wouldn't have been embarrassed. We could have helped her feel good about some of her other great qualities instead of making fun of her weakness.

It's easy to put other people down. And when we say things without really thinking, we aren't following Jesus' command to love each other. We need to use our words to build each other up.

WHAT ABOUT YOU?

:: *Think about a time you might have hurt someone with your words. Write a "script" of what happened. Now, rewrite the script so that your words build the person up instead of hurting them.*

:: *Tell God about the times you've hurt people with your words and ask for his forgiveness.*

MAY :: 4

READ LUKE 15:1-7

Reaching Out

The Pharisees and the teachers of the law muttered, "This man welcomes sinners and eats with them."
LUKE 15:2

One of the greatest personal criticisms ever made about Jesus was that he was a friend of tax collectors and sinners. Tax collecting was the lowest job a Jewish man could do, because he took money from his own Jewish people and turned it over to the Romans. The worst thing a woman could be was a "sinner," a polite way of saying "prostitute." So when people accused Jesus of being friends with tax collectors and sinners, they associated him with the rejects, the lowest of the low. And Jesus didn't mind! That's who he came to identify with. That's who he came to save!

If Jesus built his kingdom around the "lowlifes," why do we try to build our groups around the superstars? We need to try to reach everyone, but we must also remember that the "tax collectors and sinners"—those people society considers losers—often understand best their need for forgiveness.

WHAT ABOUT YOU?

:: Who in your school or neighborhood would most likely fit in with the kind of people Jesus hung out with? Next time you go to youth group, talk about what you all could do to reach out to a few of these people who need to know about Jesus.

:: Ask God to give you creative ways to expand your social group to include even those nobody loves.

MAY :: 5

Instructions Worth Reading

Wisdom calls aloud in the street, she raises her voice in the public squares.
PROVERBS 1:20

Almost everything you buy comes with instructions—you know, that piece of paper or that paragraph on the box you never read with all the important stuff on it? Well, if there were ever instructions for how to live right as a teenager (or any ager), they are in the book of Proverbs. Most of the book was written by the wisest, smartest man who ever lived: King Solomon.

In Proverbs, wisdom is treated as if it were a person. "She" speaks and teaches and helps those who listen to "her." Some people have taken this writing technique and made a whole belief system out of it. They say Wisdom is a goddess. That's goofy, to say the least. "Wisdom" is simply the smarts of God. The writer of Proverbs wants to get our attention so that we will pursue wisdom with a passion.

WHAT ABOUT YOU?

:: *Sometimes the best way to understand a Scripture passage is to put it in your own words. Try writing your own personal Proverbs 3:1–6. Use language you and your friends use every day.*

ROBYN, AGE 13

READ PROVERBS 16:2; 1 CORINTHIANS 4:5

Channel Surfing

All a man's ways seem innocent to him, but motives are weighed by the LORD.
PROVERBS 16:2

A lot of things that seem harmless to me might not be so harmless in God's eyes. Take TV, for example. I usually don't think much about what I watch. Of course, I know there's some bad stuff out there, and I should be more careful. It's just so easy to watch whatever I want.

Today's verses make sense to me. I can pretend I'm innocent as long as I don't pay too much attention to what I'm doing. That's the wrong attitude. When I do that, I'm not looking at television with the best motives. I'm just being lazy and watching whatever I can get away with. And that's definitely not what God wants for me. He wants me to do things that honor him and help me to grow as a Christian— not settle for what seems "harmless."

WHAT ABOUT YOU?

:: Turn off the TV for 3 days. At the end of that time, ask yourself: What did I miss about TV? What did I learn about myself? About God? Use what you learn to help you decide what to watch in the future.

:: Ask the Holy Spirit to help you make wise choices.

MAY :: 7

MICHAEL, AGE 13

READ PROVERBS 20:1; 23:20-21

Alcohol Abusers

Wine is a mocker and beer a brawler; whoever is led astray by them is not wise.
PROVERBS 20:1

My dad's best friend killed himself, and it had to do with drinking. So when I hear people talking about how bad it is to drink too much beer and wine, I know they're serious. This guy had started drinking a lot because he didn't know how to handle his problems, but then he realized that his drinking was the biggest problem of all. Now he's gone, and his family is stuck with the problems.

Drinking is a terrible thing to get started on because it can ruin your life. Once you're into it, it's really hard to get out. God can help you stop drinking, if you ask him, but some major damage might already be done. So don't drink—it's not worth it!

WHAT ABOUT YOU?

:: Why do you think drinking is such a big temptation for so many people?

:: Have a serious talk with your parents about drinking. Find out what they think about alcohol and why. If you want to, you can all write and sign a "contract" where you promise to follow your parents' rules about drinking.

:: Ask God to help you and your friends resist the temptation of alcohol.

READ PROVERBS 21:13; 22:9

Smelly Clothes

If a man shuts his ears to the cry of the poor, he too will cry out and not be answered.
PROVERBS 21:13

My youth group did a missions project in the inner city. I was excited about it at first, but when we actually got to the place we'd be working, I saw all these people with old, dirty clothes, smelling like they hadn't taken a shower in weeks. I couldn't help but be kind of grossed out.

It didn't take long for me to realize they were real people who needed love. And when I showed them love, I found myself receiving love in return.

I went on the missions trip thinking I could make a difference in people's lives. But the people I met made a difference in my life too. They taught me that God wants me to show love to other people, no matter who they are. He wants me to be thankful for what I have and use it to help people who don't have much. He wants me to reach out to all of his people, not just the ones with nice houses and clean clothes.

WHAT ABOUT YOU?

:: *Why do we tend to resist helping poor people?*

:: *List 5 ways you can help someone less fortunate than you. Choose one to do in the next 2 days.*

:: *Ask God to help you reach out to the needy.*

MAY :: 9

SARAH, AGE 14

Slippery Slope

A little sleep, a little slumber...and poverty will come on you like a bandit.
PROVERBS 24:33–34

Right now my grades are really bad. I knew they were going downhill, but I kept thinking, *They're not that bad.* Well, now they are that bad and improving them is going to take a lot of work. It would have been easier if I'd put in a little extra effort when my grades first started slipping.

Grades aren't the only thing that can go downhill fast. When I push God aside or think other things are more important than praying or reading my Bible, it doesn't take long for my relationship with God to slip. I need to make God a priority in my life all the time.

These verses have a lot to say about keeping on top of the things that are important in my life. Leaving things for later—whether it's my homework or spending time with God—always leads to more work and trouble.

WHAT ABOUT YOU?

:: *What are some things you avoid doing? What happens when you let those things slide?*

:: *Make up a daily schedule and plan a time for the things you need to do every day, like quiet time, homework, and chores. Stick with your schedule for the remainder of this week. How does it feel to stay on top of things?*

MAY :: 10

AMBER, AGE 13

READ PROVERBS 22:11; 27:17

The Buddy System

As iron sharpens iron, so one man sharpens another.
PROVERBS 27:17

I have this friend who sometimes dresses, well, in a way that shows off her body. I've never said anything to her about it, but after reading this verse, I think I need to talk with her about my concern. I want her to start thinking about honoring God by dressing in a less suggestive way.

One of the reasons God gives us Christian friends is so we can help each other want to get stronger in our faith. We need to confront each other in a loving way when we see stuff happening that shouldn't be happening. Being corrected isn't a pleasant experience, but when our friends correct us, God's using them to help us grow. And God can use us to help them grow too.

WHAT ABOUT YOU?

:: *How have your friends helped your faith grow? How have you helped them?*

:: *Think about something you want to do to get closer to God, like read your Bible more often, get more involved in your youth group, or just be more bold about your faith. Now, ask your best friend to let you know when you've messed up and to encourage you when you're making progress.*

:: *Thank God for friends who encourage you to grow closer to God.*

MAY :: 11

Gray Areas

Everything is permissible for me—but not everything is beneficial.
1 CORINTHIANS 6:12

This week 3 "gray areas" have come up—issues that are not clearly black or white, right or wrong. Television, alcohol, clothing styles—how do you know what to do in these areas? Of course, for kids alcohol is clearly out, since it's illegal. But what about the others?

There are 2 extremes to avoid. The first one is *license*—that's the party-on attitude that says, "Hey, if it's not illegal, it's fine." Christians get into all kinds of trouble if their standards aren't higher than this.

The other extreme is just as dangerous. It's called *legalism*, which is thinking that you have to obey a huge list of do's and don'ts in order to be close to God.

Between these 2 extremes is real *liberty*, the ability to enjoy what's good in life while avoiding what's bad.

WHAT ABOUT YOU?

:: *List some issues in your life that are gray areas (activities that the Bible doesn't specifically say are right or wrong).*

:: *Using the questions above, try to develop some guidelines to help make good decisions in these gray areas. Then talk to your parents or a youth group leader to get their opinions.*

:: *Ask God to give you wisdom to live well in a gray world.*

MAY :: 12

Discerning What Is Pleasing to God

There are six things the LORD hates, seven that are detestable to him.
PROVERBS 6:16

Everybody has their pet peeves: fingernails on the chalkboard, "up" toilet seats, that kind of stuff. Some people even have things they can't stand: racism, pollution, animal extinction. Did you know God has a list of things he truly, massively hates? These things make his wrath erupt like a solar flare. Note from our verse today that 2 of them have to do with lying. Uh oh.

But when it comes to some things, it is not always easy to tell right from wrong. To help figure it out, ask yourself these 4 questions:

>> Will it please God? Avoid anything that God will eventually judge and destroy.

>> Will it help me? Think about whether the activity is beneficial for your health and spiritual growth.

>> Could it enslave me? If the activity is tempting, addicting, or really time-consuming, watch out.

>> Will it hurt someone else? How would it feel to be in their shoes? Put your questionable activities to these tests, and you're likely to find your way through life's gray areas.

MAY :: 13

BECCA, AGE 12

READ ECCLESIASTES 3:1-11

A Lil' Bit of Everything

There is a time for everything, and a season for every activity under heaven.
ECCLESIASTES 3:1

God gives us work to do on earth. Most of the time, God doesn't automatically make the work easy. We'll have many difficulties. God will provide for our needs, though, and we need to accept the work he has for us—even if it's hard.

This is a great passage to remember when you're having a hard time. It reminds us that there is a time for everything. Life won't always be easy and perfect, but that doesn't mean God has lost control. He has special work cut out for each of us as Christians. He can see the whole picture, so he knows how the good and bad will fit together in the end. We just need to obey him, do his work, and trust him always!

WHAT ABOUT YOU?

:: *Think of all the different things you do in a typical day. What would your life be like if you just did the same thing over and over again?*

:: *Thank God for being in control of everything that happens—good and bad.*

STACY, AGE 15

READ ECCLESIASTES 4:9-12

Dynamic Duo

Two are better than one.
ECCLESIASTES 4:9

When I was in 4th grade, I didn't have a single friend. Every day I would get picked on and teased because I wasn't very athletic or popular. Day after day I'd go to school feeling like a nobody.

Then 5th grade started, and there was a new girl in class. She was athletic, pretty, and very talented. There was no way she'd ever be my friend—or so I thought. One day when the boys were picking on me (as usual), the new girl walked over and chased them off. She stuck around and hung out with me that day at recess, and we started hanging out together every day. I wasn't lonely any more!

There's a lot of truth in what these verses say about friends. Life can be tough without them. So appreciate the friends you have, and reach out to people who need friends. It really can make a difference!

WHAT ABOUT YOU?

:: *What's the nicest thing a friend has ever done for you?*

:: *Do something special for a close friend this week, like bringing them their favorite food or just saying, "Thanks for being there for me!"*

:: *Pray for your friends and thank God for them.*

MAY :: 15

A.J., AGE 13

READ ECCLESIASTES 5:10-11

More, More, More

Whoever loves money never has money enough.
ECCLESIASTES 5:10

I love baseball cards. Whenever I make a little money, I go to the card shop and buy another pack to add to my collection. But then I look at the cards in that pack, and I wonder if I could get better ones if I just bought another pack or 2. Soon I've bought several packs of cards, and I've spent all my money!

You'd think I would know better by now. It's not like I set out to waste all my money. I guess I trick myself by thinking that I'll be happy if I get the right cards or if I buy more of them. Lots of people try to make themselves happy with cars or clothes or other material possessions, but that just doesn't work. More stuff doesn't ever make us really happy. The only thing that will satisfy us is more of God.

WHAT ABOUT YOU?

:: *What things make you happy? Why won't material things ever make you truly happy?*

:: *The next time you really want to buy something, wait a week. Why? Waiting a week will keep you from buying on a whim. And it'll give you time to think about how God wants you to spend your money.*

:: *Ask God to help you trust in him, not material things, for your happiness.*

MAY :: 16

READ ECCLESIASTES 7:14; 2 CORINTHIANS 9:8

Dashed Dreams

When times are good, be happy; but when times are bad, consider: God has made the one as well as the other.
ECCLESIASTES 7:14

Right before 9th grade, everything was going great for me. I had tons of Christian friends, and I considered them my "brothers" and "sisters." After years of home schooling, I was all set to join my friends at a public high school. Four years of good times were right around the corner.

Then I found out my family was moving. One minute everything was awesome, and the next minute my dreams were all taken away. But from that experience, I've learned that God doesn't always give us "Hollywood" lives. He guides us through trials and bad times too, so we can learn how to put our trust in him. God's the one with the perfect plan for our lives—not us.

WHAT ABOUT YOU?

:: What's usually your first reaction when something doesn't go your way? Does that reaction help the situation or make it worse?

:: Make a small sign that says "God's in control!" and put it someplace where you'll see it often.

:: Thank God for being in control of your life.

MAY :: 17

READ ECCLESIASTES 10:1-15

Making the Most of It

The heart of the wise inclines to the right.
ECCLESIASTES 10:2

When I became a Christian, I had some friends who weren't exactly helping me live my new faith. For a while I thought I could still hang around with my old friends and just stay away from anything that didn't fit with my faith. But that didn't work. I knew I needed friends who would build me up and encourage me to grow in my faith.

I thought it would be easy to find Christian friends at my church, but even there I had to look hard to find people who were serious about their faith. Eventually, I found a few people I really trusted—Christian friends who help me build a better relationship with God.

Yeah, it was hard to let go of my old friends. But my first loyalty is to God. If I'm really going to live for him, he has to be first in my life. I figure, I've got one life to live for Christ. I've got to make the most of it.

WHAT ABOUT YOU?

- *Think about your closest friends. How do they help or hurt your Christian life?*

- *Write down some ways you can help your Christian friends grow in their faith.*

- *Ask God to help you live out your faith more, no matter who you're around.*

MAY :: 18

READ PROVERBS 12:26; 27:6

Good Friends, Bad Friends

A righteous man is cautious in friendship.
PROVERBS 12:26

Stacy, Susanna, and Chris each mentioned how important friendship is. Finding and keeping good friends is important now and always. Good friends are difficult to find and keep for anyone, regardless of their age.

What's a good friend? It's simple. A good friend is someone you can trust to tell you the truth, even when you don't want to hear it. A good friend likes you, likes being around you, and is loyal to you. Jesus knew how to be a good friend. He called his disciples friends.

What is a bad friend? It's simple. A bad friend is a friend you can't trust. A bad friend is someone who doesn't respect what matters to you. A bad friend is someone who tries to get you to do things he or she knows you don't believe in. Here's the deal: It's better to have no friends than have friends who don't care what happens to you.

So keep looking for friends. But the writer of Proverbs warns you to be careful! Not all friendships are good for you. Uh...remember Judas?

WHAT ABOUT YOU?

:: Who is one of your good friends and why?

:: Write a letter to this friend, telling him or her why you appreciate your friendship.

:: Ask God to show you how to be a better friend.

MAY :: 19

Anti-angst

A man can do nothing better than to eat and drink and find satisfaction in his work. This too, I see, is from the hand of God, for without him, who can eat or find enjoyment?
ECCLESIASTES 2:24–25

Every day on the radio you can hear all kinds of angry and depressing songs about the meaningless-ness of life. It seems like all you need is a tune and a 'tude and you can make millions—and still not be happy. The dark and depressing tone (often called angst) of a lot of music reminds us that money, pleasure, and popularity are powerless to satisfy the soul. So what can we do?

That's what Ecclesiastes seeks to answer. The author was a guy who saw it all and did it all, but still wasn't happy. So he wrote all his frustrations down in his journal. Many of his 3,000-year-old themes you hear coming through in today's hit songs. This book sounds pretty familiar.

Even though he saw lots of bad stuff, he also saw the good stuff. Of course, this Bible writer did have some great thoughts. Since life is short and pretty senseless, he said you ought to do 3 things: Keep everything in balance, honor God, and enjoy what you can. That's not the final word on what it means to be godly, but it's not a bad start. Especially if you've come down with a nasty case of teen-age angst.

The Right Time

Do not arouse or awaken love until it so desires.

SONG OF SONGS 2:7

Recently this boy asked me to be his girlfriend. I told him no, because I think I'm too young to get into that kind of thing. And my mom doesn't want me to date until I'm 16 anyway. I knew it just wasn't the right time.

It's important to realize that love isn't something to play around with. This verse in Song of Songs makes that clear. We shouldn't run into a dating relationship simply because everyone else thinks it's okay. God wants us to wait for the right person, not because he doesn't want us to have a good time but because he wants us to have the best time.

WHAT ABOUT YOU?

:: Think about a time in your life when you had to wait a long time for something you were really excited about. When you finally had the experience, how did the waiting make it even better? Think of waiting for real love the same way.

:: Talk to your parents about their rules for dating. Write them down, in the form of a contract, and then have everyone sign it.

:: Ask God to help you be patient while you wait for him to bring true love into your life.

MAY :: 21

STACEY, AGE 13

READ SONG OF SONGS 8:6-7

True Love

Many waters cannot quench love; rivers cannot wash it away.
SONG OF SONGS 8:7

I suppose it's pretty normal for a junior high girl to think about love. These verses describe the kind of love I hope to find one day, because it's the real thing.

Sometimes I think love is taken so lightly. People talk about being in love with someone, then 2 weeks later, they're in love with someone else. But real love, the kind King Solomon and his beloved had in this book of the Bible, is a strong commitment. It's a solemn promise that lasts forever, not a few weeks. It's the kind of love God has for us. It can never die.

WHAT ABOUT YOU?

:: How is lasting love different from the "2-week" kind?

:: Think of a married couple who really love each other. Watch them carefully and list some of the ways they show their love for each other.

:: Ask God to help you wait patiently for real love.

MAY :: 22

READ ISAIAH 1:18; JEREMIAH 33:8

The Big Clean-up

Though your sins are like scarlet, they shall be as white as snow.
ISAIAH 1:18

When I think of someone who's "dirty," I think of a garbage collector, or a little kid playing in mud, or maybe someone in a really poor country where people don't have showers. But inside, I'm as dirty as the dirtiest person on the planet. Or at least I would be if God hadn't cleaned me up.

My sins—the things that make me dirty inside—are all washed away because of my faith in Jesus Christ. I don't have to carry them anymore, because he carried them all with him to the cross.

This is one of my favorite verses in the whole Bible. It reminds me of everything Jesus did for me, and it reminds me to thank God for his forgiveness. My life would be a mess if I was stuck with my sins. But instead I'm free, clean, happy, and forgiven.

WHAT ABOUT YOU?

:: *Imagine what life would be like if no one ever said, "I forgive you." Why is forgiveness so important in your relationship with God?*

:: *Thank God for his forgiveness.*

MAY :: 23

Send Me!

I said, "Here am I. Send me!"
ISAIAH 6:8

On the last night of our youth retreat, our youth pastor opened the mic up to us and invited us to talk about what God had done in our lives. We all just sat there. I finally went up, hoping God would have something to say through me. As I opened my mouth, I felt God giving me the words to say. I ignored my fears about talking in front of people and found out that I have a gift for sharing God's Word with others. Now I'm a regular speaker at my school's Fellowship of Christian Students.

That experience showed me that anyone willing to say, "Lord, send me" will be sent. Everyone has gifts. And God, the Creator and Ruler of the universe, uses the gifts of ordinary people to do his work. What a privilege!

Be open to God's plans for you and tell him you want to be called. And hang on tight, because when God starts using you, you move fast!

WHAT ABOUT YOU?

:: *Why are we sometimes afraid to let God use us? How can you get over your fears and get ready to be used by God?*

:: *Ask your youth leader how you can become more involved in your youth group and church. Find a way to use your gifts.*

:: *Tell God if you're ready to go wherever he leads you.*

M A Y :: 2 4

LAURA, AGE 12

What Child Is This?

For to us a child is born, to us a son is given.... And he will be called Wonderful Counselor, Mighty God, Everlasting Father, Prince of Peace.
ISAIAH 9:6

If you ever think that maybe God's forgotten the world, this is the passage for you. Way back when the Old Testament was written, this prophet named Isaiah knew that people felt pretty hopeless. They had been through a lot of pain and suffering and thought it would never end.

But Isaiah promised them things would get better. He told the people about a baby who would save the world from sin. He told them that this baby would be the Son of God and that he would bring everlasting peace. Maybe the people thought Isaiah was crazy for talking that way.

But we know Isaiah wasn't crazy. God *did* send his Son to live and die for us. When we accept Jesus as our Savior, we will have everlasting peace.

WHAT ABOUT YOU?

:: *What are 2 things that make you feel hopeless? How can trusting God help you find hope?*

:: *As you read through Isaiah, look for other prophecies about Jesus. Write down the things Isaiah says about Jesus. The next time you read any of the Gospels, look for the ways Jesus fulfills Isaiah's prophecies.*

:: *Thank God for keeping his promises and giving us hope for an incredible life with him.*

MAY :: 25

READ ROMANS 7:15–8:4

Once a Sinner, Always a Sinner

Therefore, there is now no condemnation for those who are in Christ Jesus.
ROMANS 8:1

How do you stop struggling with sin? You don't. Aaron talked in his devotion about getting clean from his sins because of Jesus Christ. Not being stuck with our sins is a very cool thing.

The apostle Paul says that he had the desire to do good but sometimes couldn't make it happen. Can you relate? Whether you are 14 or 97, you struggle with sin. But the key word is *struggle*. Hopefully you'll always resist. Never give up *fighting* sin in your life.

And here's the good news: No matter how many times you fail, "There is now no condemnation for those who are in Christ Jesus." Jesus is more than willing to forgive you if you're willing to ask him to forgive you. That's why grace is amazing and why the love of Jesus is awesome.

WHAT ABOUT YOU?

:: *Do you really believe God will forgive you no matter how many times you sin?*

:: *Ask an adult you respect for ideas on how to overcome a sin you are struggling with.*

:: *Ask God to help you to keep from sinning in that area of your life.*

MAY :: 2 6

READ ISAIAH 9:2; 11:1-2

God's Megaphone

The people walking in darkness have seen a great light.
ISAIAH 9:2

Prophets were people chosen by God to speak for him. And Isaiah was a super-mega-prophet—one of the greatest prophets ever. If they had dictionaries in Jerusalem in 700 B.C. and you looked up the word prophet, it would talk about Isaiah! Isaiah was God's megaphone to the people of Judah (remember, the country split in 2: Israel became the northern part, and Judah the southern part).

And while Isaiah did a lot of preaching about turning from sin, he also made some major prophetic predictions—even about Jesus Christ! Even the structure of the book is prophetic in some ways: It has 66 chapters, just like the Bible has 66 books. The first section of 39 chapters starts with Israel's sin. The first 39 books of the Bible (the Old Testament) begin with Adam and Eve's sin. The last 27 chapters of Isaiah offer forgiveness and hope to everyone, just like the last 27 books of the Bible (the New Testament) offer Jesus Christ, our only source of forgiveness and hope, to the whole world. Isaiah wrote this hundreds of years before the New Testament books were even written. Cool, huh?

MAY :: 27

READ ISAIAH 24:1-3

Judgment Day

The LORD is going to lay waste the earth and devastate it.
ISAIAH 24:1

There are a lot of verses in the Bible that tell us about God's love. But there are other parts of the Bible that aren't so nice to read. This is one of them.

Sometimes we forget just how powerful God is and how easy it would be for him to destroy everyone on the planet. This passage tells us that God will judge human beings one day. It won't matter if someone is rich or poor, strong or weak, a master or a servant. People who haven't given their lives to God will feel God's powerful judgment and wrath.

When I read these verses and hear what God will do to the earth one day, it makes me thankful that I've given my life to him. I know God's forgiven me and will have mercy on me when he judges the earth. I hope that's true for you too.

WHAT ABOUT YOU?

:: *What does this passage tell you about God?*

:: *Read the rest of chapter 24, then read chapter 25. Draw a picture or write a poem about Isaiah's vision of heaven and earth.*

:: *Thank God for his amazing gift of salvation.*

MAY :: 28

READ ISAIAH 26:3-4

Give It Up

You will keep in perfect peace him whose mind is steadfast, because he trusts in you.
ISAIAH 26:3

Every day I struggle with trusting God. I try to fix my problems by myself, which never works, and I end up worrying my head off!

Then I remember to give all my problems to God. I feel so much better after that, because I know God's in control. I always wish I'd prayed and given all my worries to God in the first place.

It is so much better to give all your worries to God. You don't have to worry about bugging him either, because he wants to hear your voice. He knows you, and he knows your future. Let him help.

WHAT ABOUT YOU?

:: What are 3 things you worry about?

:: Pick up something really heavy, like a backpack full of books, and carry it around for a few minutes. Think of it as the weight of your problems. Notice how good it feels to finally put it down—like the feeling you get when you give your problems to God.

:: Give your worries to God in prayer.

READ ISAIAH 30:1-3

My Way

"Woe to the obstinate children," declares the LORD, "to those who carry out plans that are not mine."
ISAIAH 30:1

I wanted to buy a bike. My parents told me to think about my decision and make sure that this was what I really wanted to do with my money. But I didn't want anybody to tell me what to do, so I just went out and bought a bike without really looking into what I wanted and how much I should pay. I made a bad decision because I was too stubborn to listen to my parents.

I'm not always so great about listening to God either. But deep down, I know God always knows what's best and that I should obey him. For every big decision we need to make, God has an answer. He wants us to live for him, to honor him and to love other people. If we do those things, we'll make good decisions.

That's what Isaiah was warning people about. If people—including me—would just realize that God's incredible wisdom can help us make good decisions, we could save ourselves a lot of trouble.

WHAT ABOUT YOU?

:: *Think about a time when you've stubbornly done what you wanted, even though you knew it wasn't smart. What was the result of acting stubborn?*

:: *Ask God to help you follow his plans for your life.*

MAY :: 30

Soaring Like Eagles

Those who hope in the LORD will renew their strength. They will soar on wings like eagles.
ISAIAH 40:31

Isaiah says God never grows weary. So I know when I get tired of school, or all the other things I have to do, the first thing I need to do is ask for God's strength. God's happy to help me out in those situations, as long as I'm willing to let him lead my life.

God loves to work in people's lives. He loves to see us victorious over sin, which gives him glory and honor. That's why he wants us to rely on his strength instead of our own. Those are the best times for us—the times we soar like eagles.

WHAT ABOUT YOU?

:: *Think of a time you felt really worn out. How did God help you?*

:: *Flip through some old magazines and look for things that represent strength or power: an athlete, a missile, a powerful political figure, a mountain.... Then shut the magazines and, with a big, black marker write the word GOD across the covers to help you remember where real strength comes from.*

:: *Ask God to help you trust in his strength.*

MAY :: 31

KATY, AGE 15

READ ISAIAH 43:1-7

He Knows Your Name

Fear not, for I have redeemed you; I have summoned you by name; you are mine.
ISAIAH 43:1

This is a verse I'd like to share with my friends. It would show them how much they matter to God. God's not just some mighty ruler who looks down at earth and sees a bunch of nameless people running around. He knows each one of us by name.

God knows our troubles and our happiness. He calls out to us by name. He made each one of us special, and he wants to have a personal relationship with each of us.

When I think of God that way, I realize that he loves me and will never leave me. And best of all, I have God's promise that he called me to come to him so I can have eternal life.

WHAT ABOUT YOU?

:: How many people at your school do you know by name? What does it feel like to have people call you by name? Why is it important that God knows us by name?

:: Read Isaiah 43:1, replacing "O Jacob" and "O Israel" with your name. How does your understanding of this verse change when you think God is talking directly to you?

:: Praise God for creating you and loving you.

JUNE :: 1

READ ISAIAH 44:1-5

You Really Know Me

This is what the LORD says—he who made you, who formed you in the womb, and who will help you: Do not be afraid.
ISAIAH 44:2

In yesterday's devotion, Katy reminded us that God knows our name, which is pretty awesome. But here's something even more awesome—God knows how you are "wired" because he *made* you!

When you like to do something, it's because you were made with certain likes and dislikes. When you're good at something, you should be grateful, not boastful (since you're good at it because of the strengths God gave you). God made you the way you are for a reason, a purpose.

Here are a few more things to think about: Your likes and dislikes will change as you get older, so be patient. No matter how old you are, you may not know what you like to do until you do it, which means you have to take risks. One more thought: Whatever you do that's worthwhile takes hard work.

WHAT ABOUT YOU?

:: *What do you like to do? Make a list. Does your list make you happy or sad? Why?*

:: *Take the time to write down some of your dreams for your life.*

:: *Ask God to give you the courage to follow your dreams. And, while you're at it, thank him for forming you the way he did.*

JUNE :: 2

READ ISAIAH 42:1-4

God's Messenger Man

Here is my servant, whom I uphold, my chosen one in whom I delight:
ISAIAH 42:1

As a prophet, Isaiah's job was to stay in close contact with God, so he could deliver messages from God to the people. In those days, prophets were pretty interesting. When the passage says this is what Isaiah "saw," it doesn't mean he was sitting on his porch, checking out the action one day. It means that this is a prophecy, or message from God, to be delivered to the people of Israel. This is kind of like when we say someone had a vision.

Isaiah was delivering a message to people about their sins. He was showing them that God was not a happy camper, and that his judgment was just around the corner. God's covenant (or promise) with Israel meant that they were supposed to obey him. Since they hadn't done that, God rightfully sent down his wrath.

But along with the judgment, there were also many messages of hope. Jesus doesn't show up in a human body until the New Testament, but Isaiah's got a ton of prophecies about Jesus.

WHAT ABOUT YOU?

:: *Why do you think Old Testament prophecy of Jesus was and is important?*

_____

_____

_____

_____

_____

_____

_____

_____

READ ISAIAH 59:1; 60:1-2

Life Raft

Surely the arm of the LORD is not too short to save.

ISAIAH 59:1

As I read this verse it reminds me of when my grandpa had cancer. He was told he had only 4 to 6 weeks to live at first. He was such a godly man, and my whole family was sad about losing him. We prayed all the time and hoped God would heal him.

In the end, my grandpa lived for 2 more years—much longer than expected. And even though God didn't heal my grandpa and his death was still really hard on our family, at least God gave us more time with him.

God really does listen to our prayers. We can ask him anything, and he'll listen to us. And even if we don't feel close to God, this verse tells us he's still close to us, close enough to reach out and help us when we need him.

WHAT ABOUT YOU?

:: Ask a bunch of Christians you know—your parents, your friends, people in your youth group—to tell you about a time God answered their prayers.

:: Thank God for hearing our prayers and reaching out to save us, no matter how far away from him we feel.

JUNE :: 4

AMY, AGE 14

READ ISAIAH 65:17-19

I'm Forgiven!

Behold I will create new heavens and a new earth. The former things will not be remembered, nor will they come to mind.
ISAIAH 65:17

When I became a Christian on a church-organized backpacking trip, my heart was immediately changed. Before the trip I had been going through a really rough time, and the bad memories haunted me almost more than I could handle. But the minute Jesus came into my heart, the pain of my old life seemed so insignificant.

God's forgiveness is complete—he treats us like we never sinned. His forgiveness is the biggest reason I became a Christian. My old life was weighing me down, and I couldn't break free on my own. God's love gave me a new life.

No matter what you've done, God will forget it all if you ask him for forgiveness. You can't change what happened in the past, but you can find a better future in him!

WHAT ABOUT YOU?

:: How is being forgiven by God better than being forgiven by people? Why do we need both?

:: Draw a line down the middle of a piece of paper. On one side, write words that describe life without God. On the other side, describe life with God.

:: Confess your sins to God and thank him for his forgiveness.

JUNE :: 5

READ JEREMIAH 1:5-8

The Young and the Useful

Do not say, "I am only a child." You must go to everyone I send you to and say whatever I command you.
JEREMIAH 1:7

One of my brother's friends was at my house one day, and we started talking. I've known this guy for a while, and I knew he was into some bad stuff. I also knew he wasn't a Christian. I really felt like I should talk to him about Jesus, but I was pretty nervous about it. But before we quit talking, God gave me the strength to tell this guy about Jesus. I don't know what he thought, but I know God used me to at least tell him the truth.

God put all of us on earth to tell other people about him—and you don't have to be an adult to do that! We are all important to God, and he can work through us, no matter how old or how young we are.

WHAT ABOUT YOU?

:: What are some things you want to do for God when you get older? Do you really have to wait? Think about some ways God can work through you right now.

:: Think of one thing you can do today to share God's love with another. Get out there and go for it!

:: Thank God for living in you and helping you share his love with others.

JUNE :: 6

LAURA, AGE 12

READ JEREMIAH 10:11-16

All You Need

God made the earth by his power; he founded the world by his wisdom and stretched out the heavens by his understanding.
JEREMIAH 10:12

I love and trust God, but sometimes I don't feel like God is powerful enough to know what's going on in my life. Those are the times when I let other things take God's place as the most important part of my life. Even meaningless things like watching TV can take the place of spending time with God. I guess this is because TV, friends, and material things feel like they're solving my problems *right now*, while God doesn't always act as fast as I want him to.

But this passage says God is more powerful and more fulfilling than any of the other things I try to put in his place. God says those things, no matter what they are, can never match his power, wisdom, or understanding. And he's right.

WHAT ABOUT YOU?

:: What are some of the idols you struggle with?

:: Look at one of your favorite possessions, like your bike or your CD player. What can that thing do? What can't it do? Now think about how silly you'd feel if you prayed to that thing or trusted it to take care of all your needs.

:: Tell God you want him to be the most important part of your life.

JUNE :: 7

CHARISSA, AGE 13

Everything About Me

I the LORD search the heart and examine the mind.
JEREMIAH 17:10

In one of my classes, I had to do a project with a partner. I was supposed to do half and my partner would do half. A few weeks after the project was assigned, my partner asked how my half was coming along. I said I was finished. But the truth was, I had hardly started. I never did do the work I'd promised to do on it, and we didn't get a very good grade.

I could lie to my partner for a while, but obviously the truth came out eventually. And that's kind of how it is with God. I can try to hide things from God, but he always knows the truth about me. He sees my heart, and he knows every thought and feeling I have.

I feel bad when I think about the sinful stuff God sees in my heart, but instead of pushing me away from God, that feeling makes me want to keep my mind and my heart closer to him. Just knowing God knows everything about me motivates me to do what he wants me to do.

WHAT ABOUT YOU?

:: *What are some thoughts or feelings you try to hide from God?*

:: *Ask God to help you have a pure heart.*

JUNE :: 8

READ MARK 4:36-41

Careful What You Pray For

He got up, rebuked the wind and said to the waves, "Quiet! Be still! Then the wind died down and it was completely calm.
MARK 4:39

In an earlier devotion, Katy talked about how God gave her more time with her grandfather. She was glad to be convinced that God listens to our prayers. She feels closer to God now. That's good to know because closeness is what prayer is all about. We don't pray to get stuff; we pray to get closer to God.

Prayer is about recognizing God's presence in your life. And when you see it, you'll be glad (of course), but also a little nervous. Notice, in the passage you read today, that the disciples were terrified! Why? Because God answered their prayers—and it made them realize just how powerful God is!

So, be careful what you ask for—you just might get it!

WHAT ABOUT YOU?

:: Have you ever been afraid of God? When? Why?

:: Make a list of what you are afraid of. Someone has said that our fears are kind of weird because they tell us what matters to us (like, if we're afraid of being ugly, we really want to be liked).

:: Ask God to help you want him, more than stuff from him.

J U N E :: 9

READ JEREMIAH 13:1–7; 27:1–2

Really Strange

This is what the LORD said to me: "Make a yoke out of straps and crossbars and put it on your neck."
JEREMIAH 27:2

Jeremiah explains God's plans for Judah in some really strange ways—strange to us, at least. One explanation God told Jeremiah to use involved a linen belt. Linen, cotton, polyester, plastic—what's the difference? In Jeremiah's time it made a huge difference. The priests' clothes were made of linen because linen was supposed to be a pure and holy fabric. When Jeremiah's linen belt got ruined and was "completely useless," that meant that Israel's holiness had wasted away. The Lord said, "In the same way I will ruin the pride of Judah and the great pride of Jerusalem."

Another visual lesson came when God asked Jeremiah to wear a yoke, which is like a leash of wood and leather, around his neck out in public. Although Jeremiah, God's messenger, looked a little strange, God's message was clear: Because of the way the Israelites bucked God's plans for them, another nation was going to become their master.

JUNE :: 10

What Would You Do?

The LORD is with me like a mighty warrior; so my persecutors will stumble and not prevail.
JEREMIAH 20:11

Like a lot of people, I sometimes wear stuff to school that shows I'm a Christian. It helps me think about the things I do and say. But deep inside, I'm scared someone will ask me what it means or make fun of me for wearing it. I have to admit, sometimes I'm embarrassed about my faith.

When I read something like these verses in Jeremiah, it helps me remember that I'm not the first person to worry about what other people will think if I talk about my faith. These verses also help me remember that God gave me a job to do—to tell people about him. I could be the only Christian another person meets. I could be their only chance to find out about Jesus. If I keep quiet because I'm afraid that person will make fun of me, I'm not doing what God wants me to do.

WHAT ABOUT YOU?

:: *When have you been afraid to share your faith? What could have helped you feel more confident?*

:: *Think of 3 things you could say to someone who asks why you're a Christian.*

:: *Ask God to help you stand strong in your faith, even if others make fun of you.*

JUNE :: 11

The Man with the Plan

"For I know the plans I have for you," declares the LORD.
JEREMIAH 29:11

Recently, I went on a short-term missions trip with my youth group to England and Wales. I was really excited about it because I've thought about being a missionary after I finish college. I couldn't wait to start leading people to Jesus Christ!

On our first day there we started going to the homes of people around the town. But all day long we were met with slamming doors and negative comments. I felt like such a failure.

Toward the end of that week, God led me to a man who desperately needed Jesus. I talked with him for 3 hours, and we had a wonderful conversation. By the time we finished, he decided he would look further into Christianity.

This whole experience proved to me that I have to trust God with my life. I don't have to stress about where I'll go to college, what kind of job I'll have, or even how I'll do in school next week. God has great plans for my life and will lead me wherever I need to go.

WHAT ABOUT YOU?

:: How do you feel when you think about your future?

:: Write out your testimony. To get started, focus on 2 or 3 times when you've really seen God take care of you.

:: Ask God to help you trust his plans for you.

JUNE :: 12

TONIA, AGE 14

READ JEREMIAH 43:1-3

Stand Your Ground

All the arrogant men said to Jeremiah, "You are lying! The LORD our God has not sent you."
JEREMIAH 43:2

Imagine a guy named Jeremy is walking down the hall at school when the fire alarm goes off. He knows that several other guys are in the bathroom smoking, so he runs in to warn them about the fire. "You need to get out of here!" Jeremy says. "This isn't a drill!"

"Yeah, right," says one of the guys, "you're just trying to get us in trouble with the principal." They refuse to leave the bathroom, no matter what Jeremy says to them.

This is kind of how the "arrogant men" in Jeremiah 43:2 responded to the prophet Jeremiah's warnings. They just wouldn't listen. But that didn't mean Jeremiah's message was false. He was right; they were wrong. If you ever feel like no one will listen to you, even though you're telling the truth, think about Jeremiah. He got blasted every time he opened his mouth, but he kept speaking God's truth. Sometimes you just have to stand your ground.

WHAT ABOUT YOU?

:: *Have you ever tried to tell somebody something important and that person just wouldn't listen? How did you feel?*

:: *Ask God for the strength to keep telling his truth, even when people won't listen.*

JUNE :: 13

SHAWN, AGE 12

READ JEREMIAH 50:19-20

Forgive and Forget

"In those days, at that time," declares the LORD, "search will be made for Israel's guilt, but there will be none."

JEREMIAH 50:20

I used to feel really lonely and selfish when I sinned. I thought God would get tired of me doing the same wrong things all the time and would eventually stop forgiving me.

Wrong! When you read about all the bad stuff the people of Israel did and all the times they turned away from God or disobeyed him, you think, *Someday God is going to get these guys for good.* But this verse says just the opposite. It says one day God's going to search for Israel's guilt and not find a thing. After everything they did wrong, God will look at them as sinless.

Because I have Jesus in my heart, my sins are gone. I just need to confess my sins and ask God to forgive me. And one day, when I see God face to face, I believe he'll say to me what he said to Israel: "I searched for your sin and there is none."

WHAT ABOUT YOU?

:: Do you feel forgiven? Why is it so hard to believe that God really forgives us?

:: Find the dirtiest piece of clothing in your laundry basket. Put a safety pin on it. After it's been through the washer and dryer, check it out and notice how much cleaner it is.

JUNE :: 14

AMY, AGE 14

READ LAMENTATIONS 3:16–24

His Love Never Fails

Yet this I call to mind and therefore I have hope: Because of the LORD's great love we are not consumed, for his compassions never fail.
LAMENTATIONS 3:21–22

Sometimes people can be really mean. They can pick on you, make fun of you, and give you such a hard time you don't even want to get out of bed in the morning. They can make you feel like you're all alone.

But God says we're not alone. God sees us walking in the halls at school. He knows when people are hurting us. And he understands how it feels, because people have hurt him too. That's why we can always trust God to be there. He can comfort us like no one else can. And he never, ever fails.

When people pick on you, remember that you have value because you are the Lord's child. And that's something no one can ever change.

WHAT ABOUT YOU?

:: Think about a time when you've been hurt. How did you find comfort?

:: Find a small stone you can keep in your backpack or pocket during the day. When you feel hurt or alone, use the stone to remind yourself that Jesus is your rock and will always be with you.

:: Start each day by asking God to be with you and to help you through hard times.

JUNE :: 15

Been There, Done That

The Word became flesh and made his dwelling among us.
JOHN 1:14

Amy's comments in yesterday's devotional were painfully true. People, including kids and teenagers, can be really mean. Amy reminded us of another important truth—we're never alone. Jesus is always with us, even in tough times.

In the passage you read today, John says that Jesus not only came down from heaven but that he also moved in right here on Planet Earth! His 33 years on earth allowed him to experience what it's like to be human, to be rejected, to be hurt, to be abandoned.

It's so cool to follow Jesus because he's not some distant, head-in-the-clouds God. Nope. You're following a genuine, in-your-life God who wants to know you and (this is the amazing part) wants to know what you experience. Jesus is way more than someone who loves us with a detached kind of love...he is a God who is with us and understands what we experience and feel. He's been there too.

WHAT ABOUT YOU?

:: When was the last time you felt really alone? How did God help you through it?

:: The next time you feel lonely or down, take time to read Matthew 26:36—27:56. Remember, Jesus knows how you feel.

:: Thank God for understanding what you feel every day.

J U N E :: 1 6

A Major Jolt

I will surely repay you for your conduct and the detestable practices....Then you will know that I am the LORD.
EZEKIEL 7:4

Sometimes it took a major jolt to get the attention of the people of Judah. More conventional methods just didn't seem to cut it. In those days King Nebuchadnezzar of Babylon was the landlord of most of the known world, including Judah. Ol' Nebby told Judah's king to behave, or else. The Jewish king didn't, so Nebby invaded, posing this rather blunt question to the king: "So what part of 'do what I say or I'll kill you' don't you understand?" Then he slit the king's throat.

The murdered king's son became the new king, and—being just as sassy as his dad—lasted all of 3 months before Nebuchadnezzar invaded Judah again. This time he didn't kill the Jewish king but instead dragged him back to Babylon as a war trophy. The only ones Neb left alive in Judah were the old and the poor.

Among the Jewish captives who were forced to set up housekeeping in Babylon was the priest Ezekiel. God told him—and he told his fellow captives—that King Nebuchadnezzar wasn't through with Judah yet. Unless its people stopped worshiping idols, God would send Nebby right back to Judah and really waste it this time.

JUNE :: 17

DREW, AGE 13

READ EZEKIEL 1:25–28

Amazing God!

This was the appearance of the likeness of the glory of the LORD. When I saw it, I fell facedown.
EZEKIEL 1:28

All I could think after I read this passage was, "God is amazing, and all the stuff he does is amazing!" God is full of light, fire, love, compassion, and forgiveness. If he can be full of all those things, I know he's huge.

The great thing about God is that he's not too big to remember us. Sure, he can do whatever he wants. But that shouldn't be scary, because what he wants is to have a relationship with us. That means he's not going to use all that power and glory to get us. He's going to use it to love us! Now that's amazing.

WHAT ABOUT YOU?

:: *Why did Ezekiel fall flat on his face when he saw the glory of God? What does Ezekiel's reaction say about God and his greatness?*

:: *What images come into your head when you think about this passage? Jot down your thoughts or draw a picture about these verses.*

:: *Thank God for his power and glory. Thank him for remembering you.*

JUNE :: 18

READ EZEKIEL 20:30-32

Under Pressure

You say, "We want to be like the nations, like the people of the world, who serve wood and stone." But what you have in mind will never happen.
EZEKIEL 20:32

I guess we all do it sooner or later. We give in to the pressure to be like everyone else. Maybe we tell a lie or drink a beer or 2. Maybe we just hide our faith so other people won't think we're too "religious."

There are times when I change myself so other people will like me. I start thinking some of my friends have cooler lives than I do, so I start acting like them. But whenever I change myself like that, I never end up happier. I just end up feeling like a fake.

Maybe that's because I know the real me is someone who wants to follow God, even when it's not the cool thing to do. All that stuff that the world thinks makes a person cool doesn't really matter to God. And in the end, he's the only one I really need to please.

WHAT ABOUT YOU?

:: *Think about the last time you gave in to peer pressure. How did you feel afterward?*

:: *What are some of the ways your friends tempt you? Write down specific ways you can resist those temptations.*

:: *Ask God to help you follow him when you're tempted to follow the crowd.*

JUNE :: 19

READ EZEKIEL 34:22-30

Rejects

The trees of the field will yield their fruit and the ground will yield its crops; the people will be secure in their land.
EZEKIEL 34:27

Sometimes I wear Christian T-shirts, and every time I do, it seems like someone makes fun of me. I know I'm doing the right thing by being bold about my faith, but it's still hard to be teased.

I get a lot of comfort from verses like this one. This verse tells me that God will reward people who choose him instead of money or popularity. It really is better for me to follow God and get teased for it than to reject God so I can try and fit in.

I know God is always looking out for me, even when other people reject me. And that's a pretty good feeling.

WHAT ABOUT YOU?

:: Have you ever been teased about your faith? What happened? What did you do?

:: What do people talk about, wear, or do that makes them look "cool"? Ask your parents what was "cool" when they were your age. Why do you think our ideas about what's "cool" change so quickly?

:: Thank God for caring about you, even when it seems like the world is rejecting you.

JUNE :: 20

KELSEY, AGE 13

READ EZEKIEL 35:1–6

Sin Comes Creepin' In

Since you did not hate bloodshed, bloodshed will pursue you.
EZEKIEL 35:6

Do you ever think about hating something? Sometimes I think I hate my brothers, school, and occasionally homework. But instead of hating this kind of stuff, God wants us to hate the things he hates, like sin, evil, and violence.

We live in a pretty violent world. Sometimes I feel kind of violent myself, like when I want to punch my brothers. But if we hate something that's wrong, like violence, then we won't be so tempted to give in to it. We need to hate violent TV shows, movies, and music as much as God does.

Think about it: If you hate something, you don't want to have anything to do with it. You want to stay as far away from it as possible. But if you don't hate it, you're more vulnerable to it and a lot more likely to let it creep into your life.

WHAT ABOUT YOU?

:: What are some things the Bible says God hates? What are some things you hate? Are there differences between those things?

:: Look through today's newspaper. Find a story that tells about something bad in the world or your community. Pray that God would bring peace, hope, and healing to that situation.

:: Ask God to help you resist violence.

JUNE :: 21

EMILE, AGE 14

READ EZEKIEL 45:9-10

Getting Even

Give up your violence and oppression and do what is just and right.
EZEKIEL 45:9

Sometimes when I'm jealous of someone or angry at something they've said or done, I find myself thinking about ways to get even. I rarely end up going through with my plans for revenge, but I know that even my desire to hurt someone is against God's commands.

So many people I know think it's a sign of strength when they fight with someone or deliberately hurt someone's feelings. But I think it's more impressive when someone is able to just walk away from someone who's trying to pick a fight. God tells us to be merciful with other people, even when we're tempted to hurt them. It takes a lot of strength to do that.

God knows we're tempted to hurt other people or take advantage of them in the name of "revenge." But God would much rather have us leave our problems in his hands.

WHAT ABOUT YOU?

:: How do you respond when someone hurts your feelings?

:: Think about someone you may have taken advantage of or hurt. How can you make things right with that person?

:: Ask God to help you resist taking revenge on people who hurt you.

JUNE :: 22

READ MATTHEW 26:47-54

I'm So Mad I Could Scream!

"Put your sword back in its place," Jesus said.
MATTHEW 26:52

When Emile talked about her anger in yesterday's devotional, all of us could relate. Anger is real. Because anger is such a strong emotion, it's easy to act on it with some kind of physical response. It happens all the time.

But Emile pointed out that there's a better way. Trouble is, the better way is not always the easy way. That's why the Bible is so great. It shows us how others reacted at tense moments when violence would have seemed like the right response.

Take Jesus, for instance. He was betrayed by his friend and disciple, and he was being arrested for something he didn't do. Peter was ready to fight, but Jesus stopped him. What Jesus said was shocking. He said something like, "Hey, I could wipe these guys out with a whole truckload of angels, but I'm not going to fight these people. I am going to trust in the power of God instead of the power of violence." Wow! Jesus resisted using violence, and he can help us do the same.

WHAT ABOUT YOU?

:: *What are 2 bad habits that you have when you get angry? Commit yourself to not behave this way the next time you feel angry.*

:: *Ask God to help you find healthy ways of dealing with your anger.*

JUNE :: 23

Daring Daniel and Co.

[The king] found them ten times better than all the magicians and enchanters in his whole kingdom.
DANIEL 1:20

A young guy named Daniel and his buddies (and a bunch of other Israelites) are captured and taken from their homes and families in Judah and forced to live in Babylon. Daniel and the guys have to make a choice. Will they say to themselves, "Poor us! God must not love us anymore!" Or will they refuse to cooperate at all, which probably would earn them a death sentence?

Well, they find a place between the two and choose to rely completely on God. Sure, they participate in the educational programs of the king, but they don't eat the food they are given. And Daniel interprets many dreams, not sparing the gory details.

You may be thinking, *Big deal! So they don't eat food and tell the truth.* But these guys are even more daring! They refuse to bow down to King Nebuchadnezzar's statue. And Daniel continues to pray to God 3 times a day, which was against the law. Their disobedience brings with it some pretty tough punishments, like being thrown into a super hot furnace or into a den of hungry lions for a sleepover. As a result of their bonus-sized faith and courage, God uses these guys to teach some kings (and us) a thing or 2 about living out our faith when things don't go our way.

JUNE :: 24

EMILY, AGE 14

READ DANIEL 2:13-16

Just a Little Respect

Daniel spoke to him with wisdom and tact.
DANIEL 2:14

I sure wish I'd thought about this verse a few weeks ago when we got a new leader in our youth group. The first time I met him, I said something pretty lame. Ever since that first meeting, he's thought of me as a troublemaker. I guess I deserve it.

I have a hard time showing respect to people in authority, and it's caused me a lot of problems. I have teachers who have never liked me because I was rude when I first met them. I've learned the hard way that when you're disrespectful, you pay the price.

God wants us to respect the people who are above us, like parents, teachers, and youth leaders. When we respect those people, we show respect for God too.

WHAT ABOUT YOU?

:: *How does it feel when someone doesn't respect you? How do you think your parents or teachers feel when people don't respect them?*

:: *Think about some ways you can show respect to authority figures. For the next week, practice being a respectful person.*

:: *Ask God to help you show others respect.*

JUNE :: 2 5

READ DANIEL 3:16-18

Hey, Obey

We will not serve your gods or worship the image of gold.
DANIEL 3:18

It was a big deal when Shadrach, Meshach, and Abednego obeyed God instead of the king. Their lives were on the line! I have trouble being obedient even with the smallest things. Like a few days ago, my mom told me not to eat anything when I got home from school so I wouldn't ruin my dinner. Well, she wasn't around when I came home, so I ate a few things. When dinner rolled around, I wasn't hungry at all. It seemed like no big deal when I disobeyed, but I felt guilty later.

Many times it is easier to disobey than to obey. It would have been much easier for Shadrach, Meshach, and Abednego. Think about it: obey God, go to the fiery furnace; disobey God, stay alive. But they obeyed anyway, because it was the right thing to do. This passage encourages me to make the right move.

WHAT ABOUT YOU?

:: When was the last time you disobeyed God? Why did you do it? How can you avoid disobeying again?

:: Decide right now that you will do the next 5 things your parents ask you to do—with no complaining.

:: Ask God to help you obey joyfully!

JUNE :: 26

ROBYN, AGE 13

On My Sleeve

Three times a day he got down on his knees and prayed, giving thanks to his God, just as he had done before.
DANIEL 6:10

A few weeks ago, I wore a Christian T-shirt to school, and I was surprised at how many people noticed. All day, people came up to me and asked about the message on my shirt. They wanted to know what it meant and why I was wearing it. It was amazing how many people I talked with about God that day, just because of a T-shirt.

I believe God put us on this earth so we can share the good news about Jesus. We shouldn't hide our relationship with Jesus—we should be proud of it. We have something other people need, and we are the ones who can tell them about it. When we stand up for our beliefs, it shows other people our faith is real. It shows them that God is real in our lives and can be real in their lives too.

WHAT ABOUT YOU?

- *What are some ways you can stand up for your faith at school?*

- *Wear a cross or a Christian T-shirt to school. How do people respond? How can you use these items to show your faith to others?*

- *Read this passage again. Ask God to give you faith like Daniel's.*

JUNE :: 27

JAMIE, AGE 14

Even When It Hurts

The LORD said to me, "Go, show your love to your wife again, through she is loved by another and is an adulteress. Love her as the LORD loves the Israelites."

HOSEA 3:1

I think one of the hardest parts of being a Christian is showing love to people who hurt you. For instance, if a friend talks about me behind my back, my first reaction is to get angry at her and never want to speak with her again.

But then I think about how often I hurt God. No matter how much I mess up, God still loves me unconditionally. He forgives me and forgets about my sins. His love for me never changes. I'm supposed to show others the same kind of love I get from God—even to friends who talk about me.

WHAT ABOUT YOU?

:: Why is it so hard to show love to people who don't love us back? Why should we show them love anyway?

:: Think of someone you've fought with in the past. How can you patch things up?

:: Ask God to help you be a loving person, even when others don't show you love in return.

JUNE :: 28

KELLY, AGE 15

READ HOSEA 6:6-7

Attitude Counts!

For I desire mercy, not sacrifice.
HOSEA 6:6

Sometimes being a Christian seems like it's all rules and no fun. We can get caught up in worrying about everything we do and everything we say.

But this verse says that following the rules isn't always the same as following God. Being a Christian isn't just about our actions; it's about our attitude. Sure, we need to live by the Ten Commandments and ask for forgiveness when we sin. But the most important thing to God is what's going on in our hearts.

We can try to live perfect lives, but unless we truly love God with our whole hearts, we're not really following God. God wants us to live completely for him, not for ourselves. He wants us to follow his commandments because we love and honor him, not just because we're supposed to.

WHAT ABOUT YOU?

:: *What are some things you do to try to please God? Do you do them out of love or because you think you should?*

:: *What are some ways you can show your faith to others?*

:: *Pray that God will show you ways to follow him with your heart, to walk your talk.*

JUNE :: 29

Big Bibles?

Woe to you, teachers of the law and Pharisees, you hypocrites!... You have neglected the more important matters of the law—justice, mercy and faithfulness.
MATTHEW 23:23

Kelly was right on when she said that attitude is more important than actions. You can do all the right things but still have a bad attitude, and the right things won't mean anything. Jesus makes it very clear that the main way people can recognize his followers is by their really huge Bibles. No, wait, that's not it—it's by, um, their church attendance. Oh—that's not it either. Oh yeah, the truth is, Jesus says people can recognize his followers by their love for each other.

What Jesus wants are disciples who love one another. Maybe your actions aren't always what you want them to be, but if you love Jesus and care deeply about him, he knows about it, and your love for him and others is what matters most.

WHAT ABOUT YOU?

:: *Would people be able to tell that you're a Christ-follower by the way you show your love for others?*

:: *Pretend Jesus is writing you a letter right now. What would he say to you about what's going on in your heart?*

:: *Ask God to help you have a better attitude toward him and other Christians.*

JUNE :: 30

Can You Say Bugs?

I will repay you for the years the locusts have eaten.
JOEL 2:25

Meet the preacher-prophet Joel. Joel has one thing on his mind: grasshoppers (aka locusts). Clouds of them, thick enough to blacken the sun. It's not like the movie Starship Troopers where a giant insect grabs you with 2 of its 6 legs and proceeds to suck out all your body fluids. Watching grasshoppers devour your crops is like watching your death warrant being signed—it doesn't kill you right then. But you know that without crops you won't eat, and within months your family will gradually die from starvation. From the earth to the sky, locusts were everywhere at one point in the 9th century BC.

But Joel looks beyond a mere grasshopper disaster to a totally worse disaster—one that will end the world as we know it: the day of the Lord. Apocalypse. Armageddon. Disaster movies have been made of this kind of stuff—final judgment on a nation, whether by terrorists, asteroids, or aliens. This is the kind of destruction that Joel's really talking about.

The prophet Joel lived this nightmare along with all his family and friends. What blows the mind is that out of the chewed up remains of a locust plague God brought a blessing to his people. God has an awesome way of bringing good out of the worst situations.

JULY :: 1

CHRISTY, AGE 13

READ JOEL 2:28-29

Anyone, Anywhere

I will pour out my Spirit on all people.
JOEL 2:28

My parents are missionaries, and we knew someone in Zambia, Africa, whose parents weren't rich enough to send their son to school past 7th grade. But even though he didn't finish school, he read everything he could get his hands on. Now he's the pastor of a growing church. I always knew about his situation, but I never thought less of him for it because he was always striving to do what he thought the Lord wanted him to do.

God is so powerful that his Spirit can work through anyone—whether it's a man who didn't finish school or a child who can barely speak. Obviously God won't work through everyone the same way. Some people talk in front of big groups, and some people just tell one other person about God's love. But everyone can make a difference.

WHAT ABOUT YOU?

:: Who's the oldest person in your church? Who's the youngest? How are each of these people important to your church and to God?

:: Try to think of the things that need to be done at your church each week, from preaching the sermon to sweeping the floor. Send a note to one of these people thanking them for their ministry.

:: Tell God you're willing to serve him, even while you're young.

JULY :: 2

MIKE, AGE 14

Should I Stay or Go?

Seek good, not evil, that you may live. Then the LORD God Almighty will be with you.
AMOS 5:14

Is it just me, or is junior high one temptation after another? Like the party I was invited to a while ago. The person having the party invited 12 guys and girls, enough to make 6 couples. And even though the person said it wasn't going to be a make-out party and that their parents would be around, I still knew there'd be a lot of temptation to pair off with some girl and make out. That's why I decided not to go.

Maybe everything would have been fine and I would've just had fun with my friends. But since I wasn't sure, I stayed away. God's pretty clear about how he wants us to live. He wants us to seek good and stay away from evil, period. It's not always easy, but it's what's right.

WHAT ABOUT YOU?

:: Think about a time you had to choose between following God and giving in to temptation. How did you make your decision?

:: Characters in movies and on TV are tempted all the time. Think about temptation as you watch TV this week. How do characters make their decisions? What can you learn from their mistakes?

:: Ask God to help you resist evil and choose good.

JULY :: 3

RUSLAN, AGE 13

READ AMOS 7:14-15

Just a Regular Guy

The LORD took me from tending the flocks and said to me, "Go, prophesy to my people Israel."
AMOS 7:15

I think about the future sometimes, and I wonder what God wants me to do. I guess I won't know all the details till I get older, but I do know this: God definitely has a plan for me, and he can use me

Amos, the guy in these verses, was just a regular guy—a shepherd who also took care of trees. He didn't have any special training or a lot of money, but God made him a prophet. God has plans for all of us, no matter how ordinary we think we are.

WHAT ABOUT YOU?

:: What are some ways you think God can use you right now? What is one way you have seen God use your life already?

:: Make a list of everything about you that's ordinary—you ride the bus, you watch TV, you eat bread, you get the idea. Then make a list of everything about you that's unique—you can sing "Amazing Grace" in Spanish, you've got 5 turtles, you run marathons. Think about ways God can use all these things about you to make a difference in the world.

:: Thank God for using "ordinary" people like you to share his love.

JULY :: 4

An Enemy in Need

You should not look down on your brother in the day of his misfortune,.nor rejoice over the people of Judah. in the day of their destruction.
OBADIAH 1:12

If there's someone you don't like very much, it's pretty easy to wish that something bad would happen to them. And if something bad does happen to them, it's pretty easy to think they deserved it—or at least not feel bad for them or not offer them any help.

But God doesn't want us to do that. God wants us to help other people when they're having a hard time, even if it's someone we don't like.

This is a verse that reminds me not to rejoice when other people are hurting. It reminds me to be kind to people who are suffering. God always comforts me when something bad happens to me, and he wants me to do the same thing for others.

WHAT ABOUT YOU?

:: *Think about a time you were secretly happy when something bad happened to a person you don't like. How would you have felt if you were that other person?*

:: *Ask God to help you reach out to people who are embarrassed or hurting, no matter who they are.*

JULY :: 5

My Fault

I know that it is my fault that this great storm has come upon you.
JONAH 1:12

This summer I looked at some things on the Internet that I shouldn't have. My parents knew someone had been looking at these bad sites and when they asked me about it, I blamed my brother. He got punished and I didn't. But after a few days, I started to feel really bad about getting him in trouble. So I told my parents the truth and apologized to my brother.

It would have been pretty easy for me to just keep my mouth shut and let my brother take my punishment, just like it would have been pretty easy for Jonah to be quiet about causing the storm that might have drowned his shipmates. But that's not right.

God wants us to take responsibility for the things we do wrong. When we admit our mistakes, God can help us keep from making the same mistakes later on.

WHAT ABOUT YOU?

:: *Why is it so tempting to blame others when we mess up? Why is it better to take responsibility for our own mistakes?*

:: *Next time you get into an argument with someone, try being the first one to say, "I'm sorry." How does your apology affect the other person? How does it affect you?*

:: *Ask God to help you learn from your mistakes.*

JULY :: 6

READ MARK 12:41–43

Ordinary People

This poor widow has put more into the treasury than all the others.
MARK 12:43

Ruslan (cool name, huh?) commented on how ordinary Amos was—he was just a shepherd who liked trees. Why would God want to use a guy like that? According to the world's standards, this guy was not on anyone's VIP list.

Luckily God doesn't have that same value system. He looks at the inside of people to see what's in their hearts. Those who think they are somebodies often ignore their own desperate need for God.

But people like Amos or the poor widow—people who have fewer distractions—tend to be more quickly drawn to God. And God is drawn to them. So the next time you're wondering if you're too young for God or too irresponsible to be a disciple, remember the people God worked through. They were often inconsistent, young, ordinary people just like you. Cool.

WHAT ABOUT YOU?

:: *What are the distractions in your life that keep you from having a closer relationship with God?*

:: *Make a list of the people who have made a difference in your life and why.*

:: *Tell God how thankful you are for the way he made you. Ask him to give you confidence and wisdom to make a difference in the world.*

JULY :: 7

Bullies

Ninevah has more than a hundred and twenty thousand people.... Should I not be concerned about that great city?
JONAH 4:11

Think about some of the meanest kids at your school. Can you picture them picking on someone because that person is younger, smaller, or just plain different?

One day you're sitting in the school cafeteria, eating your lunch, minding your own business, when suddenly you sense God telling you to walk over to the table where those bullies always sit. So you do, and once you're standing in front of them you realize God wants you to warn these guys that, if they don't shape up, the principal is going to expel them from school. What would you do?

Jonah is faced with a similar problem. God tells him to go to a city called Nineveh and warn the Assyrians that they'd better change their ways—or else! Well, Jonah freaks out and tries to run away—not only from the assignment God has given him but also from God.

You know what? God isn't through with Jonah yet. In fact, all God needed was a storm, a really big fish, a vine, a worm, and some hot air to teach Jonah a few little lessons about God's great love and mercy for all people—even a table full of mean and nasty bullies.

JULY :: 8

JEFF, AGE 15

READ MICAH 6:6-8

What God Really Wants

What does the LORD require of you? To act justly and to love mercy and to walk humbly with your God.
MICAH 6:8

I feel really encouraged when I read this passage. It tells me that God doesn't expect us to be perfect. What matters to God is that we are really living for him.

To me, the key point is that we should walk humbly with God. If we really surrender ourselves to God and his will, we can be the people God wants us to be. We will be just and merciful. And, most important, we will be obeying God.

Sometimes I feel too busy to read the Bible or pray, but that's where humility comes in. When I humble myself before God, I know that nothing else in my life is as important as God, and I can't do anything without him. The more time I spend with God, the more I want to live my life for him.

It's good to know that God doesn't expect perfection from me, because I'm definitely not perfect. All God asks is that I live for him. And I'm really trying to.

WHAT ABOUT YOU?

:: *What do you think it means to act justly? To love mercy? To walk humbly with God? How can you do those things?*

:: *Ask God to show you ways you can act justly, mercifully, and humbly.*

JULY :: 9

READ MICAH 7:18-19

Off a Cliff

You...hurl all our iniquities into the depths of the sea.
MICAH 7:19

When I read these verses in Micah, I get a mental picture of God pushing my sins off a cliff where they'll never be seen again. What a great God!

God doesn't want anyone to sin, but he knows we will. He provided a way for us to have complete forgiveness through his Son Jesus. And he not only gives us a way out, he's also excited about forgiving us. The Bible says he delights in showing us mercy.

If you're like me and you sometimes wonder if God can really forgive you, remember that God will always forgive us when we are sincerely sorry and believe that Jesus took our sins away when he died on the cross and rose from the dead.

WHAT ABOUT YOU?

:: How does it feel to be forgiven? Why do you think God wants to forgive us?

:: Look around your room. What are some of the things that delight you—you know, that really make you happy? Next time you ask for forgiveness, think of that feeling of delight; it's just a tiny glimpse of the delight God feels when he shows mercy toward you.

:: Thank God for his never-ending forgiveness.

JULY :: 10

Why, God?

The LORD is good, a refuge in times of trouble.
NAHUM 1:7

I'm old enough to know that bad things happen to good people. But when I found out my grandfather had cancer, I couldn't understand what God was doing. My grandfather had lived a good life, and he had never smoked or done harmful things to his body. Now he goes to the doctor all the time for radiation treatment, and he feels so sick sometimes he can hardly move.

In the verses for today, Nahum explains that God is just, no matter what we think about him. Everything is in his hands, and nothing gets by him. That's hard for me to handle at times, because my grandfather's cancer doesn't seem fair. If I didn't know better, I would want to blame God for my grandfather's sickness. But my grandfather himself doesn't do that. He hasn't given up, and he's stayed strong. More than that, he's put his trust in God to take care of him. That helps me to see that even in hard situations we can't explain, God is always with us.

WHAT ABOUT YOU?

:: *How do today's verses help you make sense out of situations you don't understand?*

:: *Thank God for caring about you. Ask him to watch over those you love.*

ERIK, AGE 14

READ HABAKKUK 1:12–2:1

Tough Situations

Why are you silent while the wicked swallow up those more righteous than themselves?
HABAKKUK 1:13

So many bad things happen to Christians all over the world, and it seems like God keeps silent. Even in my own life there have been times when I've asked God, "Why is this happening to me?"

But even though these bad situations are really hard, they have a purpose. My pastor says they're a test of our faithfulness and trust. God allows these tests so we'll see how much we need to cling to Jesus. God knows that our faith won't get very deep if our lives are always easy. So the things that make us ask God what he's doing actually bring us closer to him. It's a hard way to learn a lesson, but it's all part of God's perfect plan.

WHAT ABOUT YOU?

:: *What are some times you've asked God, "Why me?" How did he answer you?*

:: *Talk to an elderly person in your extended family or in your church about some of the hard times they've lived through. As they tell their stories, ask what they learned from each experience.*

:: *Ask God to help you trust him, even when life is hard.*

JULY :: 12

BRIAN, AGE 14

READ HABAKKUK 3:17-19

Those Bad Days

The Sovereign LORD is my strength; he makes my feet like the feet of a deer.
HABAKKUK 3:19

My life hasn't been easy. One of my parents died, and I have had a lot of bad days since then. People try to help me feel better, but it doesn't always work. Sometimes I feel completely alone, with no one to talk to. But even in those bad times, I know God is there for me.

I guess it's normal to get down sometimes. And it's normal to feel like your life is a big mess, especially when something awful happens. That's why God wants us to know we can count on him even when it seems like the whole world is against us.

No matter how down we feel, God is there. He has seen me through some really tough times, and I know he will do the same for anyone who asks for his help.

WHAT ABOUT YOU?

:: *Think about a time you felt nothing was going right. How did you feel about God during this time?*

:: *Write down some things that are really good about your life. The next time you feel down, take a look at that list and thank God for those good things.*

:: *Ask God to help you find joy in him, even in tough times.*

JULY :: 13

Is He There?

Would he oppose me with great power? No, he would not press charges against me.
JOB 23:6

On several days of this week, Colleen, Erik, and Brian basically raised the same question: "Where is God when we need him?" It's a question you might ask in lots of different ways. *Why doesn't God show up when I'm hurting? Why doesn't God rescue me from trouble or help me get rid of my pain? If God is always with me then why do I feel lonely?*

Job admits that if he could find God, he knows God would be sympathetic to his plight. The trouble is he can't find him. Colleen, Erik, Brian, and all of us are in good company when we ask these questions.

It's important for us to remember, when we don't "feel" like God is close by that he's still in control. Our faith in him, in his existence, in his goodness, can give us strength to carry on.

WHAT ABOUT YOU?

:: Think of a time you experienced God giving you strength even when you didn't "feel" like he was there.

:: Try this. Sit down in your room alone. Stay silent for a few minutes. Think of God being present in the room with you. Begin writing what you think God is saying to you right now. See what happens.

:: Ask God to help you notice his presence in your life.

JULY :: 14

Dead Meat

Be silent before the Sovereign LORD, for the day of the LORD is near.
ZEPHANIAH 1:7

Here's what the nation of Judah was like before Zephaniah showed up on the scene: The times were good. Businesspeople were making good money, then putting their earnings into new houses, so there was a lot of construction going on. Homeowners built bigger vineyards and farms too, creating jobs for just about everybody.

Meanwhile, they believed in God, sure. But they didn't believe they should get bent out of shape over whether God actually did anything anymore. (They were pretty sure he didn't.) But that's not quite the whole story either.

In the middle of their cash bonanza and their who-cares attitude about God, these same folks sacrificed their children to Molech, the fire god. Ritual prostitution as an act of worship was common, as was the worship of sun, moon, planets, and stars. City officials were filling their pockets with bribes. Not pretty. Downright evil, in fact. Enter Zeph. "You're dead meat," he says for openers to the lunchtime crowd in the middle of the mall. "The day of the Lord is just around the corner, and you're the targets." Believe it or not, something clicked. Thanks in part to Zeph's preaching, the young king of Judah (Josiah) triggered a spiritual and moral turnaround, something the people of Judah hadn't seen in a generation. (Read more about that one in 2 Kings 22—23.)

JULY :: 15

TYLER, AGE 14

READ ZEPHANIAH 3:16-20

The Best Love

He will quiet you with his love, he will rejoice over you with singing.
ZEPHANIAH 3:17

Remember when you were little and you did something wrong? You were probably terrified your parents would find out because you knew you'd get in trouble. Sometimes I think of God that way. I'm afraid to tell him about my sins and ask forgiveness because I'm scared of the punishment I'll get.

But no matter what I do, God is ready to forgive me if I'm truly sorry. He wants me to come to him with all my problems and sins because he loves me so much

God's love is so much greater than we can even understand. His love is deep and pure. It's the best love we will ever experience. And he doesn't just love us, he delights in us. He rejoices over us. And he wants us to love him too.

WHAT ABOUT YOU?

:: Have you ever wanted to hide from God? What happened when you finally confessed to God?

:: Make a list of the ways God shows his love to you.

:: Confess your sins to God. Be honest and open with God as you ask for forgiveness.

JULY :: 16

READ HAGGAI 2:20-23

Who Do I Belong To?

I will make you like my signet right, for I have chosen you.
HAGGAI 2:23

My 6th grade class was really small. There were only 5 girls in the whole class, and our friendships were changing weekly. I often felt like the "odd one out." When the other girls chose their friends, it seemed like they never chose me.

I would have felt a lot better if I had remembered that even when nobody else paid much attention to me, God still thought I was worthwhile. Today's verse says God looked at Zerubbabel like a signet ring. That's a ring with the owner's initials on it. A signet ring shows who it belongs to. And that's how God thinks of us. Just like a person's initials are on a signet ring, God's name is written all over us.

Knowing how important I am to God reminds me of his eternal plan and my place in it. It's awesome!

WHAT ABOUT YOU?

:: *Think of something you own that you'd never want to lose, like an antique necklace that belonged to your grandmother or a stack of rare baseball cards your dad gave you. Why is this possession so important to you? How much more do you think God values you?*

:: *Thank God for loving you and calling you by name.*

JULY :: 17

MARISSA, AGE 14

READ ZECHARIAH 7:8-10

True Cool

Administer true justice; show mercy and compassion to one another.
ZECHARIAH 7:9

I look around my school and I see a lot of lonely people. There's one guy in particular who is always sitting by himself. I know I need to reach out to him and to the other lonely kids I see. The hard part is that I want to look cool. So how do I look cool and still be a friend to this guy who's always alone?

I probably can't. But God's got a different idea of what's cool. To him, it's cool when we reach out to people who are lonely and hurting.

It's cool when we do what's right instead of what will impress other people. It's cool when people know that the Lord is first in our lives.

So when I see that guy sitting alone at lunch or in the hall after school, I can walk up to him knowing I have nothing to lose because God is with me. And that's really cool.

WHAT ABOUT YOU?

:: *Have you ever had to choose between looking cool and doing what's right? What did you do?*

:: *What is one way you can reach out to a person who is lonely or needs a friend? When can you do this?*

:: *Ask God to help you show compassion and love to people who are hurting.*

JULY :: 18

LAURA, AGE 12

The Words You Choose

These are the things you are to do: Speak the truth to each other, and render true and sound judgment.
ZECHARIAH 8:16

You wouldn't believe the number of kids at my school who lie, swear, and say awful things to each other. One time, some kids came up to the boy whose locker is next to mine and started shouting at him, swearing at him, and shoving him. Finally I said, "Hey guys, cut it out!" They just laughed at me and kept swearing and yelling. But before long, they stopped and walked away.

Whenever we hear people swearing or see them acting mean, we should not be afraid to tell them to stop. Most people, even if they're not Christians, know it's not right to abuse or swear at people.

Christians need to be good examples of using our words to build other people up. We need to try to be kind and fair in the things we say. That's something no one can argue with.

WHAT ABOUT YOU?

:: Why do you think so many people are comfortable with lying, swearing, and saying mean things about others?

:: Next time you're at school, spend the day listening for all the ways people use their words. Which do you hear more often: hurtful words or helpful words?

:: Ask God to help you use words that heal instead of hurt.

JULY :: 19

NIKKI, AGE 15

READ MALACHI 1:6–14

Your Best Shot

"I am a great king," says the LORD Almighty, "and my name is to be feared among the nations."
MALACHI 1:14

I think it's pretty common for people my age to kind of slack off when it comes to God. I know I don't always make God my top priority. Take Sunday mornings, for example. I have one hour set aside during the week when I can go to church with my family, worship God, and spend time with other Christians. But almost every week I'm late for church. And when I'm late, I cheat God out of my time and attention.

God is so good to us and deserves our very best. Even if no one is looking, even if there are no immediate rewards for giving God our best, that's what we need to do.

When we cheat God out of our best, we're really cheating ourselves out of the best possible relationship with him.

WHAT ABOUT YOU?

:: What are some ways you cheat God out of your best? What changes would you need to make to really give God your very best?

:: Make a list of your "bests": your best talent, best possession, best personality trait. How can God use these things?

:: Ask God to help you give him your very best.

JULY :: 20

Written All Over Us

You also are among those who are called to belong to Jesus Christ.
ROMANS 1:6

What a great statement by Kate in her devotion: "God's name is written all over us." That's a pretty radical statement. And it's important to understand what it means—and what it doesn't mean.

It doesn't mean God makes us into religious zombies who walk around like robots and say "Hallelujah" all the time. And it doesn't mean we live perfect lives. No. God's name is written all over us in the way we are made—our gifts, our personalities, our strengths and weaknesses, our likes and dislikes, our desire to know God better. All those things come from God, all of them draw us closer. When we give ourselves to God, we are coming home to God! Since we belong to God, we never feel really whole or full or completed until we come back to where we belong.

WHAT ABOUT YOU?

:: *Think back to the time you first asked Jesus to come into your life. Write down how you felt.*

:: *Take some time to write down what you think Kate meant by saying that "God's name is written all over us." Look at it each day this week.*

:: *Then pray, "God, help me to see you in me every day this week. Help me to show others your name written all over me."*

JULY :: 21

Just Like Old Times

But for you who revere my name, the sun of righteousness will rise with healing in its wings.
MALACHI 4:2

Malachi is probably the last of the Old Testament prophets. God's people are now back in their home-land after nearly 100 years of forced time in Babylon. Through Malachi, the Lord Almighty (that's what Malachi usually calls God in his book) starts off gently—"I have loved you"—but quickly dips into all the ways that Judah has ignored and rejected him.

Malachi has some pretty strong words for the Jews who have returned from Babylon to the ruins of his homeland. There in Judah they rebuild and settle down to life as their grandparents once knew it. The problem is that they also settle back into their old ways—not only ho-hum, boring worship, but total spiritual badness. Just like old times.

In today's verses, it sounds like God is really picky about the gifts we give him, but think about it. You wouldn't consider giving your best friend a broken game or a book with pages torn out of it as a birthday present, would you? These people were giving God beat-up sheep and blind goats. No wonder he wasn't impressed. He was about to give them his only Son.

Malachi closes out the Old Testament with a chapter of hope. God says, "Here's what's gonna hap-pen someday, and most of you are gonna like it." God is always desiring to draw us close to himself. Therefore, Jesus, the ultimate sacrifice. Drum roll please....

JULY :: 22

KRISTEN, AGE 13

READ MATTHEW 1:1-17

Jesus' Relatives

A record of the genealogy of Jesus Christ the son of David, the son of Abraham.
MATTHEW 1:1

When I first read these verses, I didn't see how they could possibly mean much of anything for me personally. It's just a list of names! But then I remembered who some of these people were, and I started to get the idea.

All the people on this list are Jesus' relatives, so you'd think they'd be pretty good people. But some of them weren't very good at all. Remember Jacob and Esau? Jacob totally tricked his brother and stole his birthright—but Jacob's on the list. Tamar was thought to be a prostitute, and Rahab actually was one. David killed Uriah in order to take his wife Bathsheba. All these people are related to Jesus!

So if you ever feel that you are worthless or good-for-nothing, this passage can help you realize that God has a special plan for everyone—including you.

WHAT ABOUT YOU?

:: *Why do you think God allowed such "imperfect" people to be a part of Jesus' family tree?*

:: *With your parents' help, write out your own family tree. Ask about the people whose names you see. What can you learn from their good and bad examples?*

:: *Thank God that he knows exactly how everyone fits into his plan.*

JULY :: 23

READ MATTHEW 4:1-10

Breakin' the Rules

Then Jesus was led by the Spirit into the desert to be tempted by the devil.
MATTHEW 4:1

One of my friends wanted me to stay over at his house one night when his parents weren't home. I knew my parents wouldn't approve, but I did it anyway. The next day, we were both in big trouble for having a sleepover without their permission.

I'm faced with temptation every day. There's always someone asking me to go out and do something I shouldn't. It's tempting to break my parents' rules. Most of the time, I can stand up to temptation. But every once in a while, I give in.

It helps to know that Jesus faced temptation too. He knows how it feels to resist the temptation to do something we shouldn't. He also knows that rules are there for a reason.

God loves us and doesn't want us to get hurt or in trouble. If I can remember that the next time I face temptation, I'll be more likely to follow God and do the right thing.

WHAT ABOUT YOU?

:: *Pick something that really tempts you. What would you say to someone who asks you to give in to this temptation? Practice, so that saying no to temptation becomes a habit.*

:: *Ask God to give you the strength to resist temptation.*

JULY :: 24

ROBYN, AGE 13

READ MATTHEW 5:11–12

No Worries

Blessed are you when people insult you...because of me.
MATTHEW 5:11

I once memorized the Beatitudes (Matthew 5:3–12), but I never noticed what this particular one was saying. If I had, I would have saved myself a lot of grief. See, I've always felt that if I dressed and acted the way God wanted me to, people at school wouldn't accept me. But if I tried to please the people at school, I knew God wouldn't be happy with me. I didn't know what to do, so I spent a lot of time worrying.

Instead of worrying, I should have spent that time thinking about God. He's the One who makes right judgments; he'll never make fun of me for doing the right thing. I need to be concerned with what he thinks of me, not what anybody else thinks.

WHAT ABOUT YOU?

:: Have you ever been insulted because of your beliefs? What happened, and how did you react?

:: Blow up a balloon as big as you can. Start squeezing it until it pops. Ask yourself: How am I like the balloon? What or who is putting pressure on my life to make me fit in? What can I do to be sure the pressure doesn't make me pop?

:: Ask God to help you stand your ground when people give you a hard time.

JULY :: 25

JESSICA, AGE 12

READ MATTHEW 6:25–34

Stress Test

Do not worry about your life.
MATTHEW 6:25

I tend to get pretty stressed out about tests. But this passage tells me not to get so worried about stuff like school. That doesn't mean I should give up studying and just wait for God to help me pass my tests. It just means that as long as God is first in my life, I can be confident that he'll give me everything I need.

I like the way the passage talks about God caring for even the smallest animals. If he looks after them, I know he'll look after me, because God loves me even more than the animals.

Seeing the way God takes care of the big things in my life, I know I can trust him to take care of the little things too. So I don't have to stress out about anything, including tests!

WHAT ABOUT YOU?

:: What are some things that stress you out? How can God help you deal with those things?

:: Write down all the things you're worried about. Now, put on a piece of clothing (like a hat, a sweater, extra socks) for each of those worries. How many "worries" can you wear before you feel totally weighed down? Now take off all those extra clothes. How does it feel to shed all those "worries"?

:: Ask God to help you give your worries to him.

JULY :: 26

READ MATTHEW 10:29-37

Safe with God

Don't be afraid; you are worth more than many sparrows.
MATTHEW 10:31

When I was about 6 or 7, I'd get really concerned about the wild animals near my house, especially during bad storms. It seemed like they had no one to take care of them. But this verse about the sparrows always helped me feel better, because it reminded me that God cares for them—and he cares for me even more.

God, the greatest Being in the universe, pays attention to little creatures like sparrows and 7-year-old girls. So no matter how stormy it gets outside or in my own life, I can take comfort in knowing God cares. Nothing is too big or scary for him.

WHAT ABOUT YOU?

:: *Think of something that's very important to you. How do you take care of it? What are some similar ways God takes care of you?*

:: *Walk around your house and notice all the things that keep you safe: locks on the doors, storm windows, maybe even a security system. How is God's protection even better than all of these things?*

:: *Thank God for caring about you and protecting you.*

JULY :: 27

Family Stuff

When his family heard about this, they went to take charge of him, for they said, "He is out of his mind."
MARK 3:21

Today's Scripture reminds us that even Jesus' family life wasn't perfect. Jesus' family thought he was crazy, and they wanted to protect him and force him to rest.

Some families have mothers or fathers who can't stand to have anything out of place in the house. Some are just the opposite. Every family has certain "rules" (behaviors that are considered acceptable or unacceptable) like: we don't cry when we're hurt, we can't express our anger, or only certain family members do certain household chores.

One of the hard parts of growing up is figuring out which of your family's habits are healthy and which are not. So pay attention. Watch how your family responds to different situations. And, when you see stuff you don't really like or agree with, remember that Jesus had family problems too!

WHAT ABOUT YOU?

:: What are some of the things that are expected of you, and what are some of the things that are not allowed in your home?

:: Ask your mom and dad what their own parents were like when they were growing up. What were the family rules?

:: Ask God to help you see the good things going on in your family. And ask him to help you with the not-so-good things.

JULY :: 28

What's in a Name?

She will give birth to a son, and you are to give him the name Jesus, because he will save his people from their sins.
MATTHEW 1:21

Abraham means "father of many." Abram's wife is 90 years old when God adds a syllable to his name and tells him he's going to become the father of many nations. Now all Jews and Arabs can count Abraham as their forefather. God picks good names (Genesis 17:1-22).

Sarah means "princess." God gives her that name when she's 90, right before she's about to have her first child! It's a great name because she becomes the very great-great-etc. grandmother of all Jews (Genesis17:15).

Peter means "rock." It's the name Jesus gives to Simon, a guy no one would ever think to nickname Rocky. No one except Jesus, that is. But Jesus sees more in Simon than meets the eye, and the disciple eventually lives up to his new name (Matthew16:18).

Now, the Best Name Ever: Jesus means "The LORD saves." Every time we say it, we're declaring, "Hey! God is salvation!" When people use the name of Jesus as a curse word, they obviously don't know what they're really saying. Jesus came to earth to tell us, "God is our salvation!" His own death and resurrection made that salvation possible.

READ MATTHEW 11:28–30

A Tough Assignment

Take my yoke upon you and learn from me, for I am gentle and humble in heart.
MATTHEW 11:29

A little while ago, my family decided to leave our big suburban church and move 30 miles away to start a sister church in a tough neighborhood in Chicago. I had to leave my friends, my school, and the only home I had ever known. I didn't want to go.

But I saw how at peace my parents were about the move and how sure they were God wanted us in Chicago. I wanted to share their peace and confidence, so I asked God to help me. I told him I wanted to do his will, but it was going to be really hard on me and I needed supernatural strength.

God gave me even more than I asked for. He completely changed my attitude about moving. I actually wanted to move. Can you believe it? He gave me supportive friends and showed me that Chicago was what he wanted for me.

When I let God take control of my life, the plan that seemed totally "out there" turned into the plan I knew was best for me.

WHAT ABOUT YOU?

:: *Why do you think God sometimes wants us to do things that are difficult for us?*

:: *Thank God for his perfect plan.*

READ MATTHEW 13:31-33

Small Wonders

Though it is the smallest of all your seeds, yet when it grows, it is the largest of garden plants.
MATTHEW 13:32

This passage could have helped me when I was at camp. I was so afraid to speak out about God in front of people who didn't share my beliefs.

After camp, I sort of made a pact with myself to be brave and stand up for God in the future. Even in situations where I feel small or unwanted, I should go ahead and try to make a difference. God doesn't just use adults or people with all the answers—he uses anyone who asks for his help and isn't afraid to speak up. That means I can do something for God, whether or not I think I can. God thinks I can, and that's what really counts.

WHAT ABOUT YOU?

:: *When was a time you felt afraid to speak up for God? What could have helped you feel more confident in that situation?*

:: *Think about how beautiful flowers come from tiny seeds. Then think about how God uses the smallest things to accomplish something great.*

:: *Thank God for being so awesome that he can use anyone to do his work.*

JULY :: 31

CAROLYN, AGE 13

READ MATTHEW 18:1-5

Think Small

I tell you the truth, unless you change and become like little children, you will never enter the kingdom of heaven.

MATTHEW 18:3

Sometimes I get so caught up in myself, like the time not too long ago that I canceled plans with my dad to hang out with my friends. Dad was really looking forward to going to a movie with me, but I didn't even think about his feelings. I just thought about what I wanted to do. It seems like the older I get, the more selfish and stuck-up I become, especially toward my family.

Small children rarely seem to push away the people they love. In this way, Jesus was kind of like a child, because he always accepted other people and thought of them first. And I think this is part of what Jesus meant when he said Christians should become like little children. We need to stop thinking we're so important and think about how important other people are instead.

WHAT ABOUT YOU?

:: What are some other characteristics of children that you think Christians should try to imitate?

:: Ask your parents to tell you some of their favorite memories of you as a child. What are some ways you wish you could be more like you were back then?

:: Ask God to help you be humble like a little child.

AUGUST :: 1

NATALIE, AGE 14

READ MATTHEW 22:34-40

Top Priority

Love the LORD your God with all your heart and with all your soul and with all your mind.
MATTHEW 22:37

There was a time I wasn't as close to God as I should have been. I started focusing on material posses-sions, and I found myself making those things more important than God. This passage shows me that God wants to be my top priority. He wants me to realize he's the most important part of my life. Without him, the rest of my life is pretty meaningless. He needs to be my motivation in everything I do.

The earthly things in my life won't last, but God's love lasts forever. His love needs to influence my thoughts, actions, and words. God's love is real and, in the end, it's the only thing that really matters.

WHAT ABOUT YOU?

:: What are some of the ways you let God know he's your top priority?

:: Write "God" in large letters on a couple of note cards. Tape the cards where you'll see them every day, like on your mirror or in your locker. Every time you see one of the cards, ask yourself if you're putting God first in your life.

:: Tell God you want him to be first in your life. Then ask him to help you make it happen.

A U G U S T :: 2

ASHLEY, AGE 12

READ MATTHEW 25:34-40

Serving Others

Whatever you did for one of the least of these brothers of mine, you did for me.
MATTHEW 25:40

If you think about it, there are a lot of opportunities for teenagers to serve others. My dad and I some-times go serve the homeless with a local inner-city ministry. I try to stand up for kids at my school who are being picked on. And I show I care by visiting my grandma and the other people at the nursing home where she lives.

There are all kinds of people around us who need help. Jesus tells us to serve them as if we were serving him. God has given me gifts like kindness, joy, time, energy, and wisdom. I can easily use those gifts to help other people.

The greatest gift God has given me is eternal life with him in heaven. When I serve others, it's my way of saying, "Thank you."

WHAT ABOUT YOU?

:: What are some of the gifts God has given you? How can you use those gifts to serve others?

:: Think about the people in your school. Whom would you consider "the least of these"? Write down 5 ways you could serve some of those people and try out some of these ways on them.

:: Ask God to help you find ways to serve other people.

AUGUST :: 3

Seize the Day

You are a mist that appears for a little while and then vanishes.
JAMES 4:14

Carolyn's devotional really makes you think. She admitted that she missed a great moment with her dad because she chose to do something else.

It seems like there will be tons of time left in life to do all those things you know you should do. All of a sudden you'll be 18 and find even more reasons to ignore those "important things."

So, just like James said in the passage you read today—take advantage of life now. Develop relationships with your parents, spend time with God, and get going with those things you're tempted to push off until you're older. You won't regret it.

WHAT ABOUT YOU?

:: *Think about an area where you waste time. What can you do to decrease wasted time in your life?*

:: *Decide you're going to take one night a week and spend time with your parents. No phone calls, no CD player, no Internet. If your parents are busy doing things, see if you can tag along with them.*

:: *Ask God to give you the courage to not waste time. Ask God to help you spend more time with him.*

AUGUST :: 4

READ MATTHEW 19:23-26

More, More, MORE!

It is easier for a camel to go through the eye of a needle than for a rich man to enter the kingdom of God.
MATTHEW 19:24

What would you give up to get 50 million dollars? Your family and friends? Money is important in life. But it causes pain and grief for so many people (rich and poor and in-between). Money will never satisfy your needs in life—only Jesus will. The Bible warns us about the love of money over and over again. Love God, love people, but be sure you never fall in love with money.

God supplies our needs, he can also supply our trust if we ask him. Children have a cool sense of trust. Have you ever noticed this? Life seems simpler for them. Most kids rely completely on parents or other adults for their care. They don't worry about life too much. Someone else provides their food, clothing, home, spending money—everything! Well, God wants us to come to him with this same trust. We can rely on him! We don't need to worry; he will care for us. Take a lesson from little children.

AUGUST :: 5

KATHRYN, AGE 13

READ MATTHEW 28:19-20

"Everyone" Means Everyone

Go and make disciples of all nations.
MATTHEW 28:19

I knew a girl named Brittany, and I really didn't like her. She was so mean to my friends and to me! I thought, *Why should I invite her to church?—I don't like being around her.*

Then I read this passage about making disciples of all nations. God wants everyone, even Brittany, to hear his amazing news. But I still didn't want to be the one to tell her.

Verse 20 changed my mind. God says he'll be with me always. However scary it might be to talk to Brittany about my faith, God will be there, helping me.

It's awesome how God gives us this huge responsibility. This is the Great Commission, after all! But when he gives us this command, he gives us a promise too: We'll never have to witness alone.

WHAT ABOUT YOU?

:: What seems more difficult to you—witnessing to people in another country or witnessing to people you already know? What's tough about each kind of witnessing?

:: Think of one person you know who isn't a Christian and invite him or her to church or a youth group activity this week.

:: Ask God to give you courage to share the gospel.

AUGUST :: 6

VIANNAH, AGE 13

Get Away From It All

Very early in the morning, while it was still dark, Jesus got up...and went off to a solitary place, where he prayed.
MARK 1:35

Sometimes a person just has to be alone. Like when my dog—my long-time friend—died. I went up to my room that night and cried and prayed. I didn't have to worry about anyone seeing. It was just me and God up there, and he cared about how I felt.

When people pray in public, they don't necessarily pray about the same stuff they would pray about in private. I like to pray with others, but there is also something great about praying to God one on one.

Jesus is our example in everything, and while the Bible tells us he prayed in front of people a lot, it also tells us he made a special effort to spend time alone with God. And if that time was a big deal to Jesus, it should be a big deal to everyone.

WHAT ABOUT YOU?

:: Why do you think Jesus liked to have time alone with his Father?

:: Take some time out of your day today—even if it's just 5 minutes—to be alone with God. Talk to him about what's going on in your life. Try to spend time with God every day this week.

:: Ask God to help you remember to pray.

BECKY, AGE 13

Heart Conditions

He taught them many things by parables.... "Listen! A farmer went out to sow his seed."
MARK 4:2-3

When the disciples first heard this parable, they didn't get it. What does a gardening lesson have to do with following God? It starts to make sense when you think of the different kinds of soil as different kinds of hearts.

Jesus is always ready to come into people's hearts, even the worst people in the world. All they have to do is invite him in, and they become like the good soil. A love for God and for other people grows in that good soil.

I used to think my heart was bad soil because I'd sinned so many times. I asked myself, *Would Jesus really want to come live in my heart*? But I found out that I could be good soil too, if I just believed in Jesus and asked for his forgiveness. I'm a growing Christian now!

WHAT ABOUT YOU?

:: *Even good soil isn't perfect. What are some times in your life when you've "withered" or struggled because your faith wasn't deep enough?*

:: *Imagine that you are pulling weeds from your yard or garden. As you pull those weeds, think about some "weeds" in your own heart that need to be pulled out.*

:: *Ask God to help you plant the "seeds" of his Word in other people's hearts.*

AUGUST :: 8

READ MARK 8:27-29

Say What?

Who do people say I am?
MARK 8:27

One night at a sleepover, 2 of my non-Christian friends were asking me and another Christian friend about our religion. They were really curious—and really confused—about Jesus. I'd always figured that people basically knew who he was and what he came to earth to do. But my friends sure didn't.

It took me and my Christian friend a long time to explain that Jesus was the Son of God and he came to earth to die for our sins. I didn't think I did a very good job explaining it, but somehow God used that conversation. Both of my friends are Christians now.

We don't have to be great speakers to tell people about Jesus, but it doesn't hurt to be prepared. Since that sleepover, I've thought a lot about what I'd say to someone else who asked me about Jesus. I'll be more ready next time.

WHAT ABOUT YOU?

:: Imagine that you've never been to church or Sunday school. Why would it be hard to understand: a. Jesus, b. God, and c. the Bible?

:: To help prepare yourself for when someone asks you questions about what you belief, write a paragraph about who Jesus is and what he came to do.

:: Ask God to help you know what to say when you share your faith.

AUGUST :: 9

RYAN, AGE 12

READ MARK 10:17-22

Give a Little, Get a Lot

Go, sell everything you have and give to the poor, and you will have treasure in heaven. Then come, follow me.
MARK 10:21

I've never had so much money or material stuff that I got distracted from God, but I used to have 2 friends who were really bad influences on me. I finally decided that even though I liked hanging out with those guys, I needed to give them up as friends. It was definitely a tough choice to make, but it made me feel much, much better inside. It helped me focus on the person who should be most important to me: Jesus.

Sometimes following God will mean giving up things that seem important. But Jesus has promised that any time we give up something for him, we'll get a reward that's way better than whatever we gave up. In my case, I gave up bad friends to get a better relationship with Jesus. Even though it was a hard decision, I know I did the right thing.

WHAT ABOUT YOU?

:: *What have you had to give up to follow Jesus?*

:: *Look around your room for some things you could give away, like clothes and games that are still in good condition. Give these items to your church, secondhand store or a local charity.*

:: *Ask God to show you what you need to give up in your life.*

AUGUST :: 10

Dare to Ask

Jesus grew in wisdom and stature and in favor with God and men.
LUKE 2:52

In her devotion this week, Amy mentions how she tried to answer some questions her friends were asking her about Jesus. Do you ever have questions too? Do you ever wonder if this Christian stuff is worth it? Do you wonder if it's real?

It's okay to ask those questions. In fact (ready for this?), it's really good to ask those questions! This time of your life (junior high, middle school, young teen—whatever you want to call it) is all about change. Your body is changing; your emotions are changing (have you noticed?); your brain is changing (you can think in new and different ways); and your faith is changing. Or, at least, your faith should be changing. You're beginning to form your own beliefs about everything, God included.

So go on, ask those tough questions. Ask your parents. Ask your youth leader. Ask your pastor. And definitely ask God. He, and his people, will help you understand and develop your own personal faith. That's a good thing!

WHAT ABOUT YOU?

:: *What are some of your biggest questions about God, the Bible, and Christianity?*

:: *Choose one question (you can choose more later) and talk about it with your parents, your youth leader, or some other Christian adult.*

:: *Ask God your question. Pray that he'll give you wisdom and understanding.*

AUGUST :: 11

Done Deal

There appeared before them Elijah and Moses, who were talking with Jesus.
MARK 9:4

Elijah and Moses show up with Jesus in this passage for important reasons. Moses was a symbol of God's promise with Israel. Elijah was a symbol of the fact that God had brought Israel back home. Having them stand with Jesus on the mountain was meant to show how the story of Jesus is tied to the story of the people of Israel. Jesus is the One who fulfills the promise God made with the Jews. And Jesus is the One who completes the project of restoring God's people. This passage is a way to show that Jesus is both the reason for the story of Israel and the completion of the story, all in one. But you would never have known he was the "end all" by his attitude.

When ancient kings arrived in cities, they would make grand entrances. Like those awards shows, where all the celebrities pull up in their limousines and step out wearing expensive gowns and tuxedos. Yet Jesus arrived in Jerusalem on the lowest form of animal—a donkey (see Mark 11:4-10). This tells us a ton about Jesus' humility.

AUGUST :: 12

JONATHAN, AGE 13

Following God

Be on guard! Be on the alert! You do not know when that time will come.
MARK 13:33

I think today's verses would be scary to non-Christians, because the passage warns us to be ready when Jesus comes back to earth. Some of my friends live like he's never going to return. They do whatever they want and not what God wants. I'd say they're spiritually asleep.

Well, I'm trying to wake them up! But when I tell them that they're living in a way that displeases God, they usually say that it's okay for now—they'll become Christians later, after they've lived it up for a while. Today's passage reminds me of why that excuse isn't good enough: We don't know how much time we've been given on this earth, so we've got to make each day count. And if we're doing that, we can look forward to Jesus' return with joy, not fear.

WHAT ABOUT YOU?

:: If you knew that Jesus was going to return next week, what things would you change about your life?

:: Imagine that you're waiting for a very important phone call. You can hardly wait to answer the phone…but when is it going to ring? How is this anticipation kind of like waiting for Jesus to return?

:: Ask God to help you live for him from now on.

AUGUST :: 13

GABE, AGE 13

READ MARK 15:16-20

Been There, Done That

Again and again they struck him on the head with a staff and spit on him.
MARK 15:19

When I was younger, I got teased a lot. Even though I'm older now, it still hurts to think about being teased by my classmates.

Now I know I can turn to Jesus when other people make fun of me or give me a hard time, because Jesus was teased too. People laughed at him, spit on him, hit him, and mocked him. So when people are mean to me, Jesus knows how I feel. I know he cries with me and feels the same pain I feel. I know he cares about me and loves me.

Jesus was put to death like a criminal so we could be saved. God's Son experienced pain because he loves us. And Jesus is ready to listen to us when we hurt. I think that's amazing.

WHAT ABOUT YOU?

:: Think about a time you were teased. How did you feel? Now think about a time you teased someone else. How do you think your words affected that person?

:: The next time you're really hurting, put a chair next to your bed and imagine Jesus sitting in that chair listening to you. Tell him how you feel.

:: Tell God about times when other people's words have hurt you. Ask him to comfort you and help you forgive those people.

AUGUST :: 14

JOANNA, AGE 12

READ LUKE 1:26-38

Just Say, "Yes"

"I am the LORD's servant," Mary answered. "May it be to me as you have said."
LUKE 1:38

Can you imagine being Mary? She was just a young girl, probably not much older than I am, when an angel showed up to tell her she was going to have a baby. That would be a big deal for anybody, but especially for a young girl who was still a virgin. But Mary didn't say, "Forget it. I'm way too young. Pick someone else." She humbly told the angel she would do whatever God wanted her to do.

God wants me to be willing to serve him. For instance, I love drawing. Even though I think God has been telling me for a long time to use my skills to glorify him, I've resisted. But after reading about Mary's willingness to serve God, I know I need to be more willing to serve him any way I can.

WHAT ABOUT YOU?

:: How can you be more open to letting God use your gifts to share his love?

:: Write down some ways you think Mary's life changed after saying yes to God. Now write down some ways your life might change if you really let God use you.

:: Ask God to help you find ways to serve him.

READ LUKE 2:51-52; 5:16

Gotta Grow

Jesus often withdrew to lonely places and prayed.
LUKE 5:16

I remember when all I wanted was to be bigger and stronger. I thought, *If I could just bench press a little more, I'd be happy*. But I realized later that there will always be someone bigger and stronger than me. And even if my muscles got huge, physical strength doesn't last forever.

What does last forever is spiritual strength. We all need to grow closer to God every day. If we're not moving closer to God, we're moving farther away. So we have to do everything we can to help our faith grow, like read the Bible and pray every day.

And if we ever think we've got our faith all figured out, we just need to look at Jesus. Even though he was the Son of God, Jesus prayed constantly. He was always seeking God's will. If we want to have a relationship with God, we have to put some work into it, no matter how strong we think our faith is.

WHAT ABOUT YOU?

:: What are 2 things you do that help you feel closer to God?

:: Do 10 push-ups in a row. As you do them, think about how your spiritual strength compares to your physical strength.

:: Ask God to help you grow stronger in your faith.

AUGUST :: 16

ELIZABETH, AGE 12

READ LUKE 4:14–21

Popular and Unpopular Alike

The Spirit of the LORD is on me, because he has anointed me to preach good news to the poor...to release the oppressed.
LUKE 4:18

It's pretty easy to be nice to our friends and to the popular people. It's a lot harder to be nice to the ones who are slow or mean or don't play sports or don't wear the "right" clothes. If someone doesn't have any friends, you don't exactly want to volunteer to be the first one.

Jesus talked to wealthy and popular people, but he paid special attention to the poor and unpopular. When many of the people of that day were ignoring these people, Jesus encouraged the poor by saying, "Hey! Know what? The Lord's favor is on you!"

Because I'm a Christian, Jesus calls me to be friendly to people who have no friends. The only way I can reach out is to stay close to God, so that he can show me what to do next. If Jesus reached out to the unpopular, shouldn't I?

WHAT ABOUT YOU?

:: *Think about a time when you've felt like you had no friends. What was it like?*

:: *At lunch, look for someone who's eating alone and invite them to your table.*

:: *Thank God for reaching out to everyone and ask him to help you do the same thing.*

AUGUST :: 17

Who You Judge

What business is it of mine to judge those outside the church? Are you not to judge those inside?
1 CORINTHIANS 5:12

In the last few devotions, could you to relate to Gabe, who was teased and made fun of when he was younger? All of us can relate to what Elizabeth said about wanting to be popular!

It's easy to judge Christians and non-Christians by the same set of standards. But Paul tells us that we are not to judge those outside of the church (non-Christians) while we should judge those inside the church. In other words, as Christians we are to hold each other accountable for living and loving like Jesus would. Your friends who don't know Jesus probably don't have the same standards you have as a Christian (they don't have a reason to!). But those friends need to be "loved into a relationship with Jesus," not "judged into one."

WHAT ABOUT YOU?

:: How can you show love for a non-Christian and at the same time disagree with the wrong things they might be doing?

:: Go to a trusted Christian friend and ask, "What's an area in my life that I could improve?" (A hot temper, a negative attitude, trouble accepting others, etc.) Then ask, "Will you help me improve in this area?"

:: Ask God to give you strength to improve a weak area in your life, and strength to love non-Christians the way he would love them.

AUGUST :: 18

The Great Physician

Since I myself have carefully investigated everything from the beginning, it seemed good also to me to write an orderly account.
LUKE 1:3

Dr. Luke, physician and historian, writes this gospel, the "Good News" about Jesus, the Great Physician. No doubt Luke found his heart beating in sync with Christ's. Both love health and wholeness. Both ooze compassion. Both care about the hurting and helpless. So Luke emphasizes the humanness of Jesus. While being fully God, Jesus still had a body that required food, needed rest, and felt pain. He also shows the Lord's care for people who are hurting, from shunned leprosy sufferers to unpopular tax collectors.

Women also play a big role in this story. Though most people of that time regarded them as second-class citizens, Jesus treats them with dignity and respect. In fact, he even counts on them to help support his work financially. That was way ahead of the times!

Some call the Gospel of Luke the most beautiful book ever written. It's a warm, human story of a God who cares enough to touch us and heal us. We constantly see Jesus teaching truths and working miracles, right where people live—often in their own homes. This Great Physician makes house calls!

AUGUST :: 19

MATT, AGE 13

READ LUKE 6:37–42

Picking at Specks

Why do you look at the speck of sawdust in your bother's eye and pay no attention to the plank in your own eye?
LUKE 6:41

I'm pretty good at picking "specks" out of my brother's eye. Just the other day, I told my brother not to do something. Then later that day I found myself doing the same thing! That wasn't a very smooth move on my part. I'd be in big trouble if God judged me for all the bad things I do. But instead of judging me—which he definitely has the right to do, since he's God—he gives me grace, because I know and believe in Jesus. He forgives my sins, no matter how bad I mess up. And he calls me his very own child. Because God's been so merciful to me, I have no excuse for judging my brother...or anyone else.

WHAT ABOUT YOU?

:: Why is it easy to judge other people for their sins? Why does Jesus tell us not to judge?

:: Get a bar of soap and use it to write the word "forgiven," on your mirror. When you look at yourself in that mirror, remember that's how God sees you—as forgiven. And he sees other Christians the same way.

:: Thank God for giving you his grace.

AUGUST :: 20

READ LUKE 7:1-10

Gotta Have Faith

"Say the word, and my servant will be healed...." When Jesus heard this, he was amazed.... "I tell you, I have not found such great faith even in Israel."
LUKE 7:7, 9

Reading about the centurion's faith reminds me of writing this devotion. At first, I didn't want to do it because I didn't think I had anything to say. But I asked God to help me think about these verses and help me understand them. When I worked on the devotion the next day, I really felt like I knew what to write. I never could have done it without God's help.

I guess that's kind of what's going on in these verses. The centurion's servant was sick. And even though the centurion had all kinds of power and authority, he couldn't do anything to help his servant. So he needed to trust in the only One who could: Jesus. God is always there to help us in hard times. We just need to trust him and have faith that he will give us everything we need.

WHAT ABOUT YOU?

:: When have you really needed to trust God about something? What did God do?

:: Ask God to give you more faith in his power.

AUGUST :: 21

ROBYN, AGE 13

READ LUKE 8:26–39

God Did It

Return home and tell how much God has done for you.
LUKE 8:39

God does a lot of good things in our lives. Take the time I broke my arm, for example. I should have landed on my left arm; but I kind of flipped over and ended up landing on my right arm. So it was my right arm that broke, not my left. Since I'm left-handed, that was about the best thing that could have happened. I really think God sort of helped turn me over as I fell, so I wouldn't break my left arm. I told many people about what a wonderful thing God did.

God's not just sitting up in heaven, ignoring the world. He does great things for us all the time, and we need to tell other people. When God helps us, he's showing us how much he cares for us. And when we tell other people about the good things God's done, they'll see that he cares too.

WHAT ABOUT YOU?

:: *What great things has God done for you this week? This month? Have you told anyone about God's goodness?*

:: *The next time you talk with a friend, tell them 1 or 2 ways you've experienced God's goodness.*

:: *Thank God for all the ways he's blessed you.*

AUGUST :: 22

READ LUKE 10:38-42

First Things First

LORD, don't you care that my sister has left me to do the work by myself?
LUKE 10:40

Sometimes when my sister and I are supposed to do the dishes, she'll make some lame excuse to get out of it. I get so mad when she does that! So when I first looked at these verses, I totally agreed with Martha.

But really, this passage isn't about doing dishes or cooking or any other chores. It's about remembering what's really important in life, and that's spending time with Jesus. I might worry that my sister doesn't spend enough time in the kitchen, but I know I don't spend enough time reading my Bible or praying. So I guess until I get my own priorities in order, I really can't complain too much about my sister's. Maybe if I keep spending more time with Jesus, I won't get so mad at little things like doing the dishes.

WHAT ABOUT YOU?

:: *How do you think Martha felt after Jesus spoke to her? Why did Jesus say what he did? What did he want Martha to understand?*

:: *Make a list of things that distract you from God. What can you do to eliminate these distractions—or at least stay focused on God despite them?*

:: *Ask God to help you focus on what's really important in life.*

AUGUST :: 23

Leave the Light On

Your eye is the lamp of your body.
LUKE 11:34

I haven't always filled my mind with the greatest things. Sometimes I watch movies or TV shows I probably shouldn't. And there's so much more junk out there in magazines, on the Internet, and on the radio that just isn't good for people who want to grow closer to God.

I need to be more careful about what I see and hear. Every day I have to make decisions about the kind of stuff I let into my life. And this passage can help me make decisions that fill me with light, not darkness. Jesus is a shining light, and his love allows me to shine too. I don't want to let the darkness of the world block out God's light in me.

WHAT ABOUT YOU?

:: *Think of some things you read, watch, or listen to that you know aren't good for you. How can you get rid of those things?*

:: *The next time you feel tempted to watch something you shouldn't, call up a friend and shoot hoops or go to the mall instead.*

:: *Ask God to help you get rid of the things that bring spiritual darkness into your life.*

AUGUST :: 24

READ 2 SAMUEL 12:7-13

A Soft Heart

David said to Nathan, "I have sinned against the LORD."
2 SAMUEL 12:13

Matt talked about being judgmental. That attitude is a reflection of the "condition of your heart." Is it "soft" (ready to be used by God; quick to respond to sin) or "hard" (ignoring sin; living for yourself)? Nothing reveals the condition of your heart more clearly than how you respond when someone (another person or the Holy Spirit) points out sin in your life.

When David got caught for doing some pretty rotten things, the condition of his heart quickly became known. David had two choices: 1. deny everything, curse Nathan, and walk away, or 2. admit that he was wrong and ask for forgiveness. David chose the second option. You may want to read Psalm 51 to see how David's heart was softened.

WHAT ABOUT YOU?

:: What's the condition of your heart—or how do you respond—when God shows you something wrong you've done?

:: Ask your parents about a time when you were little and did something wrong. How did you respond to their correction? Did you learn anything from that situation?

:: Ask God to help reveal the condition of your heart when you do something wrong. Ask him to make your heart soft. Thank him for helping you see yourself as you really are.

A U G U S T :: 2 5

READ LUKE 1:52-55

Fill Me Up!

He has filled the hungry with good things but has sent the rich away empty.
LUKE 1:53

"Filled" the hungry? Sent the rich away empty? Huh? Remember when that girl or guy you have been wanting to notice you noticed you? Or when you opened that present and got exactly what you wanted? Or the last night of camp and you felt like you could touch God? That is what "filled" means. Filled means inside you feel like you just can't feel any better.

In this verse, when Jesus filled the hungry, do you think it was just with food, or do you think it went deeper?

Jesus often told his disciples, "Hey, guys, life is not about getting a bunch of stuff. Life is about following me, loving me, seeking after me! You don't need to worry about the small stuff like everyone else worries about—a great-looking body, cars, boyfriends, and girlfriends. I'm looking out for you—seriously." Jesus wanted his disciples to know that it wasn't stuff that would fill them up and bring satisfaction; he would.

MEGAN, AGE 14

READ LUKE 15:3-7

Lost and Found

Rejoice with me; I have found my lost sheep.
LUKE 15:6

I think there's a time in everyone's life when they feel far away from God. Bad things happen, or you just start to feel like God doesn't care about you. I know I've felt that way sometimes. But for me, something always happens that lets me know God hasn't forgotten me. God won't forget you either. God loves us and he'll never leave us.

It's just like the sheep in this passage. The shepherd leads the whole flock together, but sometimes a few of the sheep wander off. Then the shepherd goes out to find the lost sheep, just like God goes out to get us when we move away from him.

God cares about each one of us. He'll never leave us behind or give up on us. He'll never forget us, because each of us matters to him. And when he finds us again, no one is happier than God.

WHAT ABOUT YOU?

:: *Think about a time you felt separated from God. How did God seek you out and bring you back?*

:: *Thank God for always looking for you, even when you wander away from him.*

AUGUST :: 27

JESSE, AGE 14

READ LUKE 17:11–19

Just Say, "Thanks!"

He threw himself at Jesus' feet and thanked him—and he was a Samaritan.
LUKE 17:16

Last year I went to Mexico on a short-term missions trip with my youth group. I really didn't like the housing conditions or the food we ate, and I complained a lot. But reading the story of the 10 lepers tells me that I need to always be thankful to God.

In the story, the only person who came back to thank Jesus was a Samaritan, a hated foreigner. I was a foreigner when I was in Mexico. I was out of my comfort zone, and I didn't like it. But I should have been thankful that I had any housing and food at all, and that God gave me the opportunity to serve other people and tell them about Jesus.

God has done so many things for me. I want to do a better job of thanking him and praising him, no matter what happens.

WHAT ABOUT YOU?

:: *What are some of the things you're thankful for? When was the last time you really told God how grateful you are for all he's done for you?*

:: *Each night for a week, before you go to bed, make a list of the things you're thankful for.*

:: *Thank God each night for the things you wrote.*

AUGUST :: 28

READ LUKE 19:1-10

A Big Change for a Little Guy

Look, LORD! Here and now I give half of my possessions to the poor, and if I cheated anybody out of anything, I will pay back four times the amount.
LUKE 19:8

This passage helped me when I got in a fight with my sister. I was upset with her because she wouldn't listen to me. So I hit her. Naturally, she started to cry. That's when I realized what I'd done. I went to my room and wrote her a note to apologize. Thankfully she forgave me.

It's pretty easy to ignore our mistakes and pretend nothing happened. But when we hurt someone or cause a problem, we need to do what we can to fix it. Zacchaeus had never been a great guy, but he figured out what he'd done wrong and what he needed to do to make it right. His heart was changed, and—right then and there—Zacchaeus was saved.

WHAT ABOUT YOU?

:: *Imagine that Zacchaeus recognized his sins but never paid back the people he'd cheated. Why was it so important for Zacchaeus to act on his new faith?*

:: *Write a note to someone you've hurt. Tell them what you did wrong, apologize, and ask for their forgiveness. Then really work at changing whatever it was that caused the problem, like anger, jealousy, pride, or whatever.*

:: *Ask God to help you fix the sin in your life.*

AUGUST :: 29

MICHELLE, AGE 14

READ LUKE 21:1-4

Giving What You've Got

"I tell you the truth," he said, "this poor widow has put in more than all the others."
LUKE 21:3

When I was about 6, I had a stuffed animal I really loved. My mom heard about an orphanage where the kids had very few toys, so she asked me to share some of mine. I didn't want to include my favorite stuffed animal, but my mom told me that it could make some little boy or girl very happy. It was hard, but I gave away my favorite animal.

I know that's not quite the same as giving God everything you have, but when you're 6, your toys mean a lot to you—at least mine did. But it didn't take long for me to realize I had plenty of other things in my life that made me happy. God has given me so much. I need to always give back as much as I can, whether it's my time, my effort—or my stuffed animals.

WHAT ABOUT YOU?

:: *Why is it hard to give away things that mean a lot to you? Why do you think this kind of giving is important to God?*

:: *Ask God to help you share the gifts he's given you.*

AUGUST :: 30

STACEY, AGE 13

READ LUKE 22:56–62

Only Human

Peter replied, "Man, I don't know what you're talking about!"
LUKE 22:60

When I read about Peter and the way he messed up, I realize that no matter how close we are to God, we're all still sinners.

Peter spent a lot of time with Jesus. He was one of Jesus' closest friends. He even promised Jesus he'd stick with him no matter how tough things got. But when someone put Peter to the test, he broke his promise.

We all break promises to Jesus. We give in to peer pressure and act like we're not Christians. Sometimes we're ashamed of knowing Jesus, just like Peter was.

We don't have to try to hide from God when we do something wrong. We can tell him anything and confess all our sins. We can ask him to help us turn away from sin and do what he wants us to do.

WHAT ABOUT YOU?

:: *Why do we feel guilty when we sin? How can guilt help us grow closer to God?*

:: *Write about a time you did something you regret. Now, rewrite the story so that you resist sin and follow God instead. How does the rest of the story change?*

:: *Tell God about your sins. Be totally honest. Tell him you're sorry and ask for his forgiveness. Ask God to help you follow him.*

AUGUST :: 31

READ PSALM 100

Thanks

Enter his gates with thanksgiving and his courts with praise; give thanks to him and praise his name.
PSALM 100:4

Even if your life's pretty tough, you still have a lot to be thankful for. A bunch of reasons to be thankful were mentioned in the last few days.

When you read Psalm 100, it's totally obvious that the writer is joyful and thankful! Verse 4 mentions giving thanks twice; and it mentions the word praise twice! Sometimes the word praise can sound like a real "churchy" word, and you might wonder what it means to praise God. The writers of the recent devotions make it simple: We praise God by giving thanks to him and telling him how much we appreciate all the things he's done for us! More importantly we thank and praise him simply for who he is: our super-loving, perfect Dad!

WHAT ABOUT YOU?

:: *How would you explain "giving praise to God"?*

:: *Remember the list of things you have to be thankful for that you started earlier? Try to write a little poem to God using that list. (Who knows, it might make a great psalm or song of praise.)*

:: *Praise God for all that he has done for you and for simply being God!*

SEPTEMBER :: 1

READ JOHN 20:29-31

An Insider's Look

These are written that you may believe that Jesus is the Christ, the Son of God.
JOHN 20:31

John is the last of the 4 Jesus Gospels. In a very important way, it's different from the first 3. All 4 of the men who recorded the story of Jesus' life wanted the story to be accurate. John was no exception. But he had another reason for writing this book.

John didn't just want us to know about Jesus and the things he did. He wanted us to know Jesus, his very special friend. John often refers to himself as "the disciple whom Jesus loved." Imagine having that kind of a close friendship with Jesus. The events John chose to describe help us know who Jesus is. They show us Jesus' kindness, gentleness, love, and care. We also see his sadness, anger, steadfastness, and joy. It's kind of an insider's behind-the-scenes look at Jesus.

When you get down to it though, John really had us in mind when he wrote the story. Right near the end of the book, in chapter 20:31, John says he wrote it so you would "believe that Jesus is the Christ, the Son of God, and that by believing you may have life in his name." Pay attention as you read John's book.... It'll introduce you to someone who could change your life.

READ JOHN 1:19-28

Play Your Part

Who are you? Give us an answer to take back to those who sent us.
JOHN 1:22

A few years ago, my friend's parents got divorced. There wasn't anything I could do about it, and I felt pretty helpless. But my friend really needed someone to talk to about how she felt, and I was able to be that person. I felt like God used me to help her get through a really difficult time.

But sometimes I feel pretty useless—like I don't really have a place in the world. Maybe John the Baptist felt like he didn't have much to offer. But John knew God gave him a special job to do anyway: to help people prepare for Jesus to arrive. God really does have a purpose for everyone. God used me in my friend's life. I wonder how he'll use me again.

WHAT ABOUT YOU?

:: *How has God used you in someone else's life? How has God used other people in your life?*

:: *Think of a tough situation one of your friends is facing. Then make 2 lists: one of things you can do to help, the other of things only God can do. Make a plan to do all you can to help your friend.*

:: *Ask God to use you in the lives of others.*

SEPTEMBER :: 3

READ JOHN 2:13-17

"Positively" Furious

He made a whip of cords, and drove all from the temple area.
JOHN 2:15

This story is kind of confusing. It looks like Jesus lost his temper and went ballistic. I mean, if I did that, I'd get into big trouble! The difference here is that Jesus was angry for a really good reason. The people he chased out of the temple were messing with God and turning a holy place into a very unholy place. No wonder Jesus got so mad!

There are some things in life worth getting mad about, like abuse and murder and people who say terrible things about God. But there are lots of things that aren't worth getting mad about, like your brother sneaking one of your CDs or your parents asking you to do something you don't want to do. The key is to ask yourself, "Would Jesus get mad about this?" If he would, ask him how you should respond. But if he wouldn't, ask him to help you get over it before you do something you'll regret.

WHAT ABOUT YOU?

:: *When is anger a good thing? When is it a bad thing?*

:: *Make a list of things that make you angry, then look at each one carefully and ask, "What should I do the next time I'm feeling angry about this?"*

:: *Ask God to help you decide what's a big deal and what isn't.*

READ JOHN 4:7-10

Prejudices

You are a Jew and I am a Samaritan woman. How can you ask me for a drink?
JOHN 4:9

In Alaska, where I live, many of the Native Americans I know have problems with drugs and alcohol, and they get into trouble at school. Whites and Native Americans often form separate cliques because of bad feelings between the 2 groups. I find myself almost expecting all of them to be troublemakers.

When I'm struggling with my prejudices, I can look at the great example of Jesus. Jesus reached out to someone who was different from him. He showed God's love to the Samaritan woman, even though he could have been ridiculed or hurt for talking to her. He took a stand against racism, and I need to do the same.

God commands us to love others as we love ourselves. Treating people like they are inferior to us is the exact opposite of God's commandment. If we want to obey God, we have to reach out to people, no matter what race or culture they come from.

WHAT ABOUT YOU?

:: What are some examples of racism at your school or where you live?

:: Why do you think people get caught up in racism?

:: Ask God to help you take a stand against racism.

SEPTEMBER :: 5

Turning From God

The words I have spoken to you are spirit and they are life.
JOHN 6:63

It takes commitment and strength to follow God. The world pressures us to ignore our commitment to God. And sometimes we give in to the pressure and let our commitment slide. There was a time when I turned away from God. I thought I'd finally be able to do what I wanted instead of being "trapped" by all God's rules. But I ended up really unhappy and feeling horrible.

Finally, a good friend asked me why I had turned from God. When I thought about it, I realized I really didn't know why. Nothing I had experienced was better than the life I had with God.

Yes, it's challenging to be a Christian. But I know there's nothing out in the world that's better than my relationship with God. There's nothing better than the joy I have when I'm growing in my faith and trying to live for him.

WHAT ABOUT YOU?

:: When have you felt like living a Christian life is just too hard? What makes being a Christian so challenging?

:: Write down 2 things you can do as you grow as a Christian in the next month.

:: Thank God for the ways he's helped you grow in your faith.

SEPTEMBER :: 6

CHRISTINA, AGE 14

READ JOHN 8:3-11

Leaving Sin Behind

Neither do I condemn you.... Go now and leave your life of sin.
JOHN 8:11

This passage means a lot to me. I can relate to the woman accused of adultery because I've also had sexual sin in my life. But because Jesus forgave this woman, I know he forgives me too.

Forgiveness is a wonderful gift from our loving, caring God. But there's a lot more to being forgiven than just having my sins washed away. Jesus tells the woman to "leave [her] life of sin." She's forgiven, but she also needs to change her life. Jesus' words remind me that I need to keep living for him, even when I've sinned. I shouldn't keep sinning just because God will keep forgiving me. I need to try not to sin.

God knows I only hurt myself and others when I do things he's told me not to do. He wants me to learn from my mistakes and leave my life of sin behind.

WHAT ABOUT YOU?

:: *Think of one sin you really struggle with. How does that sin affect you, other people, and your relationship with God?*

:: *When you're ready to get rid of this sin, write a letter to God. Tell him you're sorry and tell him you need his help to change. Thank him for his forgiveness.*

:: *Read your letter out loud as a prayer to God.*

SEPTEMBER :: 7

READ JOHN 8:48–59

Follow, Follow

"I tell you the truth," Jesus answered, "before Abraham was born, I am!"
JOHN 8:58

In yesterday's devotional, Christina said that Jesus' words helped her remember that she needed to "keep living for him." Living for him means following him and trying to do what he does (like loving people and stuff like that). But sometimes it's hard to know what he would do!

It's important to remember (and Jesus says this in these verses) that Jesus Christ was not "sort of" God or somehow a second-level God or a good man with godly qualities. His statement here is pretty much the same as what God said to Moses in Exodus 3:14: "I AM WHO I AM. This is what you are to say to the Israelites: 'I AM has sent me to you.' "

The fact that Jesus is God, not just a good man, is exactly why we should live for him and try to be like him. He's the King!

WHAT ABOUT YOU?

:: *How would your friends who don't go to a church describe Jesus?*

:: *Ask God to give you confidence to follow him during the coming week.*

SEPTEMBER :: 8

READ JOHN 4:7-9

Far Out

When a Samaritan woman came to draw water, Jesus said to her, "Will you give me a drink?"
JOHN 4:7

Jesus punched a hole in the dividing wall of hatred between the Samaritans and Jews when he asked a Samaritan woman for a drink. He was willing to go against what everyone thought to help a Samaritan woman in need, regardless of where she came from.

He let her give him a drink, and then he gave her living water for eternity.

Hardly anybody could figure Jesus out—not his family, not his disciples, not the religious leaders, not his friends, and not his enemies. There are examples all over the Gospels (the 4 Jesus stories) where people either misunderstood his teaching or didn't get it at all, questioned his actions, and just basically missed the point. His actions were so different, his claims so outrageous, his words so strange, and his talk about God so "way out" that people were confused at best and totally ticked off at worst.

Everywhere Jesus went he shattered people's ideas of what he *should* do and how he was *supposed* to act. Jesus gave us our example of how to love, he gave us a new definition of "normal."

SEPTEMBER :: 9

SHANNON, AGE 13

READ JOHN 10:7-10

God's No Party Pooper!

I have come that they may have life, and have it to the full.
JOHN 10:10

I used to think that being a Christian was about the most boring thing in the world. It seemed like it was a bunch of do's and don'ts. I thought God didn't want me to have any fun.

But when I see all the problems sin causes in people's lives, I realize there's a reason God wants us to live life his way. God wants us to stay away from the stuff that seems fun but really only gets us into trouble, like sex outside of marriage and drugs and drinking. God's way is so much better.

When we follow God, we avoid problems like drunk driving, an unwanted pregnancy, sexual diseases and drug overdoses. Instead, we get to live free from those things and enjoy life to the fullest.

WHAT ABOUT YOU?

:: Why do you think God warns us to stay away from things that the world says are "fun"?

:: Think of 3 things that help you enjoy life to the fullest as a Christian. Try to do at least 1 of those things this week.

:: Tell God how great it is to have him in your life.

SEPTEMBER :: 10

MINDY, AGE 14

READ JOHN 13:34–35

His Love in Us

By this all men will know that you are my disciples, if you love one another.
JOHN 13:35

One day, my friend told me she'd been paying attention to the way I treated people. She said one of my best traits was that I never hated anyone, or at least never acted like I did.

From that day on, she began to talk to me more about my faith. Finally, right before Christmas, she gave her life to the Lord!

I feel fortunate that God used me as an example of the love Christians have for other people. Whenever we show our love to our friends and family, we show people that our relationship with Jesus Christ is based on love. And there's not a person in the world who doesn't need love.

God tells us to love others so that they'll see his love in us. When we show God's love to people, powerful things can happen. Just ask my friend!

WHAT ABOUT YOU?

:: What are some of the ways other Christians have shown you God's love?

:: Think of a person at your school who could use a dose of God's love. What can you do to show love to this person?

:: Ask God to help you show his love to others.

SEPTEMBER :: 11

MALACHI, AGE 12

READ JOHN 14:5-7

It's the Truth!

I am the way and the truth and the life.
JOHN 14:6

Last Friday night, I went on a hayride with my friend's youth group. We played games, ate sloppy joes, and made s'mores over a campfire. It was an outreach night, so there were lots of non-Christians there. During the hayride, my friend and I tried to talk to some kids who weren't Christians. It was hard trying to talk to them about God. I didn't know what to say. I wish I had thought of telling them this verse.

This verse tells us that the only way to know God is through Jesus. We have to trust in him alone. That means doing good things or going to church won't make you a Christian. If anyone tells you that they will, they don't know what they're talking about.

Jesus said, "I am the truth." So when Jesus tells us he's the only way, we'd better believe him.

WHAT ABOUT YOU?

:: Have you ever tried to earn favor with God? Why doesn't that work?

:: Memorize John 14:6. The next time you get a chance to witness to a friend, share this verse with him or her.

:: Thank Jesus for showing you the way to God.

SEPTEMBER :: 12

MICHAEL, AGE 14

READ JOHN 16:5–15

A Holy Guide

When he, the Spirit of truth, comes, he will guide you into all truth.
JOHN 16:13

I don't think the disciples had a clue what Jesus was talking about when he said he was sending them the Spirit. All they knew was that Jesus was going away. They were sad for themselves and their problems, because they thought Jesus was leaving them alone.

The disciples forgot that Jesus always keeps his promises. He promised them a Counselor who would always be with them in times of need. That's exactly what he gave them. And when we commit our lives to God, the Holy Spirit is there for us too.

We don't have to be sad because Jesus is in heaven and is no longer here on earth with us. The Holy Spirit will guide us the rest of the way.

WHAT ABOUT YOU?

:: What does a counselor do? How is the Holy Spirit like a counselor?

:: Ask your parents or your youth leader how they've seen the Holy Spirit's guidance in their lives.

:: Thank God for sending the Holy Spirit to be with you always.

STACY, AGE 15

READ JOHN 20:24-29

No Doubt About It

Blessed are those who have not seen and yet have believed.
JOHN 20:29

I asked one of my unsaved friends if she believed God existed. She said no, because she doesn't believe in things she can't see.

I started trying to think of something she couldn't see, but believed in anyway. She believed in gravity, obviously, and molecules and TV signals and satellites. "But those things are different," she argued. Well, they are different, but it got her thinking. I invited her to a youth group activity scheduled for the next day. She has started coming to youth group with me sometimes, but she hasn't accepted Jesus as her Savior yet.

It's not always easy to believe in things we can't see. That's why Jesus says, "Blessed are those who have not seen and yet have believed." I guess that means us, because we haven't seen Jesus the way Thomas did. We will, though, in heaven—no doubt about it!

WHAT ABOUT YOU?

:: *What are some things you believe in that you've never seen?*

:: *We can't see wind or electricity, but we know both exist and that they can be very powerful. How could these examples be a bridge to discussing your faith?*

:: *Thank God for working in your life.*

SEPTEMBER :: 14

READ JOHN 21:5-11

More Than Enough

He called out to them, "Friends, haven't you any fish?"
JOHN 21:5

When Shannon wrote earlier that God is no party pooper, she said that God wants us to "enjoy life to the fullest."

It's kind of like this: Your mom says she's got dinner ready for you, but when you get to the table there are 2 lousy, cold french fries on the plate—that's it! Your mom wouldn't do that, right? But that's how we often think God's going to treat us.

Jesus didn't just give the disciples 2 little guppies (in today's passage). He knew the disciples had been up all night doing what they usually did—trying to fish but, in this instance, never really catching anything. Here comes Jesus, and—wham!—they catch so many fish they have to sit on the beach and count 'em! 153 FISH!! He wants to give you the same—not necessarily lots of "stuff" but other kinds of good things.

WHAT ABOUT YOU?

:: *Think about it—on a 1 (low) to 10 (high) scale, how much do you think God wants to do for you? Do you believe that, as he did for the disciples, he wants to give you far more than you could ever need?*

:: *When's a time that God surprised you—when he gave you more than you asked for?*

SEPTEMBER :: 15

READ ACTS 2:1-4

Spreading the Jesus-news

Suddenly a sound like the blowing of a violent wind came from heaven and filled the whole house.
ACTS 2:2

Imagine that you and a couple hundred kids from your school are sitting in the gym. A teacher has just finished explaining a little trick he stumbled onto that makes each of you able to wiggle your ears. And now you all have been asked to get the news about his discovery out to the world. You can't drive, and you have no access to TV, radio, newspapers, magazines, or the Internet. What do you do?

This is kind of like the job a few hundred early Christians had—except their news was much more important. Their news was about Jesus. Matthew, Mark, Luke, and John—the first 4 books of the New Testament—tell the story of Jesus. And most of the rest of the New Testament is made up of letters that were written to different churches and groups of believers. Luke, a medical doctor, wrote the book of Acts, as well as the book of Luke. He recorded the spread of the Jesus-news and the beginning of the church (at least the really important stuff). Starting with when the Holy Spirit came to earth to live in all Christians.

This same Spirit who came 2,000 years ago is still with us today.

READ ACTS 1:7-9

Gotta Have Guts

But you will receive power when the Holy Spirit comes on you.
ACTS 1:8

Have you ever had an experience at youth group where you get all excited about telling your friends about Jesus? But then by the time you're at school the next day, you can't even open your mouth!

I'm never going to get up the courage to witness to people if I have to do it alone. That's why I need to remember that I'm not alone. I have the Holy Spirit with me to help me know what to say—and to have the guts to say it. When we have the Holy Spirit, we have the power of God to do amazing things.

WHAT ABOUT YOU?

:: *What was one time that you were afraid to do something, but God gave you the courage and power to do it?*

:: *Sit down with your youth leader or some of your Christian friends and think of some ways you can be a witness at school.*

:: *Thank God for the power he's given you in the Holy Spirit, and ask him to help you use it.*

READ ACTS 2:42-47

A Good Place to Be

They devoted themselves to the apostles' teaching and to the fellowship, to the breaking of bread and to prayer.

ACTS 2:42

There are lots of times I really don't feel like going to church. But a few weeks ago, something happened that showed me how important church really is.

I had been in an argument with some of my friends for a few days. Well, I went to church the next Sunday morning and the sermon was on the importance of loving each other and being kind to each other. I realized that my friends and I weren't being very kind by arguing and being mad at each other. So after church that day we got together, talked about the situation, and fixed our friendship.

Even though church can seem kind of boring sometimes, it's our chance to be with other Christians, to learn more about God, and to worship him and get fired up about sharing the good news of Jesus Christ to others. That's the stuff that helps our faith grow. And if we really pay attention, we might even learn something.

WHAT ABOUT YOU?

:: What do you like about your church? What don't you like? How can God use you in your church?

:: Thank God for giving you a place where you can grow in your faith.

SEPTEMBER :: 18

DAVID, AGE 14

READ ACTS 4:32–5:11

Wrestling with a Lie

You have not lied to men but to God.
ACTS 5:4

Wrestlers compete in different weight classes, with a maximum weight for each one. If you get too heavy for one class, you get bumped up into the next one, where you have to face bigger guys. So some guys will do almost anything to lose a few pounds and keep from getting bumped up. I was one of those guys.

For 2 weeks before a big meet, I starved myself. My friends saw what I was doing and tried to get me to stop, but I lied to them and said nothing was wrong. When they didn't believe my lies, I got angry with them and wouldn't talk to them.

When you lie, you hurt yourself emotionally and, like me, sometimes physically too. You hurt the people who love you, because they can't get close to you when you won't tell them the truth. Worst of all, you hurt God because lying is sinning. Being honest isn't always easy, but it's always better than telling a lie.

WHAT ABOUT YOU?

:: *Have you ever thought to yourself,* It's only a little lie? *How can "little lies" cause "big problems"?*

:: *Have you hurt someone with a lie you told?*

:: *Ask God to help you tell the truth, even when it isn't easy.*

LAUREN, AGE 15

READ ACTS 8:9-23

Fakey Faith

When Simon saw the Sprit was given at the laying on of the apostles' hands, he offered them money.
ACTS 8:18

I see a lot of people at my school wearing Christian T-shirts and jewelry. Then I see them do all kinds of stuff I know Jesus would never do, like make fun of people or swear or gossip.

It's pretty easy to pretend you're a great Christian. You just have to throw on a cross necklace, lead a few youth group discussions and show up at church every week. Those things are great if they're backed up with real faith. But sometimes people just do that kind of stuff to impress other people.

Being a Christian isn't about putting on a show. It's about loving God with your whole heart. Anyone can act like a Christian on the outside, but unless you're right with God on the inside, none of those things matter.

WHAT ABOUT YOU?

:: *Write down several things that make a person a "genuine Christian." What is one change you can make in your life that will make your own faith more real and genuine?*

:: *Ask God to help you keep your faith real.*

A genuine christian is someone who is living for Christ and enjoying what He has done. The genuine christian lives for God no matter what anyone says.

One change I can make in life is to act more like Christ and not have an attitude and try to get up on time.

READ ACTS 10:34-35

No Favorites

I now realize how true it is that God does not show favoritism.
ACTS 10:34

I'm embarrassed to admit it, but there have been times when I've been tempted to distance myself from people because they were "different" or didn't fit in.

But this passage tells us that God doesn't play favorites. He loves all people equally, no matter what race they are, how smart they are, or how much money they have. Since we're supposed to be like Jesus, we shouldn't show favoritism either. We need to share God's love with all people, even people who are different from us.

God wants all people to know him, not just a select few. He judges us all the same and offers salvation to all of us. If God, who knows us best, can look past our differences, we should too.

WHAT ABOUT YOU?

:: *Choose a culture that's different from your own and read more about it. Ask your parents to help you make a typical meal from that culture or find some music that comes from that culture. What do you think your life would be like if you'd been born into that culture?*

:: *Thank God for creating all kinds of people.*

If I were born into a different culture, I would probably not have some of the opportunies I have today. I wouldn't go to a church. I would probably go to chapel or synagouge. I wouldn't wear the clothes I wear today. Even if I did like a different culture God would still love me for who I Am.

SEPTEMBER :: 21

READ ACTS 15:36-41

Loving Disagreement

They had such a sharp disagreement that they parted company.
ACTS 15:39

Earlier Lauren talked about those who pretend to be "great Christians." Her devotional reminded us not to "put on a show" but to love God with our whole hearts. But what happens when there are disagreements between people who really love God?

Acts 15 shows us that from the very beginning, the disciples had disagreements (and even fights) with each other. There were 2 ways disciples of Jesus handled disagreements in chapter 15: figuring it out together (the first 21 verses), or going in separate directions (today's passage).

Both of these examples are good reminders that Christians need to try to get along and work together. God tells us to love each other even when it's hard. That's the most important thing to remember when you struggle with other Christians. It's okay to disagree, but never forget to love!

WHAT ABOUT YOU?

:: *Do you think that 2 people who love Jesus can "agree to disagree" and stay close, even in a conflict?*

:: *Think of a person you are having a struggle with right now. Go to that person, either one-on-one, or with a few friends or an adult to help, and try to come to an agreement.*

:: *Ask God to help you love a Christian you don't like or agree with.*

Well the friend is not A Christian but we Are
having a conflict on christianity. She desn't
believe that God created the universe and
everything in it. I keep trying to tell her
but its kinda difficult becaose I don't
have the right words to say so I need Gods
help so I can help her get saved.

S E P T E M B E R :: 2 2

READ ACTS 15:1–21

Painful Extra Credit

Unless you are circumcised...you cannot be saved.
ACTS 15:1

Tons of people got cut off from their families when they became Christ-followers. You'd think this rejection, persecution, and even torture would have snuffed out Christianity like a candle. But instead, the people who got kicked out of their homes kept talking about Jesus while they were moving to their new cities! Because of their excitement and witness, lots of people joined them—and Christianity grew.

But in a city called Antioch, the disciples had to clarify what it meant to be a Christian. The Jews were incorrectly saying that if any non-Jew wanted to be saved, they'd have to do some extra credit. And the extra credit was—ouch!—circumcision (a really painful surgery performed on a, um, sensitive area for guys).

Doing Christian stuff doesn't make someone a Christian, just like going to a fast-food place doesn't turn you into a hamburger or a taco! The only way to be a Christian is to invite Jesus Christ to come into your heart and take away your sins.

SEPTEMBER :: 23

AMY, AGE 14

READ ACTS 16:22-25

Praise? Now?

Paul and Silas were praying and singing hymns to God, and the other prisoners were listening.
ACTS 16:25

I was at a Christian music concert with a bunch of my friends. They were all praising God, singing along and dancing to the music. But I was having a hard time enjoying myself. My 17-year-old sister thought she might be pregnant, my family was fighting constantly, and one of my good friends was flirting with the guy I really liked. I couldn't stop thinking about everything that was going wrong.

But as the concert went on, I realized I had to give up my problems to God. Trusting God was the only way I was going to survive. So I said a little prayer and thanked God for being in control of my life.

Soon I was dancing and singing with everyone else at the concert. God had wanted me to give him control of my situation all along. I'm so glad I did.

WHAT ABOUT YOU?

:: *When is it toughest for you to praise God?*

:: *Imagine you were the prison guard in charge of Paul and Silas. Write down what you saw, heard, and felt when they started singing.*

:: *Say a prayer of praise to God.*

It is toughest for me to praise God when I
things on my mind that are constantly
bothering me.

I felt like the word of God had touched
my heart and it filled me with joy.

SEPTEMBER :: 24

CINDY, AGE 13

READ ACTS 20:22-24

The Unknown Future

I consider my life worth nothing to me, if only I may finish the race and complete the task the LORD Jesus has given me.
ACTS 20:24

My family moved when I was 8 years old, so I remember what it was like not knowing what you'd find in a new place. I didn't know what kind of church we would join or what my new school would be like. I wondered if anyone would even notice the new girl who didn't have any friends.

God helped me see that popularity wasn't really very important, as long as he was my best friend. I was lonely at times, but I was never really alone. Moving taught me that I can't always know what's ahead in my life. But whatever it is, God will be there.

WHAT ABOUT YOU?

:: *Why do we sometimes wish we knew what would happen in the future? Why do you think God only lets us see one step at a time?*

:: *Paul's big challenge was going to Jerusalem, but yours will probably be different. Rewrite these verses in a personal way, describing how God will be with you in a difficult situation.*

:: *Thank God for his promise to always be your friend.*

So we could prevent bAd things from happening.
He hAs something plAnned for us in the future.

READ ACTS 26:9-18

Switcheroo

I am sending you to them to open their eyes and turn them from darkness to light, and from the power of Satan to God.

ACTS 26:17-18

If I meet someone who isn't living a Christian life, that doesn't mean they'll always be that way. God loves everyone, even his enemies, and he can turn people's lives completely around. He totally changed Saul. Saul's life changed so much that God even gave him a new name—Paul.

I also need to learn to love the people I don't like. Instead of looking down on them or getting mad, I should pray for them. Maybe someone seems like a bad person to me, but he or she wouldn't always be that way if they got to know God. And if I can help them do that, I'll feel great about myself because I helped change someone's life.

WHAT ABOUT YOU?

:: Who are your enemies? What can you do to help them know more about God?

:: Find some of your baby pictures. See how much you've changed? Now, if people can change that much physically, think about how much they can change spiritually.

:: Pray for people you don't like, that God would come into their lives and change them.

People At my school who've called me mean nAmes in the pAst. I can pray for them.

SEPTEMBER :: 26

ASHLEY, AGE 12

READ ACTS 27:33-44

Back to the Basics

Now I urge you to take some food. You need it to survive.
ACTS 27:34

God has always taken care of the basic needs in my life. I've never had to sleep in the cold or go hungry. I've never been without water to drink or medicine to help me get well. Since I don't have to worry about the basics, I have the energy to do something more with my life, like help other people.

I think God wants us to be like Paul and pay attention to other people's physical needs, as well as their spiritual needs. If someone is cold or hungry or sick, the best way we can show them God's love is to make sure they have food and shelter. That's what Paul did, and that's what we need to do too.

WHAT ABOUT YOU?

:: What are some ways God has taken care of your physical needs? How do those things help your spiritual life?

:: Ask your parents or your pastor to help you find a soup kitchen or homeless shelter where you can volunteer. Hey, you could even bring some friends or your whole youth group along.

:: Ask God to help you reach out to people in need.

God has blessed me with a radio so I can listen to songs that worship God and a bible so I can read more about the word of God.

READ ROMANS 1:16–17

Share the Excitement

I am not ashamed of the gospel.
ROMANS 1:16

When I first became a Christian, I was afraid to tell some of my non-Christian friends. I didn't know what they would think, and I was scared they might make fun of me.

But I've learned that I need to be excited about my faith. If I say I'm a Christian, I'm saying I believe what the Bible says and that I want to give my life to God. That's a serious commitment. So if I believe in the gospel enough to base my whole life on it, I should believe in it enough to share it with other people.

If somebody gave you a really cool present for your birthday, you'd tell other people about it, right? Well, the salvation God gave us through Jesus is the greatest gift ever. And we need to be excited about sharing it with our friends so they can have the same great gift we've been given.

WHAT ABOUT YOU?

:: *Think about a time you were embarrassed to tell people about your faith. What could you have said or done differently?*

:: *Ask God to help you be bold about your faith.*

I could have Asked God to help choose
the right words to say so I could get
through to that person And help them
understand more About Jesus.

SEPTEMBER :: 28

READ LUKE 23:26-34

How Do You Look at Others?

Jesus said, "Father, forgive them, for they do not know what they are doing."
LUKE 23:34

Isn't it amazing how God looks at people with loving eyes? This week Melinda talked about how God can turn lives completely around and how we need to be careful not to look down on people.

Think about what Jesus said, right before he was crucified: "Father, forgive them, for they do not know what they are doing." Even when he was in extreme pain and suffering greatly, Jesus looked on people with compassion and love. No doubt he was mad about their sin, but he still loved them—he even died for them.

Allow God to use you to love people. God knows how to balance love and judgment. We don't—so stick to loving instead of judging.

WHAT ABOUT YOU?

:: Is there someone you don't get along with because of something they did?

:: Talk with a friend. Tell them how you are trying to change the way you view sin in others. It will help you think it through.

:: Ask God, "How do you do it? Teach me to love others like you do."

Yes, because they mock the Word of God And
Also direspect it.

SEPTEMBER :: 29

READ ROMANS 8:37-39

Hard Times Ahead

In all these things we are more than conquerors through him who loved us.
ROMANS 8:37

If you combined the business muscle of New York City with the political leadership of Washington, D.C., you'd have something like ancient Rome. It was the center of its world, with the "biggest and best" of everything. In the middle of this, a little group of new Christians swelled into a large Christian church. Paul's letter to these Christians reads like a lawyer's argument. On trial is the human race, and Paul proves that we're all pretty useless when it comes to living right with others and with God, but that the death and resurrection of Jesus changes all that.

Paul wanted to make sure that Christians in this busy, smart capital city started off on the right foot spiritually. Paul may have sensed some darker days coming. Christianity was already getting blamed for stuff it had nothing to do with. And soon Christians would be persecuted in ways they couldn't imagine, including group killings and being forced to "fight" hungry lions for the entertainment of the entire city. Paul himself would eventually be executed in Rome because of his faith.

With this just around the corner, Roman Christians really needed to hear that nothing in all creation will be able to separate us from the love of God.

SEPTEMBER :: 30

KENT, AGE 13

READ ROMANS 3:22-24

A Bunch of Sinners

This righteousness from God comes through faith in Jesus Christ to all who believe.
ROMANS 3:22

This is one of those passages I want to share with every new Christian I meet. A lot of people think you can earn salvation.

God knew we were all sinners and that we would suffer because of our sins. But he loved us so much that he sent Jesus to suffer for us. God did what was needed to save us. Jesus' death and resurrection took care of our sins. We didn't have anything to do with it. But we do have to accept this truth. We do that by trusting in Jesus our Savior. All that other stuff, like going to church and reading the Bible, is important, because it helps us grow in our faith. But we can't earn salvation by trying to be the very best Christian in the world. All we have to do is accept what God did for us.

WHAT ABOUT YOU?

:: *Why is it impossible to "earn" God's love?*

:: *Ask your parents or another adult you're close to why they love you. Do their reasons have anything to do with how good you are or how well you do things? How is God's love like that?*

:: *Thank God for his incredible gift of salvation.*

Because Gods love is pure love And strong love.
Gods love is powerful. That is why Gods love is
impossible to "Earn".

OCTOBER :: 1

AMY, AGE 13

He Loved You First

Just at the right time, when we were still powerless, Christ died for the ungodly.
ROMANS 5:6

One time when I was telling a friend about Jesus, she didn't understand what I was saying. She kept thinking that she had to be good first and then maybe God would love her. But I showed her these verses in Romans, and she started to understand that God already loved her—enough to send Jesus to die for her. My friend was amazed that anyone would love her that much.

God's love amazes me too. Romans 5:7 talks about how unusual it is that anyone would die for someone else. But Jesus died for us, before we knew him or cared about him at all. The truth is, Jesus even died for murderers and the worst of criminals. No one else would have done that. Only Jesus. Knowing that Jesus loves me so much has helped me love him too. I'm going to keep telling my friends about Jesus' love, because I don't want them to miss out!

WHAT ABOUT YOU?

:: *How would you tell a non-Christian friend about Jesus' love?*

:: *Praise God for his amazing love!*

OCTOBER :: 2

SARAH, AGE 13

READ ROMANS 8:35–39

Love, Always

Who shall separate us from the love of Christ?
ROMANS 8:35

I recently went through a month when I got really depressed. Even when I was with my friends, I felt like no one cared about me. I could barely get out of bed in the morning.

Somehow I had forgotten the truth of these verses. I needed someone to remind me, "Don't think that no one cares about you, because God does!" God still loved me, and nothing was going to change that.

God must really care for us if there isn't anything that can separate us from his love. Knowing that I can always turn to him keeps me going during hard situations. He is even there when things in my life are fun and easy. He is there with me through the worst of times and the best of times.

WHAT ABOUT YOU?

:: *How do you feel when you know you're loved?*

:: *Think of someone you know who's hurting and needs a little love. What is one thing you can do to encourage this person this week?*

:: *Thank God for his constant love.*

OCTOBER :: 3

LISA, AGE 13

READ ROMANS 12:1-2

Perfectly Willing

Offer your bodies as living sacrifices, holy and pleasing to God.
ROMANS 12:1

I learned a lot about giving myself to God and living for him when I went on a missions trip to a very poor part of the United States with my youth group. The work was hard and we were a long way from home. If I had been doing it all for myself, I would have just given up. But I knew I was working for God, and he was there with me during the whole trip. He helped me through the hard times, and he helped me make some great new friends.

Living to please God isn't always easy. Sometimes following him means looking uncool in front of other people. Sometimes it means giving up what I want and doing what he wants instead. But it's worth it because I know God's will is perfect—why would I want to do anything else?

WHAT ABOUT YOU?

:: *Think of a time when you had to choose between what you wanted and what God wanted. Which did you choose? Would you make the same choice today?*

:: *Tell God you're willing to live your life for him and ask him to guide you. If you find it difficult to pray this, ask God to change your heart.*

OCTOBER :: 4

Stumbling Block

Let us stop passing judgment on one another.
ROMANS 14:13

I was on a retreat and met this guy who really bothered me. I saw him hanging around with all the girls and pegged him as a big flirt. I told my friends what I thought of him and pretty soon he had a reputation that he probably didn't deserve. None of the girls wanted to talk to him and neither did the guys.

Afterward, I realized I'd really messed up. Because of me, he didn't get the chance to make some great new Christian friends. He didn't get to leave the retreat feeling charged up about his faith. Instead, he probably left thinking there were a lot of judgmental, unfriendly people there.

Even if he was flirty, it wasn't my place to turn everyone against him. Whenever we judge people, we become their stumbling blocks. If we don't show them love and kindness, we can't show them Jesus.

WHAT ABOUT YOU?

:: *Ask a friend how you can help him or her grow closer to God. Do what your friend asks for the next month and see how God works through you.*

:: *Pray that you will be a good example of living for God.*

OCTOBER :: 5

READ 1 TIMOTHY 1:6–11

What the Law Can't Do

Law is made not for the righteous but for lawbreakers.
1 TIMOTHY 1:9

In the September 30 devotion, Kent got it right. No matter what activity you do—pray, go to church, read your Bible—these things won't get you to heaven.

When a builder constructs a wall, he uses a level to make sure the wall is straight. If it's crooked, he uses his saw and hammer to repair the studs inside. If he didn't repair from the inside first, no matter how hard he pushed on the outside, the wall would always go back to its original crooked state.

Pushing on the outside of the wall is like trying to fix your guilty behavior on your own. Just like the level, God's law reveals the problem of sin but doesn't repair the problem. The repair is found in Jesus. He, in sacrificing himself, nailed your guilt and sin onto the cross.

You have to be repaired from the inside by Jesus. This happens when you put your faith in him every day.

WHAT ABOUT YOU?

:: *Looking back, have you ever allowed Jesus to come into your life? When was it? If you haven't, talk with your parents or pastor about this once-and-for-all commitment.*

:: *Ask God to help you. Pray that he'll continue to repair you from the inside.*

OCTOBER :: 6

Clean Up and Hang On

He will keep you strong to the end.
1 CORINTHIANS 1:8

Ever get a bad report card—one with a D or even worse? That's what happened to the church at Corinth. Paul was the founder and teacher of this church for a year-and-a-half, but then left to start other churches. He heard that the church was not doing well. In fact, they were flunking Christianity 101. They were acting just like all the other people in their busy city. And the people in their city had a totally sleazy reputation. They were caught up in all kinds of garbage—arguing, getting drunk on communion wine, and sleeping around. Paul wasn't happy about any of this, and he let them know it.

But Paul didn't just scold the church and move on. He gave them lots of solid advice for cleaning up their act. He told them how to relate to each other as Christians. He told them how to hang on to God, even when they were tempted. And in one of the most famous chapters in the Bible (chapter 13), he wrote down the qualities of real love—the kind of love the church at Corinth (and all of us) need to show each other.

OCTOBER :: 7

BEN, AGE 16

READ 1 CORINTHIANS 1:10–17

Get It Together

Agree with one another so that...you may be perfectly united in mind and thought.
1 CORINTHIANS 1:10

Recently I was talking to a non-Christian friend, and a Christian friend overheard me and started answering all my non-Christian friend's questions before I could. I got frustrated that this other Christian was "interrupting" me. But then I realized that God could work through my Christian friend as much as he could work through me. It didn't really matter who was doing the talking.

God likes it when his children are at peace with each other. He is glorified when we work together to build his kingdom. All Christians have the same mission: to lead people to Jesus. We might have different personalities or different ways of saying things, but we shouldn't let that keep us from working together to share Jesus Christ with others. We need each other if we want to change the world for Jesus.

WHAT ABOUT YOU?

:: What are some of the things that keep your youth group, or another Christian group you hang out with, from working together all the time?

:: Ask your leader to help you plan an activity that can help your group become more unified.

:: Thank God for your brothers and sisters in Christ.

READ 1 CORINTHIANS 3:10–15

Rock-solid Faith

By the grace God has given me, I laid a foundation as an expert builder.... Each one should be careful how he builds.
1 CORINTHIANS 3:10

At the beginning of 7th grade, I had bad grades and started getting into trouble. Things that should have been important to me just didn't seem to matter, I wasn't paying attention to the kind of life I was living. God wants me to do better than that. After all, he's given me a great foundation in Jesus, who is as solid as a rock. My job is to build on his example, making sure my choices are pure and holy. And when I'm not sure what to choose, I can ask God for help and know that his answer is true.

If I want my faith to be strong, I need to get serious about it every day.

WHAT ABOUT YOU?

:: What are some big decisions in your life right now? How can you make sure you're choosing wisely?

:: Think of one "weak spot" in your faith. Write about how you do in that area every day for a week. Then set a specific goal to do better the next week.

:: Ask God to help you make wise decisions.

OCTOBER :: 9

READ 1 CORINTHIANS 6:18-20

It's Everywhere!

Flee from sexual immorality.
1 CORINTHIANS 6:18

Sex is everywhere. And wow is it ever a big temptation for teenagers like me.

You wouldn't know it from watching movies, but God created sex to be something special to share with the person you marry, the person you give your whole life to. Sex outside of marriage causes serious problems and pulls us away from God. That's why God wants us to stay away from sexual immorality. He wants us to keep our minds on him, not on sex.

God has every right to ask us to obey him. After all, he paid for our salvation with the blood of his Son. Our lives and our bodies belong to God.

WHAT ABOUT YOU?

:: What sexual sins do you struggle with? How can you avoid being tempted to give in to those sins?

:: Find a small wooden or clay bead and a cord to make into a necklace or a bracelet. Think of it as your "flee" bead. Whenever you are tempted by sexual sin, use your bead as a reminder to get away from that temptation—fast!

:: Ask God to help you be strong and resist sexual temptation.

OCTOBER :: 10

MARISSA, AGE 14

READ 1 CORINTHIANS 9:24–25

High Priority

Run in such a way as to get the prize.
1 CORINTHIANS 9:24

I can't believe how busy I am! When I started 9th grade, I got involved with all kinds of extracurricular activities. With all of those, plus the increased homework load, I thought I'd never find time for everything—and I didn't. The first thing that slipped was my relationship with God. I'd skip my Bible reading time or forget to pray.

These verses help me remember that I need to find time for God, even though it's not always easy to do that. God is waiting for me at life's finish line, and I need to keep my focus on him, no matter how busy my life gets. When my schedule gets crazy and my calendar gets full, I need to make sure my relationship with God stays on top.

WHAT ABOUT YOU?

:: What are some time-wasters you could get rid of?

:: Write down some of your favorite verses on note cards. Stick a card in your locker, in your backpack, and in some of your textbooks. Whenever you see them, take a quick moment to think about God and about his love for you.

:: Ask God to help you manage your time wisely.

OCTOBER :: 11

SARAH, AGE 14

READ 1 CORINTHIANS 10:12-14

A Way Out

God...will not let you be tempted beyond what you can bear.
1 CORINTHIANS 10:13

Ever since the Garden of Eden, people have faced temptation. For Adam and Eve, it was the forbidden fruit. For me, it could be drugs or sex or cheating or lying. Each of these things is a test of my faith, and I have to rely on God to keep from falling.

Fortunately, God makes 2 important promises for me to remember when I'm being tempted. First, he'll make sure the temptation is never more than I can bear. It might be more than I can handle by myself, but it can't possibly be more than God can handle. He's always there for me to lean on.

Second, God promises to give me a way out of the temptation. He'll show me the way if I ask. He's already given me a lot of advice in the Bible. Memorizing his Word helps me to know the right thing to do. With God, I know I can stand strong.

WHAT ABOUT YOU?

:: *What are some ways God helps you escape temptation?*

:: *Memorize 1 Corinthians 10:13 and repeat it to yourself when you feel tempted.*

:: *Talk to God about the temptations you feel; ask him to help you resist them.*

OCTOBER :: 12

READ 1 CORINTHIANS 11:6-10

Put Your Fruit-hat Away

If a woman does not cover her head, she should have her hair cut off.
1 CORINTHIANS 11:6

There are lots of people who misunderstand what this passage is about.

Here's the deal: Paul was writing about some women who were being a distraction in worship services. This would be like a woman sitting in your church wearing a 4-foot-tall hat with all kinds of fruit stuck all over it. That would definitely take away your focus from God.

Earlier this week, when Tommy talked about following God, he made it clear that he wasn't paying attention to what God wanted. Sure, God wants you to worship, and he wants to say stuff to you in church. But he also wants to say stuff to the people sitting around you—so don't be a distraction!

WHAT ABOUT YOU?

:: Have you ever noticed someone being a distraction during the service? What did he or she do?

:: Look back at the last month and think about how you acted in worship. Is there anyone you sit next to that you probably shouldn't?

:: Begin your worship time with a prayer to God asking him to help you get the most out of your worship time.

OCTOBER :: 13

READ 1 CORINTHIANS 12:1, 4-11

Start Rippin'

Now about spiritual gifts, brothers, I do not want you to be ignorant.... All these are the work of one and the same Spirit, and he gives them to each one, just as he determines.
1 CORINTHIANS 12:1, 11

Don't you just love opening presents? The excitement of not knowing what's inside and the joy of see-ing what you got is awesome. Well, God has given each of us special talents and abilities as gifts.

All of us Christians are good at different things, and God uses each of us in special ways. Together we make up a pretty good thing. It's like your body. All the parts do different things, and together they make up a whole working, living, breathing you. Christians need to work together the same way. All the different things we do should work together and bring honor to God.

Finding out what your gifts are is like tearing back the wrapping paper—you see a little bit, then a little more, until you see the whole gift. So start rippin' that paper and explore the gifts God has given you.

OCTOBER :: 14

DANIELLE, AGE 12

READ 1 CORINTHIANS 12:12-27

God's Bod

You are the body of Christ, and each one of you is a part of it.
1 CORINTHIANS 12:27

There's a kid I know from church who gets picked on a lot at school because he's a little weird. Well, one day, I saw some people picking on this kid, and I wondered why no one was doing anything about it. Finally, I told them to leave him alone. After that, I got teased too. But I don't regret sticking up for this kid. He might be different, but he deserves care and respect as much as anyone else.

Christians are all part of the body of Christ. So we need to remember that God made all of us different for a reason. Just like no part of your body is more important than the other parts, no person is more important than other people. In God's eyes, every person he created is special and has a purpose. It doesn't matter what color you are or how much money you have—in God's eyes, you matter.

WHAT ABOUT YOU?

:: Who are some of the people our society tells us are "important"? Who are the people God thinks are "important"?

:: Praise God for creating all kinds of people.

OCTOBER :: 15

READ 1 CORINTHIANS 13:4-8

You Call That Love?

Love is patient, love is kind...it is not self-seeking.
1 CORINTHIANS 13:4-5

I was dating this guy named Keith, and he seemed like a totally great guy—a strong Christian involved in church and youth group. Then one night on a retreat we were all playing a night game where we hid in the woods while people looked for us with flashlights. I hid with Keith, and my friend Katie and her boyfriend hid with us.

We'd only been hiding a few minutes when Katie started making out with her boyfriend. Suddenly, Keith wanted to get real friendly with me too. Well, I got out of there in a hurry. I didn't want anything to do with that kind of stuff!

God wants us to think about what we can put into a relationship to build the other person up. He wants us to love the way he loves, with patience, kindness, and respect. Knowing about God's perfect love makes me want to be more like him in my relationships too.

WHAT ABOUT YOU?

:: *What are some false definitions of "love"?*

:: *Write down all the qualities of love in 1 Corinthians 13:4-8, then write a way you could show each quality to people you love.*

:: *Praise God for his perfect love.*

OCTOBER :: 16

READ 1 CORINTHIANS 15:14-17

He's Alive!

If Christ has not been raised, our preaching is useless and so is your faith.

1 CORINTHIANS 15:14

Some people don't believe the resurrection happened. But think about this: If Jesus didn't come back to life, our Christian faith would be useless. There wouldn't be any Easter. In fact, we would have nothing true to live for!

When Jesus died for us, all of our sins were forgiven. If he hadn't died, we'd still be stuck in our sins. And if he hadn't risen, it would be like sin won the battle—like death was stronger than God. That's not the kind of God we have!

Because Jesus rose, we can have faith in a living God, not a dead guy who's still in a tomb. Jesus' resurrection gives me something to live for. He took the punishment for my sins, and now I can spend eternity with him in heaven.

WHAT ABOUT YOU?

:: *Why is Jesus' resurrection the most important miracle in the Bible?*

:: *Imagine you were one of the people who saw Jesus after he came back to life. Write a letter to a friend describing what it was like to see him.*

:: *Praise God for his awesome power over death!*

EMILY, AGE 14

READ 1 CORINTHIANS 15:33–34

Peer Pressure

Do not be misled: "Bad company corrupts good character."
1 CORINTHIANS 15:33

Some of my friends and I used to hang around with a couple of girls who were always getting into trouble. It didn't take us long to realize we didn't want to be associated with them. They didn't respect anyone, including themselves.

The people you hang out with affect the things you do. It's like being with someone who's got a cold. If you hang around with that person long enough, eventually you're probably going to catch a cold too.

My 3 best friends are strong Christians. They're the kind of friends who help me grow closer to God. And they're the best kind of friends to have.

WHAT ABOUT YOU?

:: *Do your friends help or hurt your faith? How can you find some friends who will encourage you to grow in your faith?*

:: *Once a week, meet with 1 or 2 other Christian friends. Talk about things you're struggling with and find ways to encourage each other during the week.*

:: *Ask God to help you find strong Christian friends, and ask him to help you be that type of friend too.*

OCTOBER :: 18

READ 2 CORINTHIANS 1:3-7

My Comforter

Just as the sufferings of Christ flow over into our lives, so also through Christ our comfort overflows.
2 CORINTHIANS 1:5

My mom is really sick right now. She's been in the hospital a lot, and the doctors ran a bunch of tests. I guess it's something about a tumor. But my parents won't even tell me how bad it is, which makes me worry even more. The only comfort I have right now is knowing God is in control.

Some people look for comfort in worldly things, but that's just a waste of time. If I go to Jesus Christ, he'll give me as much love and support as I could ever possibly need. Jesus gives us comfort to help us, but also so we can pass it on.

I might not understand why all this is happening to me. But I do know where to find comfort, no matter how bad it gets.

WHAT ABOUT YOU?

:: What are some ways God uses other people to comfort you?

:: Do you know anyone who might need comforting? Think of something you can do this week to share Christ's love with that person.

:: Thank God for the ways he comforts you, and ask him to help you comfort others.

OCTOBER :: 19

READ LUKE 23:44-49

Big-time Dead

Jesus called out with a loud voice, "Father, into your hands I commit my spirit."
LUKE 23:46

Some people say Jesus never rose from the dead, others say he never even died. An example of this is the Koran (the Muslim bible), which says that Jesus only pretended to be dead.

Here's what you need to understand to know that Jesus really died:

»»   Jesus survived a Roman scourging. This beating ripped open the skin and exposed muscles.

»»   A crown of thorns was pushed into his head.

»»   Jesus had nails driven through his wrists, which damaged major arteries.

»»   Jesus was stabbed in the side with a spear by a Roman soldier. This was enough to kill him!

»»   Finally Jesus...hung his head down, breathed his last breath...and died.

Jesus really died (and rose again)! There are too many recorded facts to ignore. If Jesus said he was going to die and then be raised, and it really happened, what else did he say that I need to know?

WHAT ABOUT YOU?

:: What would you say to a person who claims they believe Jesus lived and died but doesn't believe he rose again?

:: Pray that God will prepare that person's heart for what you will share with them.

_____

_____

_____

_____

_____

OCTOBER :: 20

READ 2 CORINTHIANS 1:13-14

Trash Talker Turnaround

You can boast of us just as we will boast of you.
2 CORINTHIANS 1:14

Ever have someone spread rumors about you or someone you know? That's exactly what was happening in the church at Corinth. As if they hadn't learned their lesson after Paul's first letter (1 Corinthians), a few people had been talking trash about Paul, the founder of their church. They were saying he wasn't good enough to be an apostle, that he thought he was better than everyone else, and that he was a big wimp!

As you might guess, Paul was pretty frustrated about this. So he sent one of his most trusted buddies, Titus, to straighten out the trouble-makers. Titus rocked—he got the job done! Most of the people admitted they were wrong (although some kept talking about Paul behind his back). Paul was thrilled about their response. He wrote this letter to thank them for their turnaround. Paul also reminds the few who are still talking about him that God has put him in charge and they'd better learn to deal with it.

OCTOBER :: 21

READ 2 CORINTHIANS 4:7–18

Jars of Clay

We have this treasure in jars of clay.
2 CORINTHIANS 4:7

I like to think I'm good at things. But one time I tried to lead a Bible study at my school, and I wasn't very good at it. I think I was trying to impress people with how much I knew, instead of just leading the discussion. These verses help me remember that it's God who's great, not me. I'm just his servant.

God wants us to serve him and share his love with everyone we meet. We are just ordinary, imperfect people, but God can do amazing things through us. That's really encouraging to me. I know that God is in me and working through me all the time.

WHAT ABOUT YOU?

:: *Why do you think God chooses ordinary people to spread his love? How do you feel about carrying the "treasure" of the gospel?*

:: *Dig around in your basement for a little clay pot or bowl. Put it where you'll see it every day. Whenever you look at it, remember that God chose you to spread his message of love.*

:: *Thank God for the great honor of serving him and sharing him with the world.*

OCTOBER :: 22

BRIAN, AGE 14

READ 2 CORINTHIANS 5:16-21

New and Improved

If anyone is in Christ, he is a new creation.
2 CORINTHIANS 5:17

Until a few years ago, I didn't know what being a Christian really meant. I would show up at church and go through the motions, but I didn't really understand what God wanted from me. Then I started getting more serious about my faith and learning more about God and how much he loves me. I read my Bible more. I prayed more. I got baptized. Now I strive to be more like him every day.

I think it's really awesome how God can turn someone's life around. When we accept Jesus as our Savior, we become totally different people. The old junk is gone, and we have the chance to start all over again.

Experiencing a new life in Jesus Christ has given me the confidence to trust God with everything. If he can change my heart, I know he can do anything.

WHAT ABOUT YOU?

:: *What were you like before you became a Christian? How are you different now?*

:: *Make a change in your life. Rearrange your room or eat something different for lunch. How does it feel to try something new?*

:: *Praise God for the new life he's given you in Christ.*

READ 2 CORINTHIANS 7:5-7

The Friendship Factor

God, who comforts the downcast, comforted us by the coming of Titus.
2 CORINTHIANS 7:6

Everybody has bad days—when they're stressed out about a decision, when someone cuts them down, or when they just don't feel very good. On my bad days, I've found that turning to a friend goes a long way. It means a lot to me when someone notices that I'm down in the dumps and cheers me up. It helps me know that my friend cares for me.

Someone once told me God speaks to us in our struggles but shouts to us in our tragedies. He's always there, but he wants to make extra sure we know he's there when we hurt. One of the ways he shows us is by sending help through our friends.

So if you have something that's bugging you, or if you feel horrible or sad about something, talk to God about it, then share it with a friend. You'll feel a lot better when you know you're not alone.

WHAT ABOUT YOU?

:: *Think of a time you cheered up a friend. Was it easy? Was it worth it?*

:: *Give someone a note or a word of encouragement this week.*

:: *Thank God for his gift of friends.*

OCTOBER :: 24

READ 2 CORINTHIANS 9:6-7

Give It Away!

Remember this: Whoever sows sparingly will also reap sparingly, and whoever sows generously will also reap generously.
2 CORINTHIANS 9:6

After our outreach events, our youth leader asks each of us to make a phone call to 2 of the new people who came to the event, whether we know them or not.

Some weeks I'm not too thrilled about spending my time and energy calling total strangers. But these verses remind me that people who give a lot are the ones who really make a difference. When I give up some of my time to call someone, that person's a lot more likely to come back to youth group. So I give up 5 minutes, but I get the great feeling that I've done something good for someone else.

Being a cheerful giver means serving others, not because you have to, but because you want to. And that's the kind of giving God really loves.

WHAT ABOUT YOU?

:: *A lot of people give money to the church as an offering. Besides money, what else can you give to your church or youth group?*

:: *Ask someone in your family what you can do to help them today.*

:: *Ask God to help you be a more cheerful giver.*

OCTOBER :: 25

MIKE, AGE 14

READ 2 CORINTHIANS 12:9-10

God's Strength

When I am weak, then I am strong.
2 CORINTHIANS 12:10

I learned a lesson about weakness when I was hit by a bus on my way home from school. I was in the hospital for a month and in a body cast for 6 weeks. I couldn't do anything by myself.

As I got better, it was clear to me that the people who stood by me were the people who really loved me and cared about me.

The same thing is true when I'm spiritually weak. This is a time in my life when I'm going through so many changes and struggles. But our God is a great God. He can use my struggles to show me how much he cares for me. When I see how God is there for me during my hard times, it gives me a passion for him and a desire to draw closer to him, even when life's good.

WHAT ABOUT YOU?

:: *Think about a time you really needed to lean on God. How did God work in your life?*

:: *Write about a time you felt God gave you the strength to do something. Read this story the next time you lose confidence.*

:: *Ask God to use you, even when you're struggling.*

OCTOBER :: 26

READ JOB 23:8-12

Mike and Job

He knows the way I take.
JOB 23:10

In yesterday's devotional, you read how Mike responded to his tragedy by talking about how great God is in the midst of pain. How could something like this happen to a good guy like him?

People have been wondering why bad things happen to good people for, like, forever. The Bible gives an example. Job's world came crashing down on him. His servants were slaughtered, his sheep were toast, and his family was killed.

The Bible doesn't always give a clear answer to the question of why people are hurting. But one thing is clear in the story of Job: God didn't cause the pain. God used Job's pain (and Mike's pain) to bring about huge spiritual growth in their lives!

When you're facing suffering, respond like Mike and Job did, and call out to God for strength. God will respond!

WHAT ABOUT YOU?

:: *How did you respond the last time you went through pain?*

:: *If Mike's story touched your heart, find someone and support him or her in the midst of their pain.*

:: *If you are suffering, go to God and tell him your pain. He's always there for you.*

OCTOBER :: 27

READ GALATIANS 1:6-9

Sound the Alarm!

If anybody is preaching to you a gospel other than what you accepted, let him be eternally condemned!
GALATIANS 1:9

The word gospel means "Good News." Paul begins this letter with a bit of a punch—he's "astonished" that the Good News of Jesus is being twisted and ignored. He was totally ticked!

Sometime earlier he'd traveled to the cities of Galatia (a region kind of like a state or big county) and preached the Good News of Jesus Christ. Churches had been started in all those cities—churches with Jewish Christians and non-Jewish (Gentile) Christians—and they believed they were saved by God's grace alone.

A bunch of Jewish Christians were preaching that the non-Jewish Christians had to follow Jewish law to be saved (more specifically, that the men had to be circumcised). Paul's not just mad because false teaching is in the air. He's ticked because the Galatian Christians are believing it!

So Paul writes this letter to all the churches in Galatia to say, "Listen up! It's God's grace alone that saves you. You can't earn your own salvation." There are certainly Christians today who need to hear this same strong message!

WHAT ABOUT YOU?

:: *What are you believing that you shouldn't?*

:: *What can you do to change that?*

OCTOBER :: 28

LISA, AGE 13

READ GALATIANS 1:6–10

People Pleasers

Am I now trying to win the approval of men, or of God?
GALATIANS 1:10

The other day, my friends and I were sitting at the lunch table, just talking and joking around. I said something kind of sarcastic about one of my friends because I thought the other people would think it was funny. But I ended up hurting my friend's feelings instead.

There are a lot of things we do to try to impress other people or make them like us. Some people start smoking because other people will think it's cool. Some people swear or gossip or make fun of other people to seem funny or smart. But those things don't please God. Every day we have to decide if we want to follow the crowd or obey God. We can't always do both.

WHAT ABOUT YOU?

:: What are 3 ways you try to please other people? Why is it so tempting to please people instead of God?

:: For one day concentrate more on pleasing God than on pleasing people. How does it affect the decisions you make and the things you say?

:: Ask God to help you obey him, even when it's not the popular thing to do.

OCTOBER :: 29

LINDSEY, AGE 12

READ GALATIANS 3:28-29

We Are Equal

You are all one in Christ Jesus.
GALATIANS 3:28

Some people in my school are looked down on. They don't have many friends, and it's easy to make fun of them. I have to admit, I've been part of the crowd that's doing the "looking down." But that's just not the way God wants things to be.

God doesn't care what color people are or how popular they are or what they look like. God cares about what's going on inside a person's heart. I shouldn't judge people by how they look. God wants me to treat all people the same and to accept, and even love, them for who they are.

Knowing God cares about people no matter what they look like or which group they belong to makes me feel better about myself too. I'm so glad we have a God who looks beyond the barriers the world puts up between people. Everyone who follows Jesus is equal in God's eyes.

WHAT ABOUT YOU?

:: Who are some of the people you don't like because they're "different"?

:: Next time you're tempted to make fun of people or judge them, imagine that you're seeing them the way Jesus sees them.

:: Ask God to help you look at people's hearts, not just their outward appearances.

OCTOBER :: 30

GUS, AGE 14

Fabulous Fruit

The fruit of the Spirit is love, joy, peace, patience, kindness, goodness, faithfulness, gentleness and self-control.
GALATIANS 5:22–23

There are lots of times when I don't really act like a Christian—like when my brother is making me mad. At those times, I need to think about this passage and try to let the Holy Spirit guide me to do the right thing.

That's what the fruit of the Spirit is all about. These qualities are the signs that God is in control of our lives. If I want to share my faith with others or just stay out of trouble, I need to look at this list of traits and I'll know how to live. The passage says we can't go wrong when we let the Holy Spirit lead us.

WHAT ABOUT YOU?

:: What would you think of a person who had all the traits listed in today's passage? Which of these traits do you look for in a friend?

:: What kinds of "fruit" do people see when they look at you?

:: Ask the Holy Spirit to help you grow great spiritual fruit.

OCTOBER :: 31

MARISSA, AGE 14

For Me, for Free

It is by grace you have been saved, through faith.
EPHESIANS 2:8

I think I understood these verses the best when I first asked Jesus into my heart. I remember thinking it was the most amazing thing in the world that God loved me so much. It was almost unimaginable. God wanted to forgive every single sin of mine. I didn't have to do anything except ask for forgiveness and invite him into my heart.

Now that I've been a Christian for a while, I think it's easy to forget just how amazing God's grace really is. Sometimes we take credit for things God has done. We brag about how strong our faith is. But it's God who makes us strong, not anything we do to make ourselves strong.

God loves me so much and gave me such a wonderful gift; it only seems right for me to live my life for him.

WHAT ABOUT YOU?

:: *What does grace mean to you? How has God shown you his grace?*

:: *Think of someone who has hurt your feelings. How can you show grace to this person?*

:: *Thank God for his amazing gift of grace.*

NOVEMBER :: 1

KATE, AGE 12

READ EPHESIANS 4:15-16

Growin' God's Way

From him, the whole body...grows and builds itself up in love, as each does its work.
EPHESIANS 4:16

I was trying to decide if I should play the piano for the kindergarten class during the second hour of church. I wanted to help out, but I wanted to hear the sermon too. I finally decided to switch off—kindergarten class one Sunday, and the sermon the next Sunday.

I need to follow Christ's example and serve people in order to mature in my faith. But I also need to get together with other Christians to worship and praise God, because this strengthens my faith too. Both of these things are part of being in the body of Christ.

By serving in church and worshiping God with other Christians, I'll be a stronger Christian. Christ is the head of the Christian body, and I need to grow so I can be more like him.

WHAT ABOUT YOU?

:: What are 2 or 3 signs that a person is growing into a mature Christian?

:: Ask your pastor or youth leader how you might be able to help out during church or at youth group.

:: Ask God to show you ways to serve in your church.

READ PROVERBS 11:2; 29:23

The World's Scariest Prayer

A man's pride brings him low.
PROVERBS 29:23

What is the world's scariest prayer? How about, "Lord, make me humble." Is this prayer going to mean that you're in for some major embarrassing moments? Probably not (at least not because of your prayer!).

A few days ago, Lisa referred to all the things we try to do to impress other people or to make them like us. In Lindsey's devotional when she was talking about loving others, she pointed out that we shouldn't judge other people. She said we should treat all people the same and love them for who they are. This is impossible if you are always worried about what others are thinking of you. Being a Christian is about being a humble servant, not being too full of pride. So...do you have the guts to pray this prayer? Go for it. Ask God to remove your pride, and he will bless you with a humble spirit.

WHAT ABOUT YOU?

:: *Think of a time when you stole the conversation and talked about yourself .*

:: *Try to go through a day putting all your effort into drawing attention to others and to God.*

:: *Pray the tough prayer and ask God to remove your pride and bless you with a humble spirit.*

NOVEMBER :: 3

READ EPHESIANS 4:29-32

Ninja Mouth

Do not let any unwholesome talk come out of your mouths.
EPHESIANS 4:29

No one was tougher than a Roman soldier. At the time Paul wrote Ephesians, these Roman soldiers had conquered the world!

Near the end of his letter, Paul tells his friends to get dressed for war. If you're thinking army boots, machine guns, and bulletproof vests, you've got the wrong idea. As Paul says, this is a different kind of battle. It's a spiritual battle with the forces of darkness! Christians are only given one offensive weapon: "the sword of the Spirit, which is the word of God" (Ephesians 6:17). How well are you trained to use this weapon?

One of the areas where we do battle is against our own tongue. This Scripture is about more than just swearing. Unwholesome talk can be a lot of things: being mean to your little sister, gossiping about people, or just spreading a lousy attitude. The last part of this passage helps us know what is important: building others up and saying only what helps people.

WHAT ABOUT YOU?

:: Is your mouth dangerous to others?

:: How do the words you speak leave others beat up on the inside?

READ EPHESIANS 6:13–18

Ready for Battle

Take the helmet of salvation and the sword of the Spirit, which is the word of God.
EPHESIANS 6:17

We need armor to fight the battle over good and evil. The devil is just way too powerful for us to fight on our own. But God wants to protect us, so he gives us enough armor to be ready for anything.

The part of the armor that I really noticed in this passage is the helmet of salvation, because it's the part that protects your head. I think your head, or actually your mind, is one of the first places the devil attacks. He can tempt you to doubt your faith or be afraid of all kinds of things you don't really need to fear. But with the helmet of salvation, you're protected. And when you know you're protected, you can have peace—even in the middle of the battle.

WHAT ABOUT YOU?

:: Look at the pieces of God's armor: truth, righteousness, readiness, faith, salvation, and the Word of God. Which of these areas are you strongest in? Which one might be a weak spot?

:: Look in an encyclopedia or an illustrated Bible for a picture of armor. Why is armor such a good way to think about God's protection?

:: Thank God for his protection.

NOVEMBER :: 5

VIANNAH, AGE 13

READ PHILIPPIANS 2:3-5

Me First!

Do nothing out of selfish ambition or vain conceit.
PHILIPPIANS 2:3

Once I was feeling really jealous of my best friend. I was so mad I sent her a note that said, "I hate you!" Afterward I felt really bad, but I was too proud to ask her to forgive me. We're still best friends, and she never brings up the subject, but sometimes I really wish I would have apologized.

Jesus didn't have to live with this kind of guilt because he never treated anyone badly. Even though he was the Son of God, he wasn't too proud to wash his friends' dirty feet. I'm just a human, but I still need to try to be humble and act like Jesus did toward other people. The least I can do is think about other people before I do something that might hurt them. I wish I'd thought about my friend's feelings before I sent that note. Maybe it's not too late to say something after all.

WHAT ABOUT YOU?

:: *Think of one person you know who is really good at putting others first. What can you do to be more like this person?*

:: *Ask God to help you be humble.*

READ PHILIPPIANS 2:12-16

Don't Be a Downer

Do everything without complaining or arguing.
PHILIPPIANS 2:14

When I was little, I always got toys for Christmas. Whatever I got, my mom told me to say thank you and at least *pretend* I liked it. She explained that it would hurt people's feelings if I complained about a gift or just ignored it. Now that I'm older and I've heard people make fun of gifts I've given them, I can totally see what Mom was saying. It really hurts when someone doesn't appreciate what you've given them!

Every time we complain about something, we're telling God we don't appreciate what he's done for us. Besides, when we complain, we're not very fun to be around. We bring ourselves down, and we bring everybody else down too.

Reading this verse reminds me that complaining makes me miserable, but being grateful makes me a happier, more Christ-like person. It's pretty obvious which option's the way to go.

WHAT ABOUT YOU?

:: What kind of stuff do you complain about? Why?

:: Ask someone like your best friend or your parents to give you a secret signal when you start whining or complaining.

:: Thank God for all he's given you today.

KAREN, AGE 12

It's All in Your Head

Finally, brothers, whatever is true, whatever is noble, whatever is right....think about such things.
PHILIPPIANS 4:8

Have you ever tried to think about 2 things at once? Your locker combination and everything you ate yesterday? Your favorite song and the capital of South Dakota? It doesn't work, does it? You can think of one thing and then the other, but not both at the same time.

That's why Paul's advice in Philippians 4:8–9 is so great. If you're thinking about things that are true, pure, and lovely, there's no way you can be thinking about stuff that's false, dirty, or ugly. Filling your mind with thoughts of God leaves no room for the trash you shouldn't be thinking about anyway.

When I keep my thoughts on God, my actions follow right along. I stay close to him, and he stays close to me—just like verse 9 says he will.

WHAT ABOUT YOU?

:: *What are some real-life situations that make it difficult for you to keep your thoughts clean? How can you avoid those situations?*

:: *Make a list of a dozen good, godly things to think about. Spend some time thinking about those things today.*

:: *Ask God to help you control your thoughts.*

READ COLOSSIANS 2:6-8

Anything Goes?

See to it that no one takes you captive through hollow and deceptive philosophy.
COLOSSIANS 2:8

In today's world a lot of people follow the popular path. This path tells them to put themselves first. It says "truth" is something that changes and anything is acceptable. Take dating, for example. For a lot of teens, dating is about getting something. People think, "What's in it for me?" But God tells us that love is not about pleasing ourselves; it's about giving to others, sharing with them, and respecting their purity in Christ.

God's Word tells us to love others, which is the opposite of putting ourselves first. It tells us that God's Word is the ultimate truth and it never, ever changes. And God's Word tells us that Jesus Christ is the only way to salvation. That's God's message—the only message people need to follow.

WHAT ABOUT YOU?

:: Why is it so easy to listen to the messages society gives us?

:: Next time you watch TV, pay extra attention to the commercials. What do they say you have to do to be happy? How is that different from what God wants you to be?

:: Ask God to help you follow his plans for your life, not society's.

Mashed Potato Ice Cream

Love the LORD your God with all your heart and with all your soul and with all your mind and with all your strength.

MARK 12:30

Isn't it amazing how awesome food can look on TV and in magazines? Well, when you see someone licking an ice cream cone on TV or in the movies they're really licking mashed potatoes (real ice cream would melt)! How about that whipped cream on top of the pie? It almost looks like shaving cream. Probably because it is!

Plain and simple, what you see on TV does not always match reality when it comes to food commercials, sales pitches, even sexual stuff. Jesus warned us that watching and looking at that kind of stuff is really dangerous: "I tell you that anyone who looks at a woman lustfully has already committed adultery with her in his heart" (Matthew 5:28).

When you find yourself drawn to shows or magazines you know aren't good for you, ask for God's strength to help you resist the temptation.

WHAT ABOUT YOU?

:: *What are some things on TV that are "too good to be true"?*

:: *Can you think of a TV show or magazine that you like but really isn't good for you? Try to give it up for one week, then try another week.*

:: *Ask God to help you focus on him when you face temptations.*

NOVEMBER :: 10

READ COLOSSIANS 2:20-23

Rule #473

Such regulations indeed have an appearance of wisdom...but they lack any value in restraining sensual indulgence.

COLOSSIANS 2:23

There are lots of rules in churches. Almost all of them are created by us—not by God. Paul points out in these verses that rules that try to make us look like we're living for God are a waste of time. God cares about us really living for him, not just looking like we are.

Yet every relationship has "rules" for how we live, communicate, and act. This is true in our families too. But the Lego bricks that make up our rules are not made of plastic; they're made of love. Wives are to submit out of love, not out of weakness. Husbands are to love as God loves (that's pretty huge love). Children are to obey out of love. And parents are supposed to be careful that they don't make their kids bitter forever.

These "love Legos" are much stronger than plastic! Our job is to invest time and energy putting them together. Not to concern ourselves with those religious rules that just make us look good.

NOVEMBER :: 11

Obey My Parents?

Children, obey your parents in everything, for this pleases the LORD.
COLOSSIANS 3:20

One night I really wanted to go to a youth group meeting with a friend, but my mom said no. I snuck out of the house and went anyway. Halfway through, my mom showed up. Boy, was she steamed!

Now I thought going to that meeting was definitely something God wanted me to do. But the fact is, I went against God's will that night by disobeying my mom. Obviously, God wants our parents to follow and obey him. But he also wants them to instruct us and guide us in the way we should live our lives. That's their responsibility. As long as the things our parents ask us to do don't go against God's commands, we need to lovingly obey them. That's our responsibility.

God gave us the Ten Commandments, and one of them is to honor our parents. By willingly obeying Mom and Dad, we're obeying God.

WHAT ABOUT YOU?

- What are some things that really bug you about your parents? What things do you appreciate about them?
- Think of 4 ways to show respect to your parents. For the next month, do one each week.
- Ask God to help you learn to respect and obey your parents.

READ 1 THESSALONIANS 1:6-7

We Can Be Heroes

You became imitators of us and of the LORD.
1 THESSALONIANS 1:6

There is a guy in my youth group who is a really strong Christian. He's a great leader who lives his life for God. I've learned a lot from him, and now I know God better than I used to.

It's great to have a role model, someone who shows you how to live out your faith. I'm trying to do the same thing for other people. I really try to show how important my faith is by how I live and what I say. Now I have the courage to talk to my best friend about God, because I want her to see that my faith really means something. She's not a Christian yet, but I hope she will be soon!

God wants everyone to know him. So if you can be a role model to someone else, do it. And if you need a role model to help live out your faith more, find one. Having someone to look up to made a big difference for me.

WHAT ABOUT YOU?

:: Who are 2 of your spiritual role models or heroes? Why do you look up to those people? What can you learn from them?

:: Ask God to help you find a great Christian role model.

God's Purity Plan

It is God's will that you should be sanctified; that you should avoid sexual immorality; that each of you should learn to control his own body in a way that is holy and honorable.
1 THESSALONIANS 4:3-4

"Avoid sexual immorality" might sound like an outdated rule, but think about it. God has always wanted us to follow his commands and save sex for marriage. But what have people done? They've dragged his plan through the mud and messed up their lives big-time.

God gives us rules about sex because he cares for us. He knows all about the unexpected pregnancies and broken hearts and other problems that happen when people don't stay sexually pure. Following God's guidelines might be tough sometimes, but not following them can get us in situations that are a whole lot tougher!

WHAT ABOUT YOU?

:: *Think about popular TV shows, movies, and songs. What do these things say about sexuality?*

:: *Ask your youth leader about the "True Love Waits" program, and find out how your group might be able to get involved in the program or others like it.*

:: *Pray for the strength to stay sexually pure.*

NOVEMBER :: 14

CHRIS, AGE 14

READ 1 THESSALONIANS 5:16–18

Joy Ride

Give thanks in all circumstances, for this is God's will for you in Christ Jesus.
1 THESSALONIANS 5:18

When bad things happen to me, my first reaction is not to be joyful. I don't feel like giving thanks when I'm hurt by a good friend or when I fight with my parents or get a bad grade on a test. I'm more likely to won-der, *What is God doing*? I feel like saying, "That's it! If God really loved me, this wouldn't be happening!"

But then I look at all the ways God has blessed me. God gives me great, amazing gifts all the time, and I hardly ever remember to say, "Thank you." If I paid more attention to praising God and less atten-tion to my problems, I'd be a much more joyful person.

WHAT ABOUT YOU?

:: Think back to a time when something bad happened to you. What were your prayers like then?

:: Start a list of the ways God has been good to you. Whenever you think of another reason to be thankful, add it to the list.

:: Offer God a prayer of pure thanksgiving, with no requests in it. Try to make this a habit.

N O V E M B E R :: 1 5

STACY, AGE 15

Prayer Power

We constantly pray for you...that by his power he may fulfill every good purpose of yours.
2 THESSALONIANS 1:11

Praying for my friends is really important to me. Every night I pray for my Christian and non-Christian friends on a list I call my "Circle of Concern." And I know my Christian friends are praying for me too.

One semester I prayed especially for my friend Heather because she hadn't been to church in a while, and I hardly ever saw her at school. I asked God to give me more opportunities to see her. The next semester, I had the same lunch period as Heather, and we ate together every day. Soon she started coming to church again, and the next thing I knew, she was telling me how she was witnessing to some of our non-Christian friends.

Praying for your friends can strengthen your relationship with them and your relationship with God. You can really see the difference prayer makes!

WHAT ABOUT YOU?

:: How does praying for others help you grow deeper as a Christian?

:: Make your own list of 5 friends and pray for them every day this week.

:: Thank God for your friends.

NOVEMBER :: 16

READ 1 SAMUEL 15:12-33

How to Impress God

To obey is better than sacrifice.
1 SAMUEL 15:22

How would you feel if you gave someone money to buy you a pepperoni pizza, and they came back with an anchovy and squid pizza? And then they told you, "I know what you asked for, but this is better." We do that all the time to God! He asks for our obedience, but we decide we've got a better plan. Remember Meredith's story earlier this week? That's exactly what she did. Meredith can tell what she did wrong now that she's looking back.

Saul ignored God's instructions and rationalized away those he thought were "no big deal." Then the prophet Samuel called him on it. Saul paid a pretty hefty price for his lame excuses. Even after he pleaded for forgiveness, God removed him from power. He lost his job as king of Israel.

WHAT ABOUT YOU?

:: *Name one of God's instructions that you have a hard time obeying.*

:: *Try writing a letter to God, telling him your plan for obeying him in that tough situation. This will make it easier for you to remember your plan when the time comes.*

:: *Pray, "Lord, help me to see when I am not following your instructions. And help me not to pretend that I know what's best for me better than you do."*

NOVEMBER :: 17

READ 1 TIMOTHY 4:11-12

Shy Guy in Charge

Don't let anyone look down on you because you are young, but set an example for the believers.
1 TIMOTHY 4:12

Imagine this: The pastor of your church is really into missions. He thinks you're a pretty sharp kid and takes you on a couple of his mission trips where you learn a ton. Then one of the churches the two of you "planted" starts having some problems. So your pastor sends you there to be their leader!

That's Timothy's story! Paul put him in charge of the church at Ephesus (the same church for whom Paul wrote the book of Ephesians). And to make it even more tough, Timothy was kind of shy!

Paul writes this letter, 1 Timothy, to give Timothy some instructions, because Paul has become Tim's spiritual "father." Paul writes this letter to encourage his "son."

It's a kickin' book for teenage readers because the main point is: Don't wait until you're old to be a leader.

BRIAN, AGE 14

READ 1 TIMOTHY 1:15–17

Unlimited Love

Christ Jesus came into the world to save sinners—of whom I am the worst.
1 TIMOTHY 1:15

My mom works with a group that goes to local prisons to share about God. One time I got to go with them. While I was there, I heard one of the prisoners say he thought of himself as "someone God no longer wanted." Then a member of my mom's group read him 1 Timothy 1:15–16, sharing God's mercy to the worst of sinners. The prisoner gave his life to Jesus that day.

No matter how much or how badly people have sinned, God's love can still reach them. Even drug dealers. Even murderers. The worst person you can imagine can receive God's forgiveness by humbly asking for it.

There's no such thing as a person God no longer wants. There are only people who haven't accepted his love.

WHAT ABOUT YOU?

:: *Think of a troublemaker you know. Imagine God looking right into that person's face and saying, "I forgive you." Imagine doing the same thing yourself.*

:: *Write today's verses down, or memorize them. You never know when they might be exactly what someone needs to hear.*

:: *Thank God for forgiving you and ask him to help you forgive others.*

ELIZABETH, AGE 12

READ 1 TIMOTHY 4:13–15

No Fear

Devote yourself to the public reading of Scripture, to preaching and to teaching.
1 TIMOTHY 4:13

When my friend and I volunteered to help organize "See You at the Pole"— a once-a-year event when people gather at the flagpole before school and pray—we were really excited. But when it came to asking some teachers to come and pray with us, we started to get nervous. Talking to teachers can be kind of scary. They could have said no or asked us all kinds of questions we couldn't answer.

We decided to go for it anyway, and we got a great group of students and teachers to meet us at the flagpole to pray. We saw how God gives young people the courage and the strength to stand up for what they believe.

WHAT ABOUT YOU?

:: *What do you think is the worst thing that could happen when you stand up for your faith at school? What's the best thing?*

:: *Wear a T-shirt with a Christian message on it to school this week, or maybe put your Bible in your backpack and read it on your lunch break. Be prepared to answer the questions people might ask.*

:: *Thank God for giving you courage as you serve him.*

READ 1 TIMOTHY 6:6–10

Gotta Have It?

For we brought nothing into the world, and we can take nothing out of it.
1 TIMOTHY 6:7

We get a lot of mail-order catalogs for clothes and other things at my house, and I love to look through them. Sometimes I think, *Oh, I'd like this*, or, *If I earned some money, I could get that*. But then I remember that I should be content with what I have. When I think about it, I really have more than I need already.

Most people want to have the latest, coolest things. But these won't last, and they sure don't bring us any closer to God. Focusing on what I don't have makes me forget to thank God for what I do have—a home, a family who loves me, food to eat, good friends. God wants us to be content with what we have. He has given us so much more than we could ever find in a catalog.

WHAT ABOUT YOU?

:: Why do you think we want material things?

:: Go through your room and find something you thought you couldn't live without. How did you feel when you got that thing? How do you feel about it now?

:: Ask God to help you be content with what you have.

NOVEMBER :: 21

JAMIE, AGE 14

Within Reach

For God did not give us a spirit of timidity, but a spirit of power, of love and of self-discipline.
2 TIMOTHY 1:7

Some of my friends and I wanted to start a Bible study at our school. I was scared to do it because I knew we'd get teased. But we started the group anyway. Sure enough, we got teased. People called us names and made fun of us. But I'm willing to put up with it because the Bible study is an important part of my life.

I think our whole purpose as Christians is to share the gospel with others. God's love is an incredible thing, and we can't be afraid to tell people about it. We have to stand up and show our faith to others.

WHAT ABOUT YOU?

:: *Have you ever hidden your faith to avoid being teased? How did you feel about hiding your faith?*

:: *Start a prayer group, a Bible study, or a Christian fellowship group at your school, and ask your youth leader to help you get started. Or, if there's already a Christian group at school, consider joining it.*

:: *Pray that God will help you be bold about your faith.*

NOVEMBER :: 22

KATE, AGE 13

READ 2 TIMOTHY 2:22-24

Truce!

The LORD's servant must not quarrel; instead, he must be kind to everyone, able to teach, not resentful.
2 TIMOTHY 2:24

I don't know what gets into me sometimes, but I start the stupidest arguments with my parents and my brother. These spats aren't even about anything important—I want to watch a different TV show or have toast instead of cereal, and all of a sudden we're fighting!

These verses make it clear that arguing is foolish and wrong. God doesn't want us tearing each other down with our words. He wants us to have pure hearts and to live in peace with each other—especially in our families, because those are the people we have to live with every day.

If I want to be close to God, I need to start by speaking kind words instead of mean ones.

WHAT ABOUT YOU?

:: Who are 2 people you tend to argue with? How can you make your conversations more positive?

:: Write a nice note to each person in your family. Place the notes someplace where they'll be sure to find them.

:: Ask God to help you use your words to build people up.

NOVEMBER :: 23

You Want Me to Do What?!

The LORD said to him, "Go, take to yourself an adulterous wife."
HOSEA 1:2

This past week, Brian and Elizabeth both shared about being a part of activities that don't come naturally. Sharing your love for Jesus Christ with prisoners or organizing prayer at your school can make you stand out and feel uncomfortable. But God calls us to obey; he has a history of asking his people to demonstrate extraordinary obedience while facing extraordinary situations. Whether you're a prophet like Hosea or a teenager facing difficult problems, God calls you to obey. Remember God's perspective. He not only sees the present situation but he also sees the outcome.

God has the view from the road map and can see every turn. Our perspective, on the other hand, is limited to what we can see at that moment. So, if God asks you to do something strange, how will you respond?

WHAT ABOUT YOU?

:: When was a time that you felt God called you to do something that seemed strange?

:: When's the last time you asked God for instructions? (How can you obey if you don't know what the instructions are?)

:: Pray to God and ask him what your instructions are. What's his message to you?

Select, Silence, Instruct

An elder must be blameless, the husband of but one wife, a man whose children believe and are not open to the charge of being wild and disobedient.
TITUS 1:6

Paul was probably in a Roman prison when he wrote Titus. Titus was one of the younger men Paul selected, mentored, and took with him on many of his trips. Paul assigned Titus to oversee and lead the Christians on the big Mediterranean island of Crete, just south of Greece.

Paul starts out saying, "I left you in Crete to straighten out what was left unfinished." There is a lot for Titus to finish. The first chore on his to-do list is to select reliable church leaders (Paul calls them elders). Then it's on to silencing some wanna-be church leaders whose "teachings" are actually lies and slander that are confusing Christians who live there. What makes these lies especially dangerous is that they sound religious—strict rules and churchy-sounding controversies that Paul says have absolutely nothing to do with Jesus or real spirituality.

The third chore on Titus's to-do list (see chapter 2:1-10) is to teach 5 groups in the church how to live with and behave toward each other: older men, older women, younger women, younger men, and slaves.

WHAT ABOUT YOU?

:: *Do you have a spiritual to-do list?*

:: *What's at the top of your list?*

NOVEMBER :: 25

LAURA, AGE 13

READ TITUS 1:15–16

Less than Meets the Eye

They claim to know God, but their actions deny him.
TITUS 1:16

I go to a Christian school, so most people claim to be Christians. But the reality is that most people don't live out this claim. Some people say one thing and do another. People who say one thing and do another are called hypocrites, and the Bible says to watch out for them. They'll make you think they're following God, but their actions don't back it up.

But before I start calling people hypocrites, I need to take a good look at my own life. I know I don't always live out what I say I believe either. Sure, I believe the Bible, but sometimes I don't do what it says. I don't want to be a hypocrite. I need to rely on God and stick close to him.

WHAT ABOUT YOU?

:: *Think about a time you said one thing and did another. Why did you do it? How can you keep from doing it again?*

:: *This week when you see someone acting like a hypocrite, pray for that person...and pray for you! Ask God to help you both resist being hypocrites.*

:: *Ask God to help you be the "real thing" in your Christian life.*

READ TITUS 3:1-2

A Good Plan

Remind the people...to be ready to do whatever is good.
TITUS 3:1

I treat most other people with respect and patience. But I don't treat my sister that way. I say mean things to her and try to get back at her when she has hurt me first. I know it's wrong to treat her that way, and this passage reminds me of why it's wrong.

God wants us to be people who love others, people who are kind and peace-loving and respectful. I know I can be that way because I treat people outside my family that way every day. This isn't a hard passage to understand, but it can be a hard passage to live out. But with God's help, I think I can be nicer to my sister, even when she's not so nice to me.

WHAT ABOUT YOU?

:: *Who is one person you have a tough time being kind to? How can you change that?*

:: *Think of that one person who really bugs you. For the rest of this week, show that person kindness and consideration. It might only take a compliment or a smile to show him or her your friendly side.*

:: *Ask God to help you live out this passage.*

JESSI, AGE 14

READ PHILEMON 4–7

Everything I Do...

I hear about your faith in the LORD Jesus and your love for all the saints.
PHILEMON 5

This verse gave me a reality check. It made me think about how others see my faith. I realized I need to pay more attention to the reputation I'm building.

Most people's reputations are based on how tough they are, or on how popular or smart or rich they are. But as a Christian, I want my reputation to be based on my faith in Jesus. I want to set an example of someone who loves God and lives to serve him. I want the people at my school to say, "Yep, Jessi's definitely a Christian."

To make that happen, I need to think about the decisions I make. I need to ask myself, "Will this choice show people I'm living a godly life? Will it change the way they view me? Will it affect the way they view God?" If I want people to know God, I need to show them God in everything I do.

WHAT ABOUT YOU?

:: What kind of reputation do you have at school? How did you earn that reputation? Are you happy to have that rep?

:: Ask God to help you be a great example of his love and grace.

NOVEMBER :: 28

ASHLEY, AGE 14

READ HEBREWS 2:14–18

When I'm Tempted

Because he himself suffered when he was tempted, he is able to help those who are being tempted.
HEBREWS 2:18

A bunch of my friends were going to a movie I knew I shouldn't see. They begged me to go with them. I knew it was wrong for me to see the movie, but I went anyway.

Instead of just giving in to my friends, I should have asked Jesus to help me resist temptation. I know he would have given me the strength to do the right thing and say no to the movie.

Sometimes I forget that Jesus was a real live human being who experienced a lot of the same things I experience, like temptation. Because of that, I know I can look to him for help and guidance when I'm facing a difficult situation.

WHAT ABOUT YOU?

:: What do you do when you feel tempted? What are some things that can help you resist temptation?

:: Ask a Christian friend to be your "bad-idea buddy"—a friend who will help you say no to something you know is a "bad idea."

:: Thank God for understanding the power of temptation. Ask him to help you say no to things that tempt you.

NOVEMBER :: 29

ROBYN, AGE 13

READ HEBREWS 4:13-14

My Friend the King

Everything is uncovered...before the eyes of him to whom we must give account.
HEBREWS 4:13

Have you ever had to go to the principal's office? Pretty scary, huh? But what if the principal of your school was your best friend?

That's how it is when God, the King of Creation, is our best friend. He's not like Henry VIII or some other historical king who might cut off your head just for walking into the room. God is glad to see us when we come to him in prayer. He is a loving, caring King who wants to help his people, and he promises he'll listen and give us grace. We can go to God with an attitude of hope, not fear. We can be confident that he hears our prayers and answers them. We never have to be afraid or ashamed to talk to our best friend, the King.

WHAT ABOUT YOU?

:: *Why do you think God wants you to talk to him? Why are we sometimes afraid to talk to God?*

:: *Write an honest letter to God, telling him stuff you might not even tell your best friend. Write a new letter whenever you're feeling anxious about talking to God.*

:: *Thank God for being a King we can talk to without fear.*

NOVEMBER :: 30

READ MATTHEW 7:24-29

Obedience Party

Everyone who hears these words of mine and puts them into practice is like a wise man who built his house on the rock.

MATTHEW 7:24

Dogs are great fun, but training them when they're puppies can be frustrating (not as frustrating as training your goldfish, but still pretty tough).

Then one day the cute little thing gets it. He obeys! And you're ready to throw a party. God throws a party too when his children finally get it and start to obey. Our devotions this week from Laura and Jessi encouraged us to live the way God wants us to; that's called obedience.

The key is putting what we hear into practice. When we live like Jesus Christ wants us to live, then we're obeying God.

WHAT ABOUT YOU?

:: What is one area of your life that you've been the most disobedient to God?

:: Think of one word that describes how you can be obedient to God in this area. Then write it in big letters on a piece of paper and tape it to your alarm clock so you'll see it first thing every day.

:: Pray that the very next time you need to obey God, you'll have the courage to do it.

DECEMBER :: 1

READ HEBREWS 4:15-16

Give Me Some Skin

We have one who has been tempted in every way, just as we are—yet was without sin.
HEBREWS 4:15

Was Jesus a man or was he God? Actually, he's both. Pretty trippy, huh? These verses mention the "humanity" of Jesus. That's another way of saying God put on skin. Why did he do that? To destroy the devil so that nothing gets in the way of us knowing God. What a great example of how much Jesus loves us!

And because Jesus put on the skin suit, any type of junk you face or think about is the same stuff Jesus went through. He would have known about it anyway because he's, well, God. But he also experienced it as a human.

The situation might look different, but the basic issues of temptation, hurt, frustration, disappointment, sadness—all that—Jesus faced them all. And the Bible says he made it through all this junk. So now he wants to use his experience, and the fact that he's God, to help us!

DECEMBER :: 2

JESSICA, AGE 12

READ HEBREWS 10:24-25

The Buddy System

Let us consider how we may spur one another on toward love and good deeds.
HEBREWS 10:24

One of my friends from church was going through a rough time. She felt like her parents didn't care about her. She thought they paid more attention to her brother and ignored her. I couldn't do much to help her relationship with her parents, but I knew she could use some encouragement. So I tried to listen to her when she needed to talk and help her see that things were probably going to get better.

I think it's really important for people to have Christian friends. My youth group is so special to me because we support each other and encourage each other to grow in our faith. Each person in the group is an important part of the other people's lives. We need each other. We just can't make it without the fellowship we find in church and the support of Christian friends.

WHAT ABOUT YOU?

:: *How have your Christian friends supported you in the past? How have they helped you grow in your faith?*

:: *Write a note or call 1 or 2 of your Christian friends and thank them for helping you get closer to God.*

:: *Ask God to help you be an encouraging friend.*

DECEMBER :: 3

His Time, Not Mine

Faith is being sure of what we hope for.
HEBREWS 11:1

About 4 years ago, my family joined a new, larger church. I didn't know anyone and I asked God to provide new friends for me. God did provide some great friends eventually, but I can't say he came through exactly the way I asked him to. It took me almost 2 years to start making solid friendships.

Part of faith is being "certain of what we do not see." For the longest time, I didn't see God working. But now that I have many good, Christian friends, I can see he was there, helping me all along.

When I feel like God isn't listening, that's when I need to take verses like this one seriously. If I have faith in God's plan for me, he will see my faith and work everything out in his time.

WHAT ABOUT YOU?

:: *Why does God sometimes make us wait for answers to our prayers?*

:: *What can we learn from Bible characters who had to wait a long time before God answered their prayers? Look at Abram (Genesis 12:1–3), Joseph (Genesis 40:23—41:13), and Job (the whole book).*

:: *Ask God to help you have faith even when you can't see him working in your life.*

DECEMBER :: 4

READ JAMES 3:11-13

It's Show Time!

Who is wise and understanding among you? Let him show it by his life.
JAMES 3:13

"Don't just talk about it" —that's what was on James's mind when he wrote his book.

Have you ever had a class where you were supposed to do a project—and it seems you could find time to do everything else but work on that project? You know what I mean. You'd rather go to the dentist, mow the lawn, change the kitty litter, do just about anything rather than complete that project. And then it gets worse. You're sitting in discussion groups in class talking about, oh no, the project! You've read the assignment, but you haven't done a single thing about the project.

If you've ever been in a jam like this, then you'll be able to relate to the original readers of the book of James. James is the teacher who gets fired up at students who don't complete their assignment. He wants to be sure that we put our faith into practice— that we're ready to live what we believe.

WHAT ABOUT YOU?

:: *Your deeds are like a big screen that shows movies from your heart. If Jesus lives in your heart, what movies are showing up in what you do?*

DECEMBER :: 5

MATT, AGE 13

Worth the Trouble

Consider it pure joy, my brothers, whenever you face trials of many kinds.
JAMES 1:2

When I was 7, my family lived in the suburbs of Detroit. I thought everything about my life was perfect. But then one day my dad announced we were moving to California. Because I had everything I wanted right there in Detroit, I didn't want to move. When we moved, though, we found a much better church, I went to a good school, and my life actually improved considerably.

God puts us through trials for a reason. He doesn't do things to hurt us—only to help us grow and develop. He knows that we really grow when we're in tough situations, because those are the times we need to work extra hard to be close to God. Trials help us mature, so we should view them with joy. They really are some of our best opportunities to become strong Christians.

WHAT ABOUT YOU?

:: *Taking tests, getting a tetanus shot, exercising...what are some other things that seem painful at first but you know are good for you?*

:: *Offer to do something that you usually hate doing, like studying your least favorite subject in school or helping out your little brother or sister.*

:: *Thank God for knowing what's best for you.*

DECEMBER :: 6

AMY, AGE 13

READ JAMES 2:14–17

Don't Just Sit There...

What good is it...if a man claims to have faith but has no deeds?
JAMES 2:14

I changed schools right before 8th grade, and when classes started at my new school, I wanted to make a good impression. I went out of my way to be nice to people and help them if I could. Now I have lots of good friends.

It makes a big difference when you put actions with your feelings. I needed to get out there and do something to show people I wanted to be their friend.

In these verses, James talks about the deeds that come from faith, like taking care of people who need clothes and food. Just like it wasn't enough for me to hope people would like me, it's not enough to hope poor people will get everything they need. My church has some programs to help people out, and I've done little things like bringing in clothes and toys to give away. It makes me happy to know I'm helping other people. And I know it makes God happy too.

WHAT ABOUT YOU?

:: *Why do "actions speak louder than words"?*

:: *Ask God to show you ways to act out your faith.*

MICHAEL, AGE 13

READ JAMES 3:3-10

Tongue in Check

No man can tame the tongue.
JAMES 3:8

When I'm mad at somebody, it's tempting to use my words to hurt them or get even. But I can keep myself from saying something mean if I remember that God didn't give me a tongue to cut other people down. He gave me a tongue so I could praise him and speak encouraging words to others.

Words are just so easy to throw around. Before you know it, you can really hurt someone's feelings without even meaning to. So it's good to look at these verses and remember that words have power. They need to be handled carefully and in a way that pleases God.

WHAT ABOUT YOU?

:: James uses a lot of word pictures, or "metaphors," in this passage—like a horse's bit and a ship. What are the other metaphors? What's the common idea in all of them?

:: Get yourself a little jar. Every time you say something God wouldn't be proud of, drop a nickel in the jar. Makes you think, doesn't it? At the end of every week, put whatever money you've collected into the offering plate at church.

:: Ask God to help you watch your words.

DECEMBER :: 8

Owls and Old Folks

God appeared to Solomon and said to him, "Ask for whatever you want me to give you."
2 CHRONICLES 1:7

Wisdom is a word usually associated with people who've lived a long time; or owls. But wisdom—understanding how to apply knowledge—comes from the Creator.

Several years ago a church was thinking about constructing a new building and had a meeting to discuss it. A thousand people were there to argue and debate whether this was a wise move. A 14-year-old asked to speak at the microphone—much to the surprise of the adults—and his eloquent words about building for the future swung the vote to put up the new building. His words rang true with wisdom, because he was in tune with God.

It doesn't matter how old you are; the Bible says you too can be wise. The test of your wisdom isn't age—it's your heart.

WHAT ABOUT YOU?

:: *Do you desire wisdom? Why or why not?*

:: *Do you know a person who seems to make really wise decisions? Ask him or her how he or she seeks godly wisdom and understanding.*

:: *Pray that God will make you a source of wisdom for others. Ask him to help you to be humble and unselfish as he uses you.*

D E C E M B E R :: 9

Mutter, Mutter

Do not let the Book of the Law depart from your mouth; meditate on it day and night, so that you may be careful to do everything written in it.
JOSHUA 1:8

Fear protects us from stuff that may hurt us. You wouldn't stand in front of a speeding truck for fear you'd get hit and die. That's because you have a deep respect for the power of that massive truck against your breakable body. In a similar way, if you "fear" God (have a deep respect for who he is and for his power), you don't need to fear his judgment.

Part of having a deep respect for God involves memorizing his word. When you need to memorize something, you say it over and over again with the idea it will stick in your brain. In Hebrew (the language this book was first written in), to meditate means "to mutter." We're supposed to mutter God's words to ourselves day and night. If we keep repeating the words of the Bible to ourselves, we will soon find them sticking where they matter most—in our hearts and minds. So mutter 'til it sticks!

DECEMBER :: 10

READ 1 PETER 1

Your Mission

Be holy in all you do.
1 PETER 1:15

"What's God want from me?" Have you ever asked that question? It's a great question—one you should be asking all the time. Peter gives you a bunch of answers to that question.

This is your mission, should you choose to accept it (are you ready for this?): Praise God, put your hope in him, be self-controlled, obedient, holy, submissive, and respectful. Don't pound on someone when they pound on you. Suffer for God, treat your friends (and one day, your spouse!) as you would treat Christ himself. *And* live in peace with everyone, be compassionate, sympathetic, and love every-one. Sound easy? Yeah, right!

The truth is, being a Christian can be really tough. In fact, there's a 0% chance that you'll pull it off all by yourself. (That's where the Holy Spirit giving you God's power comes in.) But this list that Peter presents gives you a good idea of some of the things that will mark you as a Christ-follower. And it all starts with giving God the credit (sometimes the Bible calls this "giving God glory") for everything.

WHAT ABOUT YOU?

:: How are you praising God?

:: What are you doing to live in peace with those around you? Ask God to help you find ways to live in peace.

LISA, AGE 13

READ 1 PETER 1:13-14

Out of Control?

Prepare your minds for action; be self-controlled.
1 PETER 1:13

When I have a ton of homework, I often get really stressed out and discouraged. It takes all the self-control I have to sit down and actually do my work.

Some of my friends struggle with self-control too, They might give in to temptation and do things they shouldn't, or they might get mad at another person and lose their temper. All of us need to practice self-control and not give in to "evil desires."

Jesus was a great example of how we are supposed to live. He was calm and forgiving. He did the things he needed to do, even when he might have wanted to do something else. Like when he was 12 and he had to leave the temple and go home with his parents (see Luke 2:41–52). Jesus always made good decisions. When we work at having self-control, we can be more like Jesus.

WHAT ABOUT YOU?

:: What are 2 ways you can increase your self-control?

:: Write a little note to yourself. Remind yourself how great it feels when you make a wise decision and follow God. Keep the note in your backpack or your locker. Read it when you feel out of "self"-control.

:: Ask God to help you live for him and not for the world.

DECEMBER :: 12

KATIE, AGE 12

READ 1 PETER 2:9-10

You're Special!

But you are a chosen people...a people belonging to God, that you may declare the praises of him who called you out of darkness into his wonderful light.
1 PETER 2:9

I remember when I was having a really bad day. I got 2 test grades back that weren't too hot. My friends were being mean to me, and my mom and I got into a fight! I remember thinking that no one really liked me.

Eventually I stopped feeling sorry for myself long enough to realize that I was so wrong—God still liked me. He cares about me! He loves me! Ever since that day, I know God has a place for me in his heart. Since God says I'm "chosen," "royal," and "holy," it's hard to mope around. It's easier to praise God!

WHAT ABOUT YOU?

:: *The next time you have a bad day, remember this: In God's eyes, you're amazing!*

:: *Look up the words "chosen," "royal," and "holy" in the dictionary. That's how God describes you! Doesn't that feel good?*

:: *Thank God for loving you as his own child.*

DECEMBER :: 13

HEATHER, AGE 13

READ 1 PETER 3:13–16

Speak Up

Always be prepared to give an answer...for the hope that you have.
1 PETER 3:15

I know a lot of people who don't go to church and probably don't know Jesus. Some people at my school follow other religions, like Buddhism and Islam. I really worry about all of these people.

Sometimes I get down because some of my friends won't come to the Lord. Even when I try to talk to them about God, it seems like they don't want to listen. That's when I pray and ask God for the confidence to keep trying anyway.

But one person I've shared with has accepted Jesus into her heart, and another one is almost there. I wish I could see all of my friends make those decisions, but I can't make people change. Only God can. All I can do is stick with it and be the best friend I can be.

WHAT ABOUT YOU?

:: *What kinds of questions might your friends have about God? How would you answer them?*

:: *Think of one person you know who isn't a Christian. How can you share your faith with him or her this week?*

:: *Ask God to give you confidence to talk about your faith.*

DECEMBER :: 14

AMY, AGE 14

READ 1 PETER 5:8-9

Stay Strong

Be self-controlled and alert.... The devil prowls around like a roaring lion.
1 PETER 5:8

Imagine you're walking down the hallways at school on a Friday afternoon. A lot of students are talking about weekend parties, how they're going to get drunk or high. You stop to talk to some people, and the next thing you know, you're invited to their party. Everybody's looking at you. Will you say yes or no?

Temptation is all around us—it fills the air. The devil wants us to fall, but we can defeat him by standing strong with Christ Jesus. God knows when we're being tempted. He'll always help us if we ask him for strength and guidance.

We can help each other fight temptation too. When one person resists the pressure, it's easier for others to resist. God gives us power to help other people to be strong.

WHAT ABOUT YOU?

∷ What are some of the toughest temptations you face? What can you do to avoid these situations?

∷ Set up an "emergency hotline" with your youth leader or a trusted friend. When you face a really tough temptation, you'll have someone to call who can help you to stay strong.

∷ Ask God to help you say "no" to temptation.

DECEMBER :: 15

READ 2 PETER 1:5-9

Skyscrapers

Make every effort to add to your faith goodness; and to goodness, knowledge; and to knowledge, self-control.
2 PETER 1:5

Growing in our faith is like building a skyscraper. You have to start small. The foundation is faith. Then goodness, knowledge, and self-control are added. You finish with godliness, kindness, perseverance, and love. It's a process done in stages, not all at once.

At recess one day in grammar school I saw a girl who was sad. I went over to her, and, although I didn't know quite what to say, I tried my best to cheer her up. But kindness wasn't enough—it took perseverance to do it! That's how we become more like Christ. We use the qualities we do have, like kindness, to build the ones we don't, like perseverance. Pretty soon, I'll have a skyscraper on display!

WHAT ABOUT YOU?

:: *Draw a skyscraper. Write the word "faith" at the foundation of your building. Divide your skyscraper into 7 floors. Label each floor with the qualities from 2 Peter 1:5-7. Let it remind you of the wonderful qualities God is building within you.*

:: *Ask God to help you add Christlike qualities to your life. Thank him for giving you the strength to do it.*

DECEMBER :: 16

Us Versus Them

Pray for us, too, that God may open a door for our message.
COLOSSIANS 4:3

Sharing our faith usually begins as an act of love. We realize that people are lost and hopeless without Jesus, so we share the gospel with them.

But what starts out as compassion can quickly become a contest. Instead of one sinner reaching out to another, our witnessing becomes one gladiator battling with another. We argue that God is real, the Bible is true, and Jesus is the only way. Our friend argues that we're crazy. Soon it's "us versus them," and we find ourselves more interested in winning the argument.

The only war we wage is spiritual, as we ask God to open doors for our message and give us courage to speak. But when it comes to witnessing to our friends, we must never fight with them.

WHAT ABOUT YOU?

:: *Use a 3 x 5 card to help keep you on track in your witnessing. Put 3 names of non-Christian friends on your card. Then pray "3-by-5"—3 names, 5 minutes a day—for their eternal salvation.*

:: *Ask God to help you avoid an "us versus them" attitude in your witnessing. Then do your battle in prayer, asking God to give you opportunities to tell others about him.*

DECEMBER :: 17

Us Versus Them, Round 2

Be wise in the way you act toward outsiders; make the most of every opportunity.
COLOSSIANS 4:5

There are 3 words in verses 5 and 6 of today's passage that describe the right approach to reaching your friends:

>> *Wise*. We need to be wise in our actions, so we don't turn people off to Jesus but rather draw them to him.

>> *Winsome*. To be winsome means to be upbeat and positive in our attitude, so that we're "full of grace."

>> *Wholesome*. Our words should be "seasoned with salt," or tasty and good. Crude talk can kill our credibility and take the focus off our message.

When your witnessing breaks down, it could be because you forgot to use one of the 3 Ws—wise actions, winsome attitudes, or wholesome language. Not treating people right is the biggest witnessing wipeout. Being a believer in Jesus has to make a difference in the way you treat all people. If it doesn't, something's not connecting between your faith and your actions.

DECEMBER :: 18

READ 1 JOHN 1:8–10

Forgiven!

If we confess our sins, he is faithful and just and will forgive us our sins.
1 JOHN 1:9

Every one of us sins, so it's a good thing God is forgiving. Like the time I wanted to pierce my ears. My mom told me I couldn't, but I disobeyed her and did it myself. Not only did my ears hurt really bad, but my mom got mad and lost her trust in me. I apologized to my mom, and I asked God to forgive me. Then I felt a lot better. I was still punished for disobeying my mom, but it felt good to be honest about my sin and ask for forgiveness.

When we sin, we can confess our sins to God and know that he'll forgive us. The Bible says God will show us mercy and make us pure again.

WHAT ABOUT YOU?

:: *What sins do you need to confess? How would it feel to be honest about your sins?*

:: *Before you go to bed tonight, kneel down and take the time to really confess your sins to God. Be as specific as you can.*

:: *Thank God for being so forgiving and loving.*

DECEMBER :: 19

READ 1 JOHN 3:1-3

Amazing Love

How great is the love the Father has lavished on us, that we should be called children of God! And that is what we are!
1 JOHN 3:1

Whenever I feel insignificant or unloved, I have to remember how God has declared his love for me. He never forgets who I am, because I'm his child. He never ignores me. He loves me more than anyone else ever could.

One of the most amazing things about God's love is that it's infinite—it never ends. And it isn't like I have to work really hard and be perfect to get this love, because he already loves me more than I can imagine.

The more I learn about God's love for me, the more I want to love him and show his love to others. His love is a model for me every day.

WHAT ABOUT YOU?

:: *What does it mean to be a child of God?*

:: *List 10 ways God has shown his love for you lately.*

:: *Thank God for his love and ask him to help you show that love to others.*

DECEMBER :: 20

AMY, AGE 13

READ 1 JOHN 4:16–18

Fearless

Perfect love drives out fear.
1 JOHN 4:18

My basketball team was playing in a championship game. I was so nervous and scared before the game that I felt sick to my stomach. I was so psyched out that I made all kinds of mental mistakes during the game. I played terrible.

That game taught me something: Don't let fear take over your life. God wants us to trust him to take care of us. If I had prayed and trusted God to help me play my best, I probably would have felt and played better.

God wants the best for us. So we don't need to be afraid of the future. God is in control. Knowing this truth can help me conquer my fears before my fears conquer me.

WHAT ABOUT YOU?

:: *What are some of your fears? How do you think God can help you conquer those fears?*

:: *Get the VeggieTales video "Where is God When I'm Scared?" (You can probably borrow it from your church.) Memorize the song, "God is Bigger Than the Boogeyman." The next time you're scared or nervous, sing the song to yourself.*

:: *Thank God for taking care of all your fears.*

DECEMBER :: 21

EMILY, AGE 14

READ 1 JOHN 5:11–14

Check It Out

I write these things to you who believe...so that you may know that you have eternal life.
1 JOHN 5:13

A few years ago I really started to doubt my salvation. To help me deal with all my questions, my dad showed me these verses. They helped me understand that we can always trust in God's promise to save us.

Whenever I start to doubt that my salvation is real, I think about checks. That's right, checks. When I babysit for someone and they pay me with a check, I know I've been paid. They haven't given me actual money; they've given me a promise of money. That's kind of how salvation works. I won't actually experience eternal life for a long time. But I trust God's promise that he has saved me and I will spend eternity with him.

God is no liar. When he says he will save those who have Jesus in their hearts, he means it.

WHAT ABOUT YOU?

:: *Have you ever had doubts about God? What did you do about those doubts?*

:: *The next time you have questions about God, dig through the Bible, talk to other Christians, and pray about your questions until you have answers.*

:: *Thank God for keeping his promises, even when you have doubts.*

DECEMBER :: 22

JESSE, AGE 14

Wholehearted Love

His command is that you walk in love.
2 JOHN 6

I grew up in a Christian family, and I heard about Jesus from the time I was a baby. If you'd asked me, I would have said, "Sure, I love Jesus." But the truth is, after Sunday I wasn't doing a very good job of following God the other 6 days of the week.

We shouldn't say we love Jesus and then turn around and do things that displease him. He wants us to obey him because we love him. And he wants us to show love to others. God's commands are there to help us live the way he wants us to live. When we obey his commands, we are showing God we trust him and love him with our whole hearts.

WHAT ABOUT YOU?

:: What are some ways you show God you love him? What are some ways you show God's love to other people?

:: Think of one way you can obey God today. Maybe it's by showing your parents or teachers more respect, not cursing, or taking more time to talk to God.

:: Think of one area in your life where you have been trying to obey God and have done a good job. Ask God to help you keep following him.

DECEMBER :: 23

READ 1 JOHN 2:3-6

Prove It

We know that we have come to know him if we obey his commands.
1 JOHN 2:3

There are a lot of different ways to play the classic basketball game "Horse." The basic rules say that when one player makes a shot and the next one misses, a letter is given. But if you play "Prove It," no letter is given right away. Instead, the player who misses has a choice. Either he can try the shot again, or he can make the first player make the shot a second time. In this way no letters are given until you "prove" a second time that they are truly deserved.

Assurance of your salvation works much the same way. Once you sincerely trust Jesus, you're saved. But your life needs to show it. Anyone who wants to know for sure that he or she is a Christian must prove it by walking, or living, as Jesus did.

WHAT ABOUT YOU?

:: *On a scale of 1 to 10, how sure are you of your salvation?*

:: *Make a simple list of the evidence for your own salvation. How has God changed your life? How has your faith made a difference to you? What do you do as a result of what you believe?*

:: *Rededicate yourself to walking as Jesus did.*

DECEMBER :: 24

READ JUDE 3-13

Beware of the Bogus

Woe to them! They have taken the way of Cain.
JUDE 11

After a New Testament full of good news—that God came to earth as a human, that he died voluntarily to save us from our sin, that his resurrection means we'll be resurrected too, that we can love and be loved by an extended family called the church—after all this, Jude drops a dark warning.

The warning is this: You've gotta look out for bogus Christians who aren't really Christians at all. These phonies say Jesus wasn't actually God. They say the forgiving grace of God means you can keep sinning—hey, God will always forgive you, right?

Jude speaks tenderly to his readers, but he doesn't hold out much hope for the phonies. He says they're like clouds without rain or dead trees. They're spiritually dead. Doomed to "blackest darkness."

Jude took them to 3 Old Testament guys who blew it in different ways. Cain (Genesis 4) was jealous and hateful, Korah (Numbers 16) was proud and uncooperative, and Balaam (Numbers 22) was greedy and selfish. If we're honest, we have to admit that each of these things could be a problem for us today too.

WHAT ABOUT YOU?

:: *Are any of these things problems for you?*

_____

_____

_____

_____

_____

_____

_____

DECEMBER :: 25

JUSTIN, AGE 13

READ JUDE 22-23

Never Give Up

Be merciful to those who doubt.
JUDE 22

I had a friend who used to say some really bad things about Jesus. He'd make fun of Christians and laugh at God. He'd make me so angry, I'd want to hit him!

But these verses remind me that a person who makes fun of God or has doubts about God needs to know the truth. When I got angry at my friend about his feelings toward God, I wasn't helping him get to know God; I was just making the situation worse.

I wish I had tried to tell my friend the truth about God instead of getting angry at him. I should have talked to him about his feelings. After all, Jesus had mercy on people who laughed at him. God still loves people who doubt him. God never gives up on anyone, and neither should I.

WHAT ABOUT YOU?

:: How can doubts about God actually work to deepen your faith?

:: Do you know someone who has doubts about God? Ask that person to talk to you about those doubts. Then ask your pastor or youth leader to help you find some answers for your friend.

:: Ask God to make you more patient with people who have doubts about him.

DECEMBER :: 26

PATRICK, AGE 16

Super Power

I am the Living One; I was dead, and behold I am alive for ever and ever!
REVELATION 1:18

When I accepted Jesus as my Savior, my itty-bitty existence exploded into true life. The everlasting Creator of the universe placed his hand on me, and I woke up from the sleep of death. Since the day I first realized Jesus hung on a cross for me, I'm constantly learning more about his amazing love and power.

God has so much more power in the fingernail of his pinky finger than I have in my whole body. He used his great power to form the world. He used that power to conquer death through Jesus' resurrection. And he used that power to reach out to insignificant little me.

The God who can do absolutely anything chooses to love me. I can't think of a better feeling.

WHAT ABOUT YOU?

:: What are some things that only God can do?

:: Write "God shows his power by…" at the top of a piece of paper, and finish the sentence with as many phrases or pictures as you can think of.

:: Praise God for his power through a song or a prayer.

DECEMBER :: 27

MINDY, AGE 14

Staying Close

Because you are lukewarm—neither hot nor cold—I am about to spit you out of my mouth.
REVELATION 3:16

At the beginning of this school year, I didn't know where my relationship with God was going. Some days I felt like I was sinning way too much, but other days I felt like I was walking right next to God. It really bothered me to have such an "iffy" feeling about my faith.

God has promised never to leave me. Unfortunately, that doesn't mean I'll always be as close to him as I should be. I made a decision to fight the "iffy" feeling. Once I did, I found out he was there all along, waiting for me to get serious.

Even now, I know that sometimes I'll still wander further away from God than I should. But I've started this journey of living for God, and I'm determined to stick with it.

WHAT ABOUT YOU?

:: Have you ever felt "iffy" about your faith? What did you do about it?

:: Rate yourself 1-5 in each of these areas: prayer life, reading the Bible, obedience to parents and other authorities, loving others, telling others about Jesus. Which one is weakest for you? How can you strengthen that area?

:: Ask God to help you stay serious about your walk with him.

DECEMBER :: 28

RACHEL, AGE 12

READ REVELATION 15:3-4

Hey, Thanks!

Great and marvelous are your deeds, LORD God Almighty.
REVELATION 15:3

How often do you take God for granted? I know I do it all the time. When I went to Colorado to go skiing, I saw the Rocky Mountains for the first time. I could have been thinking, *Wow! These are so beautiful, and God made them! He's awesome!* Instead, I was worrying about falling off my skis and looking stupid in front of everybody.

You'd think that with all the gifts God has given us—food to eat, air to breathe, people to love—it wouldn't be hard for us to remember to thank him once in a while. Plus, he loves it when we thank him and worship him. He loves it so much that we're going to be worshiping him with the angels forever in heaven. We might as well start now!

WHAT ABOUT YOU?

- Why do you think it's so easy to take God for granted?
- Think of 10 ways God shows his love, mercy, and forgiveness toward you and people you know.
- Pray the words of Revelation 15:3-4.

DECEMBER :: 29

No More Tears

He will wipe every tear from their eyes.
REVELATION 21:4

When my uncle died, I kept asking God why it happened. But I realized that my uncle was going to the perfect place: heaven.

I don't think about heaven very often. But this verse makes it sound like a pretty amazing place. There will be no more tears or death or any of the other things that make life hard for us on earth. Now, when something bad happens to me or to someone I love, I can think about heaven and remember that my life here is only part of God's plan for me. I can look forward to a happy, perfect life with God that will last forever.

WHAT ABOUT YOU?

:: *What do you think heaven will be like? How can your thoughts about heaven help you right now?*

:: *As you read through the rest of Revelation, make a list of the things that make heaven such a perfect place. Once you're done, draw a picture, write a poem, or compose a song that describes heaven the way it is portrayed in the book of Revelation.*

:: *Thank God for creating such a perfect place for you.*

DECEMBER :: 30

READ REVELATION 7:9-12

A World Full of Christians

Before me was a great multitude...from every nation, tribe and people and language, standing before the throne.
REVELATION 7:9

Rachel asked us to read a song of praise from Revelation 15 this week. The lyrics mention "all nations" worshiping God. That reminds us that God's kingdom is not single-colored. It's made up of all kinds of people.

Revelation 7 makes the same point. Do you realize what that means? Heaven is completely integrated. Christians from all over the world will be united in heaven. How cool! The God who created an infinite variety of beetles, birds, and butterflies has also called a wide variety of believers to populate his heaven. When you think about it, life would be pretty boring on *earth* if we were all the same too.

WHAT ABOUT YOU?

:: *Do you have any friends who are a different race then you? Does it matter what's on the outside compared to what's on the inside?*

:: *Next time you're in a store, make a point to notice people from other ethnic groups. The world is full of all kinds of races. Heaven will be too!*

:: *Pray for good race relations in your community and for opportunities to be around people who are different from you.*

DECEMBER :: 31

READ REVELATION 19:11–15

I Hardly Recognized You

His eyes are like blazing fire, and on his head are many crowns.
REVELATION 19:12

In the Greek language (which is the language people spoke where this part of the Bible was written), the first letter of the alphabet was "alpha" and the last letter was "omega." When Jesus says "I am the Alpha and the Omega," he is saying that he is the beginning and the end (Revelation 1:8). In English he might have said, "I am the A and the Z." This was especially important because this book deals with end-of-the-world stuff, and Jesus wanted us to understand that he will still be in charge.

Think of the Jesus you got to know in the stories of his years on earth. He was a simple carpenter, walking where he went, hanging out with poor people, and, in the end, nailed to an ugly cross. In these verses, he's back where he came from—in heaven and in charge. The One on the white horse with fire in his eyes and crowns on his head—that's your friend, Jesus. He promises he's coming to take you to heaven someday soon. Can you think of anything more awesome?

A plan for Bible reading to take readers through the New Testament and Psalms twice a year, and through the rest of the Bible once each year.

J A N U A R Y

1st	Genesis	1	Matthew	1	Ezra	1	Acts	1
2nd	Genesis	2	Matthew	2	Ezra	2	Acts	2
3rd	Genesis	3	Matthew	3	Ezra	3	Acts	3
4th	Genesis	4	Matthew	4	Ezra	4	Acts	4
5th	Genesis	5	Matthew	5	Ezra	5	Acts	5
6th	Genesis	6	Matthew	6	Ezra	6	Acts	6
7th	Genesis	7	Matthew	7	Ezra	7	Acts	7
8th	Genesis	8	Matthew	8	Ezra	8	Acts	8
9th	Genesis	9–10	Matthew	9	Ezra	9	Acts	9
10th	Genesis	11	Matthew	10	Ezra	10	Acts	10
11th	Genesis	12	Matthew	11	Nehemiah	1	Acts	11
12th	Genesis	13	Matthew	12	Nehemiah	2	Acts	12
13th	Genesis	14	Matthew	13	Nehemiah	3	Acts	13
14th	Genesis	15	Matthew	14	Nehemiah	4	Acts	14
15th	Genesis	16	Matthew	15	Nehemiah	5	Acts	15
16th	Genesis	17	Matthew	16	Nehemiah	6	Acts	16
17th	Genesis	18	Matthew	17	Nehemiah	7	Acts	17
18th	Genesis	19	Matthew	18	Nehemiah	8	Acts	18
19th	Genesis	20	Matthew	19	Nehemiah	9	Acts	19
20th	Genesis	21	Matthew	20	Nehemiah	10	Acts	20
21st	Genesis	22	Matthew	21	Nehemiah	11	Acts	21
22nd	Genesis	23	Matthew	22	Nehemiah	12	Acts	22
23rd	Genesis	24	Matthew	23	Nehemiah	13	Acts	23
24th	Genesis	25	Matthew	24	Esther	1	Acts	24
25th	Genesis	26	Matthew	25	Esther	2	Acts	25
26th	Genesis	27	Matthew	26	Esther	3	Acts	26
27th	Genesis	28	Matthew	27	Esther	4	Acts	27
28th	Genesis	29	Matthew	28	Esther	5	Acts	28
29th	Genesis	30	Mark	1	Esther	6	Romans	1
30th	Genesis	31	Mark	2	Esther	7	Romans	2
31st	Genesis	32	Mark	3	Esther	8	Romans	3

F E B R U A R Y

1st	Genesis	33	Mark	4	Esther	9–10	Romans	4
2nd	Genesis	34	Mark	5	Job	1	Romans	5
3rd	Genesis	35–36	Mark	6	Job	2	Romans	6
4th	Genesis	37	Mark	7	Job	3	Romans	7
5th	Genesis	38	Mark	8	Job	4	Romans	8
6th	Genesis	39	Mark	9	Job	5	Romans	9
7th	Genesis	40	Mark	10	Job	6	Romans	10
8th	Genesis	41	Mark	11	Job	7	Romans	11
9th	Genesis	42	Mark	12	Job	8	Romans	12
10th	Genesis	43	Mark	13	Job	9	Romans	13
11th	Genesis	44	Mark	14	Job	10	Romans	14
12th	Genesis	45	Mark	15	Job	11	Romans	15
13th	Genesis	46	Mark	16	Job	12	Romans	16
14th	Genesis	47	Luke	1:1–38	Job	13	1 Corinthians	1
15th	Genesis	48	Luke	1:39–80	Job	14	1 Corinthians	2
16th	Genesis	49	Luke	2	Job	15	1 Corinthians	3
17th	Genesis	50	Luke	3	Job	16–17	1 Corinthians	4
18th	Exodus	1	Luke	4	Job	18	1 Corinthians	5
19th	Exodus	2	Luke	5	Job	19	1 Corinthians	6
20th	Exodus	3	Luke	6	Job	20	1 Corinthians	7
21st	Exodus	4	Luke	7	Job	21	1 Corinthians	8
22nd	Exodus	5	Luke	8	Job	22	1 Corinthians	9
23rd	Exodus	6	Luke	9	Job	23	1 Corinthians	10
24th	Exodus	7	Luke	10	Job	24	1 Corinthians	11
25th	Exodus	8	Luke	11	Job	25–26	1 Corinthians	12
26th	Exodus	9	Luke	12	Job	27	1 Corinthians	13
27th	Exodus	10	Luke	13	Job	28	1 Corinthians	14
28th	Exodus	11–12:21	Luke	14	Job	29	1 Corinthians	15

M A R C H

1st	Exodus	12:22–50	Luke	15	Job	30	1 Corinthians	16
2nd	Exodus	13	Luke	16	Job	31	2 Corinthians	1
3rd	Exodus	14	Luke	17	Job	32	2 Corinthians	2
4th	Exodus	15	Luke	18	Job	33	2 Corinthians	3
5th	Exodus	16	Luke	19	Job	34	2 Corinthians	4
6th	Exodus	17	Luke	20	Job	35	2 Corinthians	5
7th	Exodus	18	Luke	21	Job	36	2 Corinthians	6
8th	Exodus	19	Luke	22	Job	37	2 Corinthians	7
9th	Exodus	20	Luke	23	Job	38	2 Corinthians	8
10th	Exodus	21	Luke	24	Job	39	2 Corinthians	9
11th	Exodus	22	John	1	Job	40	2 Corinthians	10
12th	Exodus	23	John	2	Job	41	2 Corinthians	11
13th	Exodus	24	John	3	Job	42	2 Corinthians	12
14th	Exodus	25	John	4	Proverbs	1	2 Corinthians	13
15th	Exodus	26	John	5	Proverbs	2	Galatians	1
16th	Exodus	27	John	6	Proverbs	3	Galatians	2
17th	Exodus	28	John	7	Proverbs	4	Galatians	3
18th	Exodus	29	John	8	Proverbs	5	Galatians	4
19th	Exodus	30	John	9	Proverbs	6	Galatians	5
20th	Exodus	31	John	10	Proverbs	7	Galatians	6
21st	Exodus	32	John	11	Proverbs	8	Ephesians	1
22nd	Exodus	33	John	12	Proverbs	9	Ephesians	2
23rd	Exodus	34	John	13	Proverbs	10	Ephesians	3
24th	Exodus	35	John	14	Proverbs	11	Ephesians	4
25th	Exodus	36	John	15	Proverbs	12	Ephesians	5
26th	Exodus	37	John	16	Proverbs	13	Ephesians	6
27th	Exodus	38	John	17	Proverbs	14	Philippians	1
28th	Exodus	39	John	18	Proverbs	15	Philippians	2
29th	Exodus	40	John	19	Proverbs	16	Philippians	3
30th	Leviticus	1	John	20	Proverbs	17	Philippians	4
31st	Leviticus	2–3	John	21	Proverbs	18	Colossians	1

APRIL

1st	Leviticus	4	Psalms	1–2	Proverbs	19	Colossians	2
2nd	Leviticus	5	Psalms	3–4	Proverbs	20	Colossians	3
3rd	Leviticus	6	Psalms	5–6	Proverbs	21	Colossians	4
4th	Leviticus	7	Psalms	7–8	Proverbs	22	1 Thessalonians	1
5th	Leviticus	8	Psalms	9	Proverbs	23	1 Thessalonians	2
6th	Leviticus	9	Psalms	10	Proverbs	24	1 Thessalonians	3
7th	Leviticus	10	Psalms	11–12	Proverbs	25	1 Thessalonians	4
8th	Leviticus	11–12	Psalms	13–14	Proverbs	26	1 Thessalonians	5
9th	Leviticus	13	Psalms	15–16	Proverbs	27	2 Thessalonians	1
10th	Leviticus	14	Psalms	17	Proverbs	28	2 Thessalonians	2
11th	Leviticus	15	Psalms	18	Proverbs	29	2 Thessalonians	3
12th	Leviticus	16	Psalms	19	Proverbs	30	1 Timothy	1
13th	Leviticus	17	Psalms	20–21	Proverbs	31	1 Timothy	2
14th	Leviticus	18	Psalms	22	Ecclesiastes	1	1 Timothy	3
15th	Leviticus	19	Psalms	23–24	Ecclesiastes	2	1 Timothy	4
16th	Leviticus	20	Psalms	25	Ecclesiastes	3	1 Timothy	5
17th	Leviticus	21	Psalms	26–27	Ecclesiastes	4	1 Timothy	6
18th	Leviticus	22	Psalms	28–29	Ecclesiastes	5	2 Timothy	1
19th	Leviticus	23	Psalms	30	Ecclesiastes	6	2 Timothy	2
20th	Leviticus	24	Psalms	31	Ecclesiastes	7	2 Timothy	3
21st	Leviticus	25	Psalms	32	Ecclesiastes	8	2 Timothy	4
22nd	Leviticus	26	Psalms	33	Ecclesiastes	9	Titus	1
23rd	Leviticus	27	Psalms	34	Ecclesiastes	10	Titus	2
24th	Numbers	1	Psalms	35	Ecclesiastes	11	Titus	3
25th	Numbers	2	Psalms	36	Ecclesiastes	12	Philemon	1
26th	Numbers	3	Psalms	37	Song of Songs	1	Hebrews	1
27th	Numbers	4	Psalms	38	Song of Songs	2	Hebrews	2
28th	Numbers	5	Psalms	39	Song of Songs	3	Hebrews	3
29th	Numbers	6	Psalms	40–41	Song of Songs	4	Hebrews	4
30th	Numbers	7	Psalms	42–43	Song of Songs	5	Hebrews	5

M A Y

1st	Numbers	8	Psalms	44	Song of Songs	6	Hebrews	6
2nd	Numbers	9	Psalms	45	Song of Songs	7	Hebrews	7
3rd	Numbers	10	Psalms	46–47	Song of Songs	8	Hebrews	8
4th	Numbers	11	Psalms	48	Isaiah	1	Hebrews	9
5th	Numbers	12–13	Psalms	49	Isaiah	2	Hebrews	10
6th	Numbers	14	Psalms	50	Isaiah	3–4	Hebrews	11
7th	Numbers	15	Psalms	51	Isaiah	5	Hebrews	12
8th	Numbers	16	Psalms	52–54	Isaiah	6	Hebrews	13
9th	Numbers	17–18	Psalms	55	Isaiah	7	James	1
10th	Numbers	19	Psalms	56–57	Isaiah	8–9:7	James	2
11th	Numbers	20	Psalms	58–59	Isaiah	9:8–10:4	James	3
12th	Numbers	21	Psalms	60–61	Isaiah	10:5–34	James	4
13th	Numbers	22	Psalms	62–63	Isaiah	11–12	James	5
14th	Numbers	23	Psalms	64–65	Isaiah	13	1 Peter	1
15th	Numbers	24	Psalms	66–67	Isaiah	14	1 Peter	2
16th	Numbers	25	Psalms	68	Isaiah	15	1 Peter	3
17th	Numbers	26	Psalms	69	Isaiah	16	1 Peter	4
18th	Numbers	27	Psalms	70–71	Isaiah	17–18	1 Peter	5
19th	Numbers	28	Psalms	72	Isaiah	19–20	2 Peter	1
20th	Numbers	29	Psalms	73	Isaiah	21	2 Peter	2
21st	Numbers	30	Psalms	74	Isaiah	22	2 Peter	3
22nd	Numbers	31	Psalms	75–76	Isaiah	23	1 John	1
23rd	Numbers	32	Psalms	77	Isaiah	24	1 John	2
24th	Numbers	33	Psalms	78:1–37	Isaiah	25	1 John	3
25th	Numbers	34	Psalms	78:38–72	Isaiah	26	1 John	4
26th	Numbers	35	Psalms	79	Isaiah	27	1 John	5
27th	Numbers	36	Psalms	80	Isaiah	28	2 John	1
28th	Deuteronomy	1	Psalms	81–82	Isaiah	29	3 John	1
29th	Deuteronomy	2	Psalms	83–84	Isaiah	30	Jude	1
30th	Deuteronomy	3	Psalms	85	Isaiah	31	Revelation	1
31st	Deuteronomy	4	Psalms	86–87	Isaiah	32	Revelation	2

JUNE

1st	Deuteronomy	5	Psalms	88	Isaiah	33	Revelation	3
2nd	Deuteronomy	6	Psalms	89	Isaiah	34	Revelation	4
3rd	Deuteronomy	7	Psalms	90	Isaiah	35	Revelation	5
4th	Deuteronomy	8	Psalms	91	Isaiah	36	Revelation	6
5th	Deuteronomy	9	Psalms	92–93	Isaiah	37	Revelation	7
6th	Deuteronomy	10	Psalms	94	Isaiah	38	Revelation	8
7th	Deuteronomy	11	Psalms	95–96	Isaiah	39	Revelation	9
8th	Deuteronomy	12	Psalms	97–98	Isaiah	40	Revelation	10
9th	Deuteronomy	13–14	Psalms	99–101	Isaiah	41	Revelation	11
10th	Deuteronomy	15	Psalms	102	Isaiah	42	Revelation	12
11th	Deuteronomy	16	Psalms	103	Isaiah	43	Revelation	13
12th	Deuteronomy	17	Psalms	104	Isaiah	44	Revelation	14
13th	Deuteronomy	18	Psalms	105	Isaiah	45	Revelation	15
14th	Deuteronomy	19	Psalms	106	Isaiah	46	Revelation	16
15th	Deuteronomy	20	Psalms	107	Isaiah	47	Revelation	17
16th	Deuteronomy	21	Psalms	108–109	Isaiah	48	Revelation	18
17th	Deuteronomy	22	Psalms	110–111	Isaiah	49	Revelation	19
18th	Deuteronomy	23	Psalms	112–113	Isaiah	50	Revelation	20
19th	Deuteronomy	24	Psalms	114–115	Isaiah	51	Revelation	21
20th	Deuteronomy	25	Psalms	116	Isaiah	52	Revelation	22
21st	Deuteronomy	26	Psalms	117–118	Isaiah	53	Matthew	1
22nd	Deuteronomy	27–28:19| Psalms	119:1–24	Isaiah	54	Matthew	2
23rd	Deuteronomy	28:20–68| Psalms	119:25–48	Isaiah	55	Matthew	3
24th	Deuteronomy	29	Psalms	119:49–72	Isaiah	56	Matthew	4
25th	Deuteronomy	30	Psalms	119:73–96	Isaiah	57	Matthew	5
26th	Deuteronomy	31	Psalms	119:97–120	Isaiah	58	Matthew	6
27th	Deuteronomy	32	Psalms	119:121–144| Isaiah	59	Matthew	7
28th	Deuteronomy	33–34	Psalms	119:145–176| Isaiah	60	Matthew	8
29th	Joshua	1	Psalms	120–122	Isaiah	61	Matthew	9
30th	Joshua	2	Psalms	123–125	Isaiah	62	Matthew	10

JULY

1st	Joshua	3	Psalms	126–128	Isaiah	63	Matthew	11
2nd	Joshua	4	Psalms	129–131	Isaiah	64	Matthew	12
3rd	Joshua	5–6:5	Psalms	132–134	Isaiah	65	Matthew	13
4th	Joshua	6:6–27	Psalms	135–136	Isaiah	66	Matthew	14
5th	Joshua	7	Psalms	137–138	Jeremiah	1	Matthew	15
6th	Joshua	8	Psalms	139	Jeremiah	2	Matthew	16
7th	Joshua	9	Psalms	140–141	Jeremiah	3	Matthew	17
8th	Joshua	10	Psalms	142–143	Jeremiah	4	Matthew	18
9th	Joshua	11	Psalms	144	Jeremiah	5	Matthew	19
10th	Joshua	12–13	Psalms	145	Jeremiah	6	Matthew	20
11th	Joshua	14–15	Psalms	146–147	Jeremiah	7	Matthew	21
12th	Joshua	16–17	Psalms	148	Jeremiah	8	Matthew	22
13th	Joshua	18–19	Psalms	149–150	Jeremiah	9	Matthew	23
14th	Joshua	20–21	Acts	1	Jeremiah	10	Matthew	24
15th	Joshua	22	Acts	2	Jeremiah	11	Matthew	25
16th	Joshua	23	Acts	3	Jeremiah	12	Matthew	26
17th	Joshua	24	Acts	4	Jeremiah	13	Matthew	27
18th	Judges	1	Acts	5	Jeremiah	14	Matthew	28
19th	Judges	2	Acts	6	Jeremiah	15	Mark	1
20th	Judges	3	Acts	7	Jeremiah	16	Mark	2
21st	Judges	4	Acts	8	Jeremiah	17	Mark	3
22nd	Judges	5	Acts	9	Jeremiah	18	Mark	4
23rd	Judges	6	Acts	10	Jeremiah	19	Mark	5
24th	Judges	7	Acts	11	Jeremiah	20	Mark	6
25th	Judges	8	Acts	12	Jeremiah	21	Mark	7
26th	Judges	9	Acts	13	Jeremiah	22	Mark	8
27th	Judges	10–11:11	Acts	14	Jeremiah	23	Mark	9
28th	Judges	11:12–40	Acts	15	Jeremiah	24	Mark	10
29th	Judges	12	Acts	16	Jeremiah	25	Mark	11
30th	Judges	13	Acts	17	Jeremiah	26	Mark	12
31st	Judges	14	Acts	18	Jeremiah	27	Mark	13

A U G U S T

1st	Judges	15	Acts	19	Jeremiah	28	Mark	14
2nd	Judges	16	Acts	20	Jeremiah	29	Mark	15
3rd	Judges	17	Acts	21	Jeremiah	30–31	Mark	16
4th	Judges	18	Acts	22	Jeremiah	32	Psalms	1–2
5th	Judges	19	Acts	23	Jeremiah	33	Psalms	3–4
6th	Judges	20	Acts	24	Jeremiah	34	Psalms	5–6
7th	Judges	21	Acts	25	Jeremiah	35	Psalms	7–8
8th	Ruth	1	Acts	26	Jeremiah	36 & 45	Psalms	9
9th	Ruth	2	Acts	27	Jeremiah	37	Psalms	10
10th	Ruth	3–4	Acts	28	Jeremiah	38	Psalms	11–12
11th	1 Samuel	1	Romans	1	Jeremiah	39	Psalms	13–14
12th	1 Samuel	2	Romans	2	Jeremiah	40	Psalms	15–16
13th	1 Samuel	3	Romans	3	Jeremiah	41	Psalms	17
14th	1 Samuel	4	Romans	4	Jeremiah	42	Psalms	18
15th	1 Samuel	5–6	Romans	5	Jeremiah	43	Psalms	19
16th	1 Samuel	7–8	Romans	6	Jeremiah	44	Psalms	20–21
17th	1 Samuel	9	Romans	7	Jeremiah	46	Psalms	22
18th	1 Samuel	10	Romans	8	Jeremiah	47	Psalms	23–24
19th	1 Samuel	11	Romans	9	Jeremiah	48	Psalms	25
20th	1 Samuel	12	Romans	10	Jeremiah	49	Psalms	26–27
21st	1 Samuel	13	Romans	11	Jeremiah	50	Psalms	28–29
22nd	1 Samuel	14	Romans	12	Jeremiah	51	Psalms	30
23rd	1 Samuel	15	Romans	13	Jeremiah	52	Psalms	31
24th	1 Samuel	16	Romans	14	Lamentations	1	Psalms	32
25th	1 Samuel	17	Romans	15	Lamentations	2	Psalms	33
26th	1 Samuel	18	Romans	16	Lamentations	3	Psalms	34
27th	1 Samuel	19	1 Corinthians	1	Lamentations	4	Psalms	35
28th	1 Samuel	20	1 Corinthians	2	Lamentations	5	Psalms	36
29th	1 Samuel	21–22	1 Corinthians	3	Ezekiel	1	Psalms	37
30th	1 Samuel	23	1 Corinthians	4	Ezekiel	2	Psalms	38
31st	1 Samuel	24	1 Corinthians	5	Ezekiel	3	Psalms	39

SEPTEMBER

1st	1 Samuel	25	1 Corinthians	6	Ezekiel	4	Psalms 40–41
2nd	1 Samuel	26	1 Corinthians	7	Ezekiel	5	Psalms 42–43
3rd	1 Samuel	27	1 Corinthians	8	Ezekiel	6	Psalms 44
4th	1 Samuel	28	1 Corinthians	9	Ezekiel	7	Psalms 45
5th	1 Samuel	29–30	1 Corinthians	10	Ezekiel	8	Psalms 46–47
6th	1 Samuel	31	1 Corinthians	11	Ezekiel	9	Psalms 48
7th	2 Samuel	1	1 Corinthians	12	Ezekiel	10	Psalms 49
8th	2 Samuel	2	1 Corinthians	13	Ezekiel	11	Psalms 50
9th	2 Samuel	3	1 Corinthians	14	Ezekiel	12	Psalms 51
10th	2 Samuel	4–5	1 Corinthians	15	Ezekiel	13	Psalms 52–54
11th	2 Samuel	6	1 Corinthians	16	Ezekiel	14	Psalms 55
12th	2 Samuel	7	2 Corinthians	1	Ezekiel	15	Psalms 56–57
13th	2 Samuel	8–9	2 Corinthians	2	Ezekiel	16	Psalms 58–59
14th	2 Samuel	10	2 Corinthians	3	Ezekiel	17	Psalms 60–61
15th	2 Samuel	11	2 Corinthians	4	Ezekiel	18	Psalms 62–63
16th	2 Samuel	12	2 Corinthians	5	Ezekiel	19	Psalms 64–65
17th	2 Samuel	13	2 Corinthians	6	Ezekiel	20	Psalms 66–67
18th	2 Samuel	14	2 Corinthians	7	Ezekiel	21	Psalms 68
19th	2 Samuel	15	2 Corinthians	8	Ezekiel	22	Psalms 69
20th	2 Samuel	16	2 Corinthians	9	Ezekiel	23	Psalms 70–71
21st	2 Samuel	17	2 Corinthians	10	Ezekiel	24	Psalms 72
22nd	2 Samuel	18	2 Corinthians	11	Ezekiel	25	Psalms 73
23rd	2 Samuel	19	2 Corinthians	12	Ezekiel	26	Psalms 74
24th	2 Samuel	20	2 Corinthians	13	Ezekiel	27	Psalms 75–76
25th	2 Samuel	21	Galatians	1	Ezekiel	28	Psalms 77
26th	2 Samuel	22	Galatians	2	Ezekiel	29	Psalms 78:1–37
27th	2 Samuel	23	Galatians	3	Ezekiel	30	Psalms 78:38–72
28th	2 Samuel	24	Galatians	4	Ezekiel	31	Psalms 79
29th	1 Kings	1	Galatians	5	Ezekiel	32	Psalms 80
30th	1 Kings	2	Galatians	6	Ezekiel	33	Psalms 81–82

OCTOBER

1st	1 Kings	3	Ephesians	1	Ezekiel	34	Psalms 83–84
2nd	1 Kings	4–5	Ephesians	2	Ezekiel	35	Psalms 85
3rd	1 Kings	6	Ephesians	3	Ezekiel	36	Psalms 86
4th	1 Kings	7	Ephesians	4	Ezekiel	37	Psalms 87–88
5th	1 Kings	8	Ephesians	5	Ezekiel	38	Psalms 89
6th	1 Kings	9	Ephesians	6	Ezekiel	39	Psalms 90
7th	1 Kings	10	Philippians	1	Ezekiel	40	Psalms 91
8th	1 Kings	11	Philippians	2	Ezekiel	41	Psalms 92–93
9th	1 Kings	12	Philippians	3	Ezekiel	42	Psalms 94
10th	1 Kings	13	Philippians	4	Ezekiel	43	Psalms 95–96
11th	1 Kings	14	Colossians	1	Ezekiel	44	Psalms 97–98
12th	1 Kings	15	Colossians	2	Ezekiel	45	Psalms 99–101
13th	1 Kings	16	Colossians	3	Ezekiel	46	Psalms 102
14th	1 Kings	17	Colossians	4	Ezekiel	47	Psalms 103
15th	1 Kings	18	1 Thessalonians	1	Ezekiel	48	Psalms 104
16th	1 Kings	19	1 Thessalonians	2	Daniel	1	Psalms 105
17th	1 Kings	20	1 Thessalonians	3	Daniel	2	Psalms 106
18th	1 Kings	21	1 Thessalonians	4	Daniel	3	Psalms 107
19th	1 Kings	22	1 Thessalonians	5	Daniel	4	Psalms 108–109
20th	2 Kings	1	2 Thessalonians	1	Daniel	5	Psalms 110–111
21st	2 Kings	2	2 Thessalonians	2	Daniel	6	Psalms 112–113
22nd	2 Kings	3	2 Thessalonians	3	Daniel	7	Psalms 114–115
23rd	2 Kings	4	1 Timothy	1	Daniel	8	Psalms 116
24th	2 Kings	5	1 Timothy	2	Daniel	9	Psalms 117–118
25th	2 Kings	6	1 Timothy	3	Daniel	10	Psalms 119:1–24
26th	2 Kings	7	1 Timothy	4	Daniel	11	Psalms 119:25–48
27th	2 Kings	8	1 Timothy	5	Daniel	12	Psalms 119:49–72
28th	2 Kings	9	1 Timothy	6	Hosea	1	Psalms 119:73–96
29th	2 Kings	10	2 Timothy	1	Hosea	2	Psalms 119:97–120
30th	2 Kings	11–12	2 Timothy	2	Hosea	3–4	Psalms 119:121–144
31st	2 Kings	13	2 Timothy	3	Hosea	5–6	Psalms 119:145–176

NOVEMBER

1st	2 Kings	14	2 Timothy	4	Hosea	7	Psalms	120–122
2nd	2 Kings	15	Titus	1	Hosea	8	Psalms	123–125
3rd	2 Kings	16	Titus	2	Hosea	9	Psalms	126–128
4th	2 Kings	17	Titus	3	Hosea	10	Psalms	129–131
5th	2 Kings	18	Philemon	1	Hosea	11	Psalms	132–134
6th	2 Kings	19	Hebrews	1	Hosea	12	Psalms	135–136
7th	2 Kings	20	Hebrews	2	Hosea	13	Psalms	137–138
8th	2 Kings	21	Hebrews	3	Hosea	14	Psalms	139
9th	2 Kings	22	Hebrews	4	Joel	1	Psalms	140–141
10th	2 Kings	23	Hebrews	5	Joel	2	Psalms	142
11th	2 Kings	24	Hebrews	6	Joel	3	Psalms	143
12th	2 Kings	25	Hebrews	7	Amos	1	Psalms	144
13th	1 Chronicles	1–2	Hebrews	8	Amos	2	Psalms	145
14th	1 Chronicles	3–4	Hebrews	9	Amos	3	Psalms	146–147
15th	1 Chronicles	5–6	Hebrews	10	Amos	4	Psalms	148–150
16th	1 Chronicles	7–8	Hebrews	11	Amos	5	Luke	1:1–38
17th	1 Chronicles	9–10	Hebrews	12	Amos	6	Luke	1:39–80
18th	1 Chronicles	11–12	Hebrews	13	Amos	7	Luke	2
19th	1 Chronicles	13–14	James	1	Amos	8	Luke	3
20th	1 Chronicles	15	James	2	Amos	9	Luke	4
21st	1 Chronicles	16	James	3	Obadiah	1	Luke	5
22nd	1 Chronicles	17	James	4	Jonah	1	Luke	6
23rd	1 Chronicles	18	James	5	Jonah	2	Luke	7
24th	1 Chronicles	19–20	1 Peter	1	Jonah	3	Luke	8
25th	1 Chronicles	21	1 Peter	2	Jonah	4	Luke	9
26th	1 Chronicles	22	1 Peter	3	Micah	1	Luke	10
27th	1 Chronicles	23	1 Peter	4	Micah	2	Luke	11
28th	1 Chronicles	24–25	1 Peter	5	Micah	3	Luke	12
29th	1 Chronicles	26–27	2 Peter	1	Micah	4	Luke	13
30th	1 Chronicles	28	2 Peter	2	Micah	5	Luke	14

DECEMBER

1st	1 Chronicles	29	2 Peter	3	Micah	6	Luke	15
2nd	2 Chronicles	1	1 John	1	Micah	7	Luke	16
3rd	2 Chronicles	2	1 John	2	Nahum	1	Luke	17
4th	2 Chronicles	3–4	1 John	3	Nahum	2	Luke	18
5th	2 Chronicles	5–6:11	1 John	4	Nahum	3	Luke	19
6th	2 Chronicles	6:12–42	1 John	5	Habakkuk	1	Luke	20
7th	2 Chronicles	7	2 John	1	Habakkuk	2	Luke	21
8th	2 Chronicles	8	3 John	1	Habakkuk	3	Luke	22
9th	2 Chronicles	9	Jude	1	Zephaniah	1	Luke	23
10th	2 Chronicles	10	Revelation	1	Zephaniah	2	Luke	24
11th	2 Chronicles	11–12	Revelation	2	Zephaniah	3	John	1
12th	2 Chronicles	13	Revelation	3	Haggai	1	John	2
13th	2 Chronicles	14–15	Revelation	4	Haggai	2	John	3
14th	2 Chronicles	16	Revelation	5	Zechariah	1	John	4
15th	2 Chronicles	17	Revelation	6	Zechariah	2	John	5
16th	2 Chronicles	18	Revelation	7	Zechariah	3	John	6
17th	2 Chronicles	19–20	Revelation	8	Zechariah	4	John	7
18th	2 Chronicles	21	Revelation	9	Zechariah	5	John	8
19th	2 Chronicles	22–23	Revelation	10	Zechariah	6	John	9
20th	2 Chronicles	24	Revelation	11	Zechariah	7	John	10
21st	2 Chronicles	25	Revelation	12	Zechariah	8	John	11
22nd	2 Chronicles	26	Revelation	13	Zechariah	9	John	12
23rd	2 Chronicles	27–28	Revelation	14	Zechariah	10	John	13
24th	2 Chronicles	29	Revelation	15	Zechariah	11	John	14
25th	2 Chronicles	30	Revelation	16	Zechariah	12–13:1	John	15
26th	2 Chronicles	31	Revelation	17	Zechariah	13:2–9	John	16
27th	2 Chronicles	32	Revelation	18	Zechariah	14	John	17
28th	2 Chronicles	33	Revelation	19	Malachi	1	John	18
29th	2 Chronicles	34	Revelation	20	Malachi	2	John	19
30th	2 Chronicles	35	Revelation	21	Malachi	3	John	20
31st	2 Chronicles	36	Revelation	22	Malachi	4	John	21

See our entire collection of books at summersidepress.com, including these 365-Day Devotional Journal titles:

Joy & Strength

MARY WILDER TILESTON

As one of the most cherished devotionals of the last century, this best-selling compilation captures biblical truths and enduring values. Daily meditations that will touch your heart are paired with lined space that invites your personal reflections. With words of time-tested encouragement, this 365-day devotional offers messages of hope and journaling space for every day of the year.

ISBN 978-1-60936-101-3
$19.99

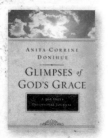

Glimpses of God's Grace

ANITA CORRINE DONIHUE

From the best-selling author whose devotionals have sold more than a million copies comes this 365-day devotional with journaling space for every day of the year. In the "everyday" and the "ordinary," she invites you to discover how our heavenly Father extends His grace into every aspect of life. Use the lined space for your own prayers and insights.

ISBN 978-1-60936-100-6
$19.99

Alone in God's Presence

Warm, authentic meditations encourage you to quiet your soul and recognize God's presence each day. He wants to enter your reality and walk through it with you. Use these moments and the writing lines provided to create a sacred space where you can hear the voice of God and sense His nearness.

ISBN 978-1-60936-102-0
$19.99

NIV Teen Devotional Journal

There are a lot of choices about the future that teenagers have to wade through. Questions and decisions wait at every turn. But you are not alone. Others want to share how God can help you through anything. Read the devotional entries then express your thoughts, ask your questions, or formulate your plans in the lined space. There is a relevant message about the stuff that really matters for every day of the year.

ISBN 978-1-60936-103-7
$19.99

Also available at your local bookseller or amazon.com, christianbook.com, and bn.com.